Writing Women's History

Credit: Les Todd, Duke University News Service

Writing Women's History

A Tribute to Anne Firor Scott

Edited by Elizabeth Anne Payne

University Press of Mississippi / Jackson

www.upress.state.ms.us

The University Press of Mississippi is a member
of the Association of American University Presses.

Color reproductions used in this volume were
made possible through the support of the College
of Liberal Arts at the University of Mississippi.

Copyright © 2011 by University Press of Mississippi
All rights reserved
Manufactured in the United States of America

First printing 2011

∞

Library of Congress Cataloging-in-Publication Data

Porter L. Fortune, Jr. History Symposium (32nd : 2007 : University
of Mississippi)
Writing women's history : a tribute to Anne Firor Scott / edited by
Elizabeth Anne Payne.
    p. cm. — (Chancellor Porter L. Fortune Symposium in
Southern History series)
"Essays in this volume were originally presented at the Thirty-
second Annual Porter L. Fortune Jr. History Symposium at the
University of Mississippi"—
    Includes bibliographical references and index.
    ISBN 978-1-61703-173-1 (cloth : alk. paper) — ISBN 978-1-61703-
174-8 (ebook)   1. Women—United States—History—Congresses. I.
Payne, Elizabeth Anne, 1943– II. Title. III. Series.
    HQ1410.P67 2007
    305.40973—dc22   2011013398

British Library Cataloging-in-Publication Data available

For Conwill

Contents

ix   Acknowledgments
          —ELIZABETH ANNE PAYNE

xiii   A Student's Perspective
          —MARKEEVA MORGAN

xv   Introduction
          —JACQUELYN DOWD HALL

3   Equally Their Due: Women's Education and Public Life
          in Postrevolutionary and Antebellum America
          —MARY KELLEY

28   Down from the Pedestal:
          The Influence of Anne Scott's Southern Ladies
          —LAURA F. EDWARDS

64   "How are the daughters of Eve punished?":
          Rape during the Civil War
          —CRYSTAL N. FEIMSTER

82   "A Quilt unlike Any Other":
          Rediscovering the Work of Harriet Powers
          —LAUREL THATCHER ULRICH

117   Taking Care of Bodies, Babies, and Business:
          Black Women Health Professionals in South Carolina, 1895–1954
          —DARLENE CLARK HINE

142   From Jim Crow to Jane Crow, or How Anne Scott and
          Pauli Murray Found Each Other
          —GLENDA ELIZABETH GILMORE

172 The Million Mom March: The Perils of Color-Blind Maternalism
    —DEBORAH GRAY WHITE

203 Writing Women's History: A Response
    —ANNE FIROR SCOTT

211 Contributors

223 Index

Acknowledgments

The essays in this volume were originally presented at the thirty-second annual Porter L. Fortune Jr. History Symposium at the University of Mississippi. Organized in 1975, the symposium honors the late Porter L. Fortune Jr., a historian who served as chancellor of the university from 1968 to 1984 and was pivotal in launching the symposium. Past symposia have covered the terrain of the American South's history and include slavery, manners, civil rights, sports, gender, religion, and Native Americans. Elizabeth Fortune has generously supported the History Symposium since its beginning, and she graciously assisted in planning this symposium on writing women's history.

Choosing Anne Firor Scott's work and its impact on women's history as the emphasis of the symposium was easy. The fruitful intersection of the publication in 1970 of *The Southern Lady: From Pedestal to Politics, 1830–1930* with the rising women's movement meant that historians responded with a keen interest to both the approach and message of the book. Using women's diaries, letters, and other personal documents, Scott demonstrated brilliantly that the familiar dichotomy of personal versus public, private versus civic, that had dominated traditional scholarship about men could not be made to fit women's lives. In doing so, she helped to open up vast terrains of women's neglected experiences for historical study. Her student Sara Evans, for example, would publish *Personal Politics: The Roots of Women's Liberation in the Civil Rights Movement and the New Left* (1980).

Anne Scott has been a mentor to many women (and men) who were not her own students, including myself. I worked at Duke University's Women's College during the academic year of 1967–68 and admired from a distance this attractive, no-nonsense female history professor who wore flat shoes, short hair, and no makeup. I continue to regret that I did not take her course during that year—I was at that point too timid—as it would have saved me detours in my career. I attended the University of Chicago Press's announcement of *The Southern Lady* in 1970, by which time I had become a student of history. I listened intently and with gratitude as Anne described southern women in a different vein and in a way that corresponded to the stories of women in my own family. Later she coedited the series on women's history published by the University of Illinois Press in which my revised dissertation was published. In that role, she challenged me to think more seriously about the nature and shape of feminist influence in the 1920s and 1930s. I will always be grateful not only for her mentoring but for her friendship, which has enriched my life.

Anne once laughingly told me that during the 1960s, when the women writing American women's history met together at the annual conventions of the Organization of American Historians and the American Historical Association, it was she and Gerda Lerner having breakfast with each other. Humor is one of her best traits. She chuckles, for example, as she recalls her first year at Duke. After teaching during the 1959–60 academic year at the University of North Carolina, she accepted a temporary position at Duke while the department sought to "find somebody." When Duke's Department of History called Harvard's asking it to send "your best man"—that's the way it was done then; no searches and no announcements—Harvard, to its credit, responded, "You've already got our best person."

She broke with the heroic understanding of historical research and scholarship as a lonely and, if not alienating, always individual experience. She eagerly promoted shared projects. She applauded the budding careers of students not her own. In one case, she snatched the manuscript of an author in danger of not receiving tenure and got permission to send it to a major press. The book became a best seller; the author's career has soared. In another case, she spent one morning a week for a year helping a student who graduated from another university reorganize her dissertation into an appealing manuscript. And in 2000, having retired from Duke in 1991, she taught a remarkable course to my students at the University of Mississippi's McDonnell-Barksdale Honors College titled "Parallel Lives: Black Women; White Women." Markeeva Morgan, whose reminiscence "A Student's Perspective" precedes the introduction to this volume, remembers Anne's teaching as a life-changing experience.

An edited volume is always built on the cooperation, commitment, and research of the authors. These historians, all leading scholars in American women's history, made editing this volume both exciting and entirely a pleasure. They responded to multiple queries from me and graciously incorporated suggestions. They participated eagerly in our symposium as a way of honoring the role that Anne Scott had played in their work; they cheerfully acknowledged how Scott's scholarship had helped to shape their own intellectual and scholarly journeys. One author revealed that she had chosen her field after reading *The Southern Lady*.

Acknowledgments

The symposium is always a communal effort. Sheila Skemp and Nancy Bercaw brainstormed with me in choosing the speakers, and Glenn Hopkins, dean of liberal arts, generously provided funds for publishing in color the two quilts described in Laurel Thatcher Ulrich's essay. Robert Haws, as chair of the history department, quickly endorsed the proposal to make the thirty-second symposium a tribute to Anne Scott and her work. Joseph Ward, his successor as chair, was especially encouraging and helpful in supporting the symposium. Betty Harness assisted in multiple ways to make the three-day event unfold gracefully. Susan Nicholas and Nichole Bourgeois cheerfully assisted. Linda Denning and other graduate students helped with myriad details of organizing the conference. The University Lecture Series generously supported the symposium financially. Bonnie Payne Davidson organized an enchanted lunch for symposium participants on the lawn of Rowan Oak, William Faulkner's home.

Much of the editing was done during my year as a fellow at the National Humanities Center in North Carolina. Geoffrey Harpham, director of the center, and Kent Mullikin, its associate director, lent the center's support in completing the work of this volume. Marie Brubaker and Lois Whittington helped in multiple ways. Karen Carroll, who does copyediting for scholars at the center, worked on several of the essays. All the authors commented on Carroll's pursuit of excellence in her copyediting of their essays.

Pamela Tyler read one section, and I especially appreciate her ear for "clunkiness." An anonymous reader provided valuable suggestions, which are gratefully incorporated here. Craig Gill, the University Press of Mississippi's assistant director and editor-in-chief, enthusiastically endorsed the project from the beginning. Brenda M. Eagles read and gave editorial suggestions that strengthened several of the essays, and I appreciate her support of this volume. William G. Henry did the final copyediting, and Tyrone Nagai indexed the book.

Kenneth Rutherford, who shares my admiration for Anne Scott, encouraged me throughout this project, as he does with all the endeavors I undertake. The book is dedicated to our daughter Conwill, who assisted me with the symposium and whose smile lights my world. I thank Anne Scott for her enthusiasm for the symposium, for her special interest in the University of Mississippi, and most of all for her inspiration over the decades.

A Student's Perspective

—MARKEEVA MORGAN

I have asked myself how I could possibly represent Dr. Scott's students, having taken one course from her that lasted a mere three weeks and was not even held at her home institution. Then I had an aha moment, a moment of clarity, even a revelation: I cannot. But if *I* can recall with such pleasure my experience in Dr. Scott's class and the passion and energy she invested in it as well as the individual interest she demonstrated in my classmates and me—she can still remember where each of us sat—during that one course, what more must there have been in her other classes for all her former students who had the benefit of learning from her for an entire semester or quarter? Perhaps, then, the story of such a short, rich interface with her provides a testimonial glimpse of what she means to us all.

I am an engineer. I will not bore you with my feeble interpretations of history or the study of it. I will, however, share with you a couple of thoughts I consider pertinent to this recollection. First, in the spirit of full disclosure, I confess that Dr. Scott gave me a B for that course at a time when Bs were foreign to me. I also confess that I initially harbored a little anger and resentment toward her for that. There is, however, a foreshadowing here.

Now, subscribing to the theory that we are the sum of our experiences and decisions filtered and complemented by our individual, congenital predispositions, one can view history as a vicarious simulation of alternative collections of experiences and decisions that could easily have belonged to each of us. Then, the *study* of history inevitably becomes an introspective evaluation of humanity, the self's effect on it, and an individual's transformation because of it. Through this introspective evaluation of that course (which is now a part of history), I realized that, in fact, Dr. Scott didn't *give* me a B in that class; I *earned* a B in that class. You

---

Markeeva Morgan, a graduate of the University of Mississippi, heads a task force charged with astronauts' safety at the George C. Marshall Space Flight Center, National Aeronautics and Space Administration.

see, what is a teacher without the nurtured hope that, through teaching, students will actually learn? While I had performed well enough, per the syllabus, to be awarded an A, I had not invested sufficient energy in *learning*. Based on what I *could* have learned, I earned a B. I can now thank Dr. Scott for having the courage to give me the grade I earned. What she may never understand is the contribution that experience has had on my life, personally and professionally.

I suspect that scores of students could tell stories similar to mine, some grander, probably. So when scholars gather to give homage to the movers and shakers of our era, when all our lives have also become alternative collections of experiences and decisions to be evaluated by some future introspective student of history, when the volumes documenting Dr. Scott's contributions to history are counted, I can only hope that the record devoted to her dedication to maturing this particular genre of historical study pales in comparison with the pages capturing the stories of her impact on the lives of the many students she has touched. While compiling such an archive would be a futile endeavor, let us hope that someone undertakes it nonetheless.

Anne Firor Scott is a woman regal in all her ways, a scholar and teacher nonpareil who, through those stories, has imprinted all of history.

Introduction

—JACQUELYN DOWD HALL

This book is a tribute to a scholar who has changed the way we see the past. Since 1970, when her first book, *The Southern Lady: From Pedestal to Politics, 1830–1930*, launched the modern study of southern women's history, Anne Firor Scott has pursued a stirring project: making the invisible visible, teaching us to hear the unheard.[1] In so doing, she has driven home the simple yet transformative point that we can never understand the history of the American South while ignoring half of its people. Likewise, Scott and the younger scholars who followed her have reversed what we used to call the "New Englandization" of women's history: the tendency to generalize from the experience of white, middle-class women in the Northeast. In place of that partial history, we now have an efflorescence of scholarship on women throughout the country and on women whose lives were shaped as much by class and race as by gender.

"Contingency is everything," Anne Scott likes to say, crediting timing and luck for her wonderful career (though I think she would admit that pluck figured as well). She was born on April 24, 1921, right after women won the vote. She grew up in Athens, Georgia, and graduated summa cum laude from the University of Georgia in 1941, just in time to walk through the doors that opened to women during World War II. Two events in particular propelled her on her way. First, she landed a job with the National League of Women Voters. That post taught her what organized women could do. It also introduced her to a group of surviving suffragists who exemplified the progressive female reform tradition she would bring to visibility in her first book. The second providential encounter was a date with Andrew (Andy) MacKay Scott, a brash young man, a navy pilot during World War II, who issued an invitation on the spot. "Come marry me and go to Harvard," he said, to which she responded, "You can't be serious."

Jacquelyn Dowd Hall, Julia Cherry Spruill Professor of History, directs the Southern Oral History Program at the University of North Carolina, Chapel Hill.

His return volley was "I've never been more serious about anything in my life." Twenty-three years later, Anne dedicated *The Southern Lady* to him. "*Sene te nihil*," she wrote, although, of course, when she had to go on without him after his death in 2005, she did, with courage and grace.[2]

While Andy pursued a Ph.D. at Harvard, Anne studied under the famous Oscar Handlin at Radcliffe College. "Sink or swim" summed up Handlin's approach to mentoring. But he paid serious attention to her, and "that attention was of the utmost importance." Too proud to sink, Anne swam.[3] By the time she finished her course work, her husband was ready to pursue his career. Following him from place to place, she had three children over the next eight years. She also found time by 1958 to complete her dissertation, "Southern Progressives in the National Congress, 1906–1916." The Scotts settled in Chapel Hill when Andy began teaching in the political science department at the University of North Carolina. After a short stint in the UNC history department, where she began researching southern women in earnest, Anne answered a call from Duke to fill a vacant position until a suitable candidate could be found.[4] That suitable candidate apparently never materialized, and Anne Scott eventually became the W. K. Boyd Professor of History and the first woman to chair the Duke history department.

In her dissertation on southern Progressives, Scott kept "stumbling over women," but she lacked the confidence or the framework to include them in the story.[5] First in an article published in 1962 and then in *The Southern Lady*, she brought those women from the margins to the center of Progressivism in the South and placed them in a narrative that swept from the antebellum period to the eve of the Great Depression. More books and gemlike essays followed, establishing Anne Scott as southern women's history's preeminent scholar.[6]

When Scott and I coauthored a historiographic essay on southern women in 1987, we were amazed at how thoroughly the men who controlled southern history had ignored women before *The Southern Lady* appeared and my generation of feminist graduate students burst through the university's previously closed doors.[7] And we wrote at length about how much the historical landscape had changed. What we did not emphasize enough was the degree to which *The Southern Lady* served as the starting point for a series of debates that defined much of the new work in the field. Did the ideal of the southern lady provide a blueprint for white women's lives? Were plantation mistresses secret abolitionists or the bulwarks of slavery? Did the Civil War shore up the patriarchy or open the way to white women's emancipation? What impact did women's voluntary organizations have on southern Progressivism and the emergence of the welfare state?[8]

Since 1987, scholars have raised a host of new questions and brought a legion of new figures onto the historical stage. Yet, as Laura Edwards points out in her essay in this book, even those who write about people and topics quite distant from Anne Scott's preoccupations often do so in her spirit. Like Anne Scott's *The Southern Lady*, these new works are filled with "imposing women of historical consequence, who left their imprint on the South and whose legacy demands our attention."[9]

Anne Scott did more than set a new field of knowledge in motion. She also helped to open the doors of the historical profession to women such as the contributors to this book. She has, moreover, set an example for us all by writing with unusual honesty and modesty about how she discovered and overcame her own blind spots—such as, for example, when she used her presidential address to the Southern Historical Association to draw attention to the black women's voluntary organizations she had not noticed in her early work.[10]

Scott retired in 1991, although retirement hardly seems the right word for years filled with teaching, mentoring, and writing and crowned with honors and awards.[11] She was eighty-seven when we gathered in Oxford for the thirty-second annual Porter L. Fortune Jr. History Symposium in March 2008, and to the surprise of no one, we found her to be as curious, as indefatigable, and as devoted to learning and teaching as she has always been. I think I can speak for all of us when I say that we are indebted to her work, grateful for her mentorship, and humbled by her unflagging energy, her bracing engagement with the world.

Notes

1. Anne Firor Scott, *The Southern Lady: From Pedestal to Politics, 1830–1930* (Chicago: University of Chicago Press, 1970).

2. "History Doyens: Anne Firor Scott," History News Network, October 8, 2006, http://hnn.us/roundup/entries/30623.html (accessed October 23, 2008). For more on Scott's life, see Anne Firor Scott, "A Historian's Odyssey," in *Making the Invisible Woman Visible* (Urbana: University of Illinois Press, 1984), xi–xxvii; Nancy Weiss Malkiel, "Invincible Woman: Anne Firor Scott," in *Visible Women: New Essays on American Activism*, ed. Nancy A. Hewitt and Suzanne Lebsock (Urbana: University of Illinois Press, 1993), 383–92; Anastatia Sims, "Anne Firor Scott: Writing Women

into Southern History," in *Reading Southern History: Essays on Interpreters and Interpretations*, ed. Glenn Feldman (Tuscaloosa: University of Alabama Press, 2001), 233–46; and Anne Firor Scott, "Chance or Choice?" in *Shapers of Southern History: Autobiographical Reflections*, ed. John Boles (Athens: University of Georgia Press, 2004), 40–61.

    3. "History Doyens."

    4. Scott, "Historian's Odyssey," xx.

    5. Ibid., xviii.

    6. Other works authored or edited by Scott include (with Andrew M. Scott) *One-Half the People* (Philadelphia: Lippincott, 1975); *Making the Invisible Woman Visible* (Urbana: University of Illinois Press, 1984); *Natural Allies: Women's Associations in American History* (Urbana: University of Illinois Press, 1991); *Unheard Voices: The First Historians of Southern Women* (Charlottesville: University of Virginia Press, 1993); and most recently *Pauli Murray and Caroline Ware: Forty Years of Letters in Black and White* (Chapel Hill: University of North Carolina Press, 2006).

    7. Jacquelyn Dowd Hall and Anne Firor Scott, "Women in the South," in *Interpreting Southern History: Historiographical Essays in Honor of Sanford W. Higginbotham*, ed. John B. Boles and Evelyn T. Nolen (Baton Rouge: Louisiana State University Press, 1987), 454–509.

    8. For these debates, see Sims, "Anne Firor Scott," 238–45. ANCE\d4

    9. Laura F. Edwards, "Down from the Pedestal: The Influence of Anne Scott's *Southern Ladies*," (this volume), 30.

    10. Anne Firor Scott, "Most Invisible of All: Black Women's Voluntary Associations," *Journal of Southern History* 56, no. 1 (February 1990): 3–22.

    11. Among these was the Distinguished Service Award of the Organization of American Historians, which Scott received in 2002.

Writing Women's History

Equally Their Due

Women's Education and Public Life in Postrevolutionary and Antebellum America

—MARY KELLEY

Practically every page of this essay bears the imprint of Anne Firor Scott. Scott's "The Ever Widening Circle: The Diffusion of Feminist Values from the Troy Female Seminary, 1822–1872" introduced historians to one of the first schools to offer women an education equal to that offered by the male colleges. Scott invited us to explore with her the social and cultural implications of this unprecedented emphasis on women's intellectual capacities. In "What, Then, Is the American: This New Woman?," the pathbreaking article she published in the Journal of American History *in 1978, Scott identified the female counterpart to Hector St. John de Crèvecoeur's "new man." Emma Willard, founder of the Troy Female Seminary, built institutions and female networks that were decisive in the rapid expansion of women's higher education in the decades before the Civil War. Equally important, Scott's* Natural Allies: Women's Associations in American History *alerted historians to the powerful role played by voluntary associations in shaping both women's subjectivities and American public life. Like so many scholars of American women's history, I have drawn on all this scholarship and in the process have incurred a lasting debt.*

❖ ❖ ❖

Standing before students and teachers at Litchfield Female Academy in the fall of 1818, Sarah Pierce called on the women who were attending the school she headed to "vindicate the equality of female intellect." Four years earlier, Pierce had introduced a curriculum that provided the tools with which her students might achieve that vindication. Grounded in the subjects then being taught at the male colleges, Litchfield's course of study focused on mathematics, moral philosophy, logic, the natural sciences, and Latin. Assigned the same texts as students at the colleges, young women were expected to master William Paley's *Principles of Moral and Political Philosophy*, Hugh Blair's *Lectures on Rhetoric*, and Archibald Alison's *Essays on the Nature and Principles of Taste*. Pierce's curriculum was gendered in one telling respect. Inaugurating a tradition that teachers and students subsequently practiced at many female academies and seminaries, the woman who identified with British luminaries such as Hannah More, Maria Edgeworth, and Hester Chapone invited her students to read books by and about learned women. Women for whom the exercise of intellect was a daily practice, the Mores, the Edgeworths, and the Chapones became the students' exemplars.[1]

With the exception of Oberlin College in 1833, America's colleges and universities began to admit women only after the middle of the nineteenth century. The earliest women's colleges, Vassar, Wellesley, and Smith, opened their doors in 1865, 1873, and 1875, respectively. Mount Holyoke College, which had been founded in 1837, continued to call itself a seminary until 1888. For nearly two centuries after the founding of Harvard College, then, female academies and seminaries were the only institutions that welcomed women into the world of higher learning. In a letter to her cousin in 1819, Maria Campbell of Virginia spoke to the difference the presence of these schools made in women's lives. "In the days of our forefathers," she told Mary Humes, who was attending the acclaimed Salem Academy in North Carolina, "it was considered only necessary to learn a female to read the Bible." Times were changing. Those who claimed that women had the same intellectual potential as men were gaining ascendancy. They were institutionalizing the claim's obvious corollary: female educational opportunities ought to reflect that equality. Now receiving what was "equally their due," women who had been educated at female academies and seminaries were dedicating that knowledge to an instrumental end: the making of public opinion.[2]

Mary Humes, a student at Salem Academy in the second decade of the nineteenth century, was one of the thousands of women who attended a female academy or seminary in the decades between 1790 and 1840. Residents of both the North and the South, women came to these schools from cities and villages and from towns large and small. In their subsequent lives, some would earn their livelihood as teachers. Others would take their places in elite planter or wealthy merchant families. Still others would join their lives with those of ministers, shopkeepers, or farmers. What these socially, economically, and regionally diverse individuals shared was as significant as what distinguished them. They were female, they were white, and regardless of their standing in property or income, they were supplied with at least a modicum of social capital. Most notably, they were claiming for themselves the cultural capital that distinguished them from their predecessors who had been taught only to read the Bible.

Female academies and seminaries taught approximately the same number of students as did male colleges. Two of the larger female academies, both of which had national reputations, taught thousands of students. Between 1785 and 1858, 3,600 women attended an academy founded by the Moravians in Bethlehem, Pennsylvania. Families from seventeen states sent more than 3,600 of their daughters to Salem Academy between 1804 and 1856. In the four decades after Sarah Pierce founded the Litchfield Female Academy in 1792, she schooled nearly 2,000 women. Two of the nation's prominent seminaries enrolled still more students. More than 12,000 students attended Emma Willard's Troy Female Seminary in the fifty years after its founding in 1821. Mary Lyon's Mount Holyoke Seminary, which opened in 1837, had one of the most impressive records. In its first twelve years, 1,400 students enrolled; three decades later, that total reached 12,500, with many students hailing from regions outside New England.[3]

Female academies and seminaries that relied on local and regional constituencies also educated large numbers of students. One of the most successful regionally based academies, Catharine Fiske's school in Keene, New Hampshire, took in more than 3,000 New Englanders between its founding in 1814 and 1837. At least 4,000 southerners attended the South Carolina Female Collegiate Institute between 1830 and 1862. Many seminaries had enrollments that numbered in the hundreds yearly. In the spring of 1823, Catherine Beecher began teaching seven students in a single room above a harness shop in Hartford, Connecticut. Eight years later, in 1831, the year Beecher resigned as principal of Hartford Female Seminary and left for Cincinnati to found the Western Female Institute, the seminary counted 223 students. Hartford's enrollment that year was more than double the number of students attending Brown and the University of North Carolina, Chapel Hill, which had 101 and 107 students, respectively. Beecher's students also exceeded those at Princeton, which had 215 in 1834 and 216 a decade later. The Alabama Female Institute in Tuscaloosa followed a similar pattern, as did the Carolina Female College in Ansonville, North Carolina. Only three years after the Alabama Female Institute had opened its doors in 1833, 184 students were attending the school. The Carolina Female College taught between 100 and 200 students a year between its founding in 1849 and the Civil War, as did other southern schools such as Aberdeen Female College in Aberdeen, Mississippi; Wesleyan Female College in Macon, Georgia; and Huntsville Female College in Huntsville, Alabama. Northern institutions, including Bordentown Female College (New Jersey), Charlestown Female Seminary (Massachusetts), Georgetown Female Seminary (Washington, D.C.), Wesleyan Female College (Cincinnati, Ohio), and Rutgers Female Institute (New York), were also schooling between 100 and 200 women yearly between 1840 and 1860. During these decades, Brown, South Carolina, Princeton, and Amherst taught a similar number of students on a yearly basis.[4]

In educational practices ranging from classroom instruction to literary societies to reading protocols to emulation of intellectually accomplished women, students were schooled in a curriculum that matched that of the male colleges. The emphasis that teachers and principals at female academies and seminaries placed on "liberal culture," or the arts and sciences, as we call them today, reminds us that there was one important distinction between female and male institutions of higher learning. Latin and Greek stood at the center of the course of study at the colleges, at least for the initial two years of a student's career. Women began with the liberal arts that men engaged fully only in the third and fourth years. The education these students were being offered more closely resembled the curriculum we associate with the modernization of the college and university undertaken in the late nineteenth century. Only then did the arts and sciences take the place that had been held by Latin and Greek, both of which were made electives.

Between 1790 and 1830, the exclusively female schools that offered more than the reading, writing, and ciphering taught in the common schools almost always called themselves academies. Despite the diversity in the course of study at these schools, they shared basic patterns in curricular organization and scholastic requirements. Nearly all the academies established between 1790 and 1820 instructed students in reading, grammar, writing, history, arithmetic, and geography. Some also taught rhetoric. The transition to a more advanced course of study that paralleled the offerings of the colleges occurred in the 1820s. Academies began to teach the natural philosophy, chemistry, algebra, botany, astronomy, and Latin that Sarah Pierce had been requiring since 1814. Circulars and catalogs of already existing and newly founded academies scattered across the United States included these courses. At the Lafayette Female Academy in Lexington, Kentucky, students were taking all these subjects as early as 1821. Their counterparts at the First Female School in Portsmouth, New Hampshire, pursued a similar course of study, as did the students at Elizabeth Academy in Washington, Mississippi, at the Mount Vernon Female School in Boston, and at Albany Female Academy in Albany, New York. Additional offerings in logic were highlighted in the catalogs for the schools in Boston and Portsmouth. Moral philosophy was taught at Elizabeth Academy. Latin was taught at Mount Vernon, and Greek, Hebrew, and French were included as electives. In addition to the academies, Emma Willard's Troy Female Seminary, Catharine Beecher's Hartford Female Seminary, and Zilpah Grant's Ipswich Female Seminary in Derry, New Hampshire—all of which had explicitly been designed to instruct students in a course of study that equaled that of the colleges—opened their doors in 1821, 1823, and 1828, respectively.[5]

The connections that principals and teachers at these schools began to forge in the 1820s accelerated the development of local, regional, and national networks. A nationally uniform curriculum was perhaps the most visible result of these collaborations. The founding of still more schools and the replication of teaching strategies were equally important institutional outcomes. In terms of the subjectivity, or sense of self, that the students themselves were fashioning, principals and teachers who constituted these networks made decisive contributions. In classrooms across the nation, they privileged intellectual achievement, transmitted knowledge in the arts and sciences, and instilled perspectives that promoted engagement in civil society. The impact of Emma Willard is telling in this regard. A survey of 3,500 of the 12,000 students who attended Troy Female Seminary in the fifty years after Willard founded the school in 1821 has shown that approximately 40 percent of these students committed themselves to teaching. Nearly 150 of them either founded or administered a school. Together they established a network of schools modeled on the "Troy idea" in Ohio, Maryland, New York, Indiana, South Carolina, Georgia, and Alabama.[6]

By the 1830s, students could expect an education resembling the curricula pursued at institutions such as Mount Holyoke Seminary in South Hadley, Massachusetts, or South Carolina Female Collegiate Institute in Columbia, two of antebellum America's leading schools for women. In a letter written shortly after Mount Holyoke opened its doors in 1837, Harriet Hollister described the school's requirements. She and the other entering students took grammar, ancient geography, history, physiology, rhetoric, geometry, and botany. The next year, they were expected to continue grammar and botany and to take algebra and physics. During their final year, Hollister and her classmates concentrated on ecclesiastical history, chemistry, zoology, logic, and astronomy. In the moral philosophy course they took that year, they read Richard Whatley's *Elements of Rhetoric*, William Paley's *Natural Theology*, and Joseph Butler's *Analogy of Religion*. Students at the South Carolina Female Collegiate Institute were schooled in a similar fashion. In the first of their four years at the institute, pupils enrolled in algebra, ancient geography, botany, ancient history, mineralogy, and composition. In the second year they studied rhetoric, chemistry, modern geography, and U.S. government; in the third year they studied logic, astronomy, modern history, geology, and natural philosophy. The final year was devoted to belles lettres, mathematics, and moral philosophy. In the last of these courses, pupils read the same books by Paley and Butler as the students at Mount Holyoke Seminary. In common with many faculty at colleges, their teachers chose the equally popular *Lectures on Rhetoric and Belles Lettres* by Hugh Blair instead of Whatley's text. They required as well Lord Kames's *Elements of Criticism* and John Milton's *Paradise Lost*. Students at either the seminary or the institute would almost certainly have concurred with Susan Allen's description of Mount Holyoke Seminary. She had enrolled in a "Brain Factory," Allen told a friend shortly after her arrival in South Hadley.[7]

In according primacy to the cultivation of intellect, "Brain Factory" was a fitting label. However, Susan Allen told only part of the tale. Principals and teachers at these academies and seminaries took on a second and, in terms of women playing a visible role in civil society, equally important instructional task—teaching students how to negotiate between the ambitions generated by their education and the constraints inherent in conventional models of womanhood. No one performed this negotiation more skillfully than Julia Pierpont Marks. Educated at Emma Willard's Troy Female Seminary, Pierpont married Elias Marks, principal of the Female Collegiate Institute, in 1833. Tradition dictated that the male Marks remain the institute's official principal; nonetheless the women attending the school and their parents understood that "Mrs. Marks is the head," as one student described the individual who was the institute's governing force. The Marks whom students looked to as their leader was also the woman who cloaked the exercise of male authority in a womanly gentility that her daughter remembered as "hospitable, generous, dignified, what we call in the South, and mean much when we use the term, lady." In its emphasis on these familiar conventions, the tribute signaled the persistence of the role that elite women had performed in the eighteenth century. Expected to preside at tea tables, musical gatherings, salons, and dinner parties, antebellum southern women used these institutions of sociability for the same purpose as their predecessors, the making of public opinion. The principal of Mount Holyoke Seminary schooled students in similar conventions of ladyhood. "Sometimes Miss Lyon gives us a description of a beautiful young lady," Lucy Goodale wrote to her sister Mary in December 1841. Meticulous in observing conventions, Mary Lyon's lady "always has her hair combed neatly, she always looks cheerful and happy, she is always in the proper place at the proper time, and when she is at work she does it in the best way." Students attending to their teacher's lessons might well have noted Lyon's final injunction—that as learned women in the making, they had "work" before them. This work was not so much in the performance of sociability as in "the cause of benevolence," as Lyon told prospective students and their parents in a circular printed two years before Mount Holyoke opened its doors. Thousands of the school's graduates took this "new direction." Committed to exercising influence in civil society, these "daughters of fairest promise," as Lyon described her students, played a prominent role in organized benevolence and enlisted in the ranks of those calling for white women's rights and black people's emancipation. Mount Holyoke's graduates were also influential actors in the antebellum missionary movement, organizing and teaching in mission schools in Africa, India, and Persia.[8]

The women who attended academies and seminaries were schooled by teachers who placed an almost equal value on the reading students did informally as on the instruction they were offered in their classrooms. Those who had been introduced to the world of reading by their parents found that world expanded and their habits of reading reinforced during their years as students. Others were welcomed into the world of reading. Whatever their situation, these learned women-in-the-making were instructed by teachers who privileged books. Sixteen-year-old Caroline Chester, who kept a commonplace book during her tenure at Litchfield Female Academy, rehearsed the convictions that Sarah Pierce taught her students. Books, as she declared in 1816, were the means by which "we learn how to live."[9]

"We learn by example," New Hampton Female Seminary's Sarah Sleeper declared in the opening sentence of a memoir honoring Martha Hazeltine, the woman who had taught her at the seminary Sleeper headed in the 1830s. The testimonial was more than rhetorical. Many students at these schools shared in Sleeper's formative experience—interacting with and adopting as a personal ideal a teacher who had already made books the vehicle for pursuing knowledge. Sarah Porter, the founder of Miss Porter's School in Farmington, Connecticut, was one such teacher. A woman who mirrored the taste of the larger antebellum literary culture, Porter integrated reading into the rhythm of daily life, spending a morning with Euripides' *Alcestis*, turning a few days later to Hildreth's *History of the United States*, setting aside an hour here and there for Wordsworth's *Excursion*, and devoting an afternoon to *Novalis's Journal*. Porter, who looked to books as "fountains of knowledge," spent evenings reading to students, introducing them to James Hamilton, Harriet Beecher Stowe, and Susan Warner. She also stocked her school's library with recently published history, biography, and fiction. "Reading," as one MSR titled a composition she wrote while enrolled at the school, was an imperative for Sarah Porter. Already instructed by Porter in the tenet that nineteenth-century Americans had inherited from colonial readers of the popular eighteenth-century British periodical the *Tatler*, MSR opened her composition with a paraphrase from Richard Steele's Isaac Bickerstaff, "Reading is to the mind what exercise is to the body as it is strengthened and invigorated by it," as Bickerstaff had told readers nearly 150 years earlier. MSR was hardly alone in rifling the pages of the *Tatler*. Students at other academies and seminaries did the same. Recording maxims such as Steele's in journals, compositions, and debates of literary societies, they testified to the persistence of reading in polite letters. MSR and her counterparts had been taught the corollary maxim: reading was more than a matter of matching mental to physical fitness. Books, as Porter's student had learned, were endowed with the same foundational purpose as they had served in colonial America, "improving their morals or regulating their conduct."[10]

In giving books to reward accomplishment, in sharing personal libraries, in sponsoring literary societies, and in using reading to strengthen bonds with students, the Sarah Porters of female schooling engaged in a host of practices that defined reading as a *woman's* enterprise. Like other teachers in postrevolutionary America, Jane Barnham Marks rewarded excellence with tokens of achievement. Some instructors presented students with elaborately inscribed certificates. Others gave them autograph albums. Marks, a teacher at the South Carolina Female Collegiate Institute during the 1820s, chose Priscilla Wakefield's aptly titled *Mental Improvement* as a gift for one of her students. On the flyleaf of Harriet Hayne's copy, an inscription dated June 4, 1821, tells us that Hayne had achieved the highest status in Third Class in Geography. Years later Harriet Hayne, following Marks's precedent, presented the volume to her sister Sarah, who carefully inscribed her name on the title page.[11]

In concert with their teachers, students embraced books, literally and figuratively. Selecting them as companions on voyages of discovery, they relished the play of ideas, delighted in unexpected insights, and pondered the implications of newly found knowledge. Perhaps most notably, they made books into sites for meditations on, and experiments with, the individual subjectivities they were fashioning. These readers explored ideas and personae, sampling perspectives and measuring relevance for their lives. Then, still using books as a primary resource, they set about making and remaking subjectivities. Julia Hyde and Lucy Goodale, both of whom entered Mount Holyoke Seminary on the day Mary Lyon opened the doors in 1837, forged an enduring bond at the intersection of female friendship and female learning. It was the learning that Hyde made the subject of a letter she sent to Goodale during the summer of 1839. She encouraged Goodale to "cultivate independence of character." In addition to instruction in the classroom, reading books and considering their merits were the vehicles Hyde chose. "Take some book," she told her friend, "and read it and form your own opinion as to its character, its influence, its beauties, and its faults." Then, she added, "You can find out what others think and compare your decision with theirs. You can do this in your studies too." Women like Hyde and Goodale were improvising, bringing their critical faculties to bear on a text and then interpreting their findings in collaboration with others.[12]

Students practiced the reading and writing that Hyde advocated in compositions they prepared for recitations, in essays they delivered at commencements, and in prose and poetry they published in newspapers and magazines sponsored by current students and alumnae. In all these enterprises, students were supported by the schools' literary societies. These organizations acted as schools within schools, providing their members with an informally constituted course of study, a fully stocked library, and a host of oral and scribal opportunities for engaging the debates taking place in civil society. While interrogating the texts they read and those they wrote themselves, students cultivated habits of reading and critical thought, writing and cultural production. Their oral and scribal performances of learning also instilled self-confidence. Simultaneously, students at female academies and seminaries undertook a related and equally relevant project, experimenting with subjectivities that were informed by the advanced education they were pursuing. For some of the members, the books read and the essays written in response sanctioned subjectivities they had already begun fashioning for themselves. For others, reading and writing together were catalysts as they changed course and set themselves to crafting alternative selves.

Literary societies were designed, as were the schools housing them, "to promote female education." Most academies and seminaries housed one circle, although students at South Carolina's Limestone Springs Female High School could choose between the Hemans and Sigourney Societies, each of which had been named in honor of women writers whom the students had claimed as models. Students at Greensboro Female College selected either the Sigourney or the Philomathusian Society. Other schools boasted Adelphean, Crystal, Philomathean, Belles Lettres, Euphrasian, and Iris Societies. Whatever name students elected, they held meetings "for improvement in Composition and Criticism," as the literary society at Wesleyan Female College in Wilmington, Delaware, announced. In focusing on composition and criticism, members of these literary societies had a tripartite objective: learning to read critically, to write lucidly, and to speak persuasively, all of which contributed to the development of their reasoning and rhetorical faculties. The records of the literary societies at female academies and seminaries indicate that these organizations competed for members. In schools where only one society existed, membership was generally open to all students. No matter the number of societies, membership was considered a privilege. Most literary societies were initiated by students, although teachers occasionally took the lead.

In 1839, shortly after her arrival at the Female Collegiate Institute of Buckingham County, Virginia, Mary Virginia Early told her mother that one of her teachers had asked a few students to join her in establishing a Young Ladies' Lyceum. Teacher and students divided the labor. Mrs. W. "framed the Constitution, and Laws"; the students chose a "President, two Vice Presidents, and a Secretary." Appointing "two of the members to write on a subject, one taking the affirmative, the other the negative, and six for disputants," Mrs. W. also determined the structure of the meetings. The forms thus established, students were left to discuss the reading and writing in which they were engaged. Early herself had been asked to present a "Moral Essay" at the lyceum's first meeting.[13] Students at Ipswich Female Seminary in the early 1830s established their literary society and set its rules. All members were expected to select an article from one of the periodicals in the society's library and prepare a commentary, which was to be delivered at a meeting. In explaining why the presentations were required, Maria Cowles spoke to the importance these women attached to the command of reason and rhetoric. Members, she said, would "learn the use of language, learn to arrange facts systematically and acquire confidence in speaking before such a company." In the process, students at Ipswich had begun to be more assertive, and, as Cowles told her brother Henry and his wife, they had also begun to "feel more interest in promoting the grand object of doing good." Cowles mapped the sites at which members of the literary society had moved beyond interest to intervention. All had already been interested in "the cause of benevolence," as she told them. With the missionary movement only beginning to take hold in the early 1830s, they had selected the obvious alternative—teaching as a means by which to proselytize the West. Three were already at their posts in Chillicothe, Ohio, one in Marietta, Ohio. Several others were bound for Edwardsville, Illinois.[14]

In a composition titled "Advantages of Education," Laura Cone, a student at Miss Porter's School, enumerated the faculties that students cultivated at female academies and seminaries. Memory, said Cone, was "to be strengthened by taxing it with new truths each day." Reason and judgment were to be "unfolded," imagination was to be "expanded," and taste was to be "formed." All of this was to be committed to education's ultimate objective, the "cultivation of the intellect." Nowhere was this commitment more strikingly visible than in a document titled "Communication" penned by the senior class of 1829 and presented to teachers and students at Ipswich Female Seminary. As they prepared for graduation, these students dedicated themselves to the pursuit of ideals that the seminary, headed by Zilpah Grant, had taught them: to "constantly aim at discipline of mind, making it an object to express their ideas with clearness and force." Promising to continue in the path marked for them, they dedicated themselves to examining "subjects for themselves, nor do they mean to admit the assertions of any author, unless convinced by fair argument, or by their own reflection." Not least, they would take special care to "cultivate the judgment as well as the memory." "Advantages of Education" and "Communication" mirrored the mental and moral philosophy articulated by Sarah Porter and Zilpah Grant, who themselves had taken their lessons from William Paley and Francis Wayland. Claiming the precepts that informed Paley's *Principles of Moral and Political Philosophy*, students at both schools placed a special emphasis on developing the reasoning and rhetorical faculties. Those at Miss Porter's had also been exposed to the teachings of Wayland, whose *Elements of Moral Science* had been published in 1835. Cone's enumeration called attention to the signal lesson Wayland taught, interrogating the self through rational reflection, or "self-examination." This continual application of reason and reflection enhanced all the faculties cited in "Advantages of Education" and "Communication." Perhaps most important, the daily interrogation of the self produced the independence of thought that the senior class at Ipswich made the ultimate objective of their education.[15]

In the letters of students who had already graduated from a female academy or seminary, one glimpses the lasting influence of the mental cultivation and pursuit of knowledge embodied in the subjects taught at these schools. Virginia Terrell bracketed her experience as a student, telling a former teacher that, in comparing life before and since, the years she had spent at an academy in Lexington, Virginia, had been "by far the happiest." Terrell did more than pay rhetorical tribute: she honored those years in the continued pursuit of knowledge. Most recently, as she told her teacher, Terrell had completed *Paradise Lost* and "found (as you once told me) that I had need of all my learning to understand some parts of it; there are others that are truly sublime." She was now immersed in the *Iliad*, with which she was "much delighted." In the three or four histories she had read recently, she had made good use of the French she had mastered as a student. The tributes of Terrell and the senior class accorded prominence to the ideals that teachers had instilled. The "Communication" written by Ipswich's students was the promissory note they issued at their graduation. Terrell's letter, written years after her graduation, was a report of her progress in meeting that note.[16]

The parents of students at female academies and seminaries left traces that reflected a deep investment in the schooling of their daughters. Various bills and receipts tucked away in collections of letters marked the material costs of education. Letters measured less tangible but equally significant costs. In a letter after her daughter had spent three years at the aptly named Daughters College in Harrodsburg, Kentucky, Josephine Downing Price underscored the value that parents ascribed to a daughter's education. Writing in January 1860, Price acknowledged that the separation from Isabella had been a difficult trial. Nonetheless, to complete the college's four-year course of study, she told her daughter, "I must let you stay one year longer." In making her decision, Price had calculated the lasting impact of the schooling at Daughters College: "A good education is so desirable as something you will always possess." Whatever her life experience and however she deployed her education, Price understood that Isabella would be taught to discipline her mind and to employ her critical faculties. That alone would bring a singular treasure—intellectual independence.[17]

In reminding daughters that these years were perhaps the most decisive of their lives, mothers and fathers registered the importance they attributed to an education at an academy or seminary. After sending his daughter to Mrs. Edwards's Seminary in Leesburg, Virginia, in 1845, Lloyd Noland counseled Ella "not to neglect one moment from your studies—this is the most important time of your life—your character hereafter may now be about to take its *cast*." Four years later, with Ella's education almost completed, Elizabeth Noland was equally emphatic: "Let nothing draw your mind off from your studies," she declared. In the second of her two years at North Carolina's Salem Academy, Mary Laura Springs received a parental injunction "to exercise your usual application and industry in pursuing your studies and be able at the examination to do yourself honor." Two years later, in 1831, the school had changed, but the admonitions had not. Now a student at Mrs. Sazarin's Academy in Philadelphia, Springs was still expected to concentrate on "the improvement of your mind and manners."[18]

The intellectual ends to which daughters were expected to commit themselves were the same at southern and northern schools, as were the courses of study and the pedagogies that principals and teachers practiced. Caroline Thayer, the head of Mississippi's Elizabeth Female Academy, which had been founded in 1818, spoke for her counterparts throughout the South. In her report to the academy's trustees in 1825, she claimed that women were now "permitted to aspire to the dignity of intellectual beings." And, as she proudly noted, that permission had been acknowledged by a learned gentleman whose address had concluded the school's public examinations. "The whole map of knowledge is spread before the female scholar," he had told the trustees, parents, teachers, and students. However, the social ends that mothers and fathers anticipated had a regional inflection. In preparing children to take their places among the planter elite, parents like the Springses wanted their daughters schooled in the conventions of ladyhood practiced by their predecessors. In the heterosocial gatherings of tea table and dinner party at which they presided, southern women were expected to display their command of social intercourse and cultural sensibility. There, as in the seasonal balls and assemblies, they were responsible for installing a lively sociability. Of course, and perhaps most notably, at all these sites southern women took for themselves a role in the making of public opinion.[19]

The different expectations that one F. R. Bentley brought to the education of his daughter also had a regional inflection. Shortly after Sophia Bentley enrolled at Lima Institute in New York in 1858, this northern father began a series of letters in which he counseled his daughter about the task before her. Sophia, who had the privilege of an advanced education, ought to make herself "decided, independent, and self-reliant." Of course, she should always "show a proper respect for the opinions of others." However, the protocols of social deportment mattered less than disciplining one's mind and sharpening one's analytical skills. Most certainly, Sophia should "not allow mere accidents and trivialities to become paramount objects of attention." Concluding with the principle that had informed all his counsel, F. R. Bentley declared: "Think for yourself, and have an opinion and a purpose of your own."[20]

Mary Lyon might well have applauded Bentley. The work in organized benevolence and social reform to which she committed her students not only required that they think for themselves but also that they respect the opinions of those who might disagree with them. The self-reliance that principals and teachers like Lyon instilled played an influential role in the lives of their students. Indeed, self-reliance and its expression in independent thought were perhaps the most important lessons they taught to women who grounded their subjectivities in associational life. These regional distinctions were more matters of emphasis than opposing dictates, however. Teachers like Julia Pierpont Marks fully expected that southern women would engage in organized benevolence. Conversely, Lyon anticipated that women who attended schools like Mount Holyoke would act as "ladies, " no matter how radical the cause to which they committed themselves. And most parents South and North expected a student at an academy or seminary to combine a rigorous academic program with some training in social skills. A daughter, if she had been properly instructed, would embody a "happy union of female gentleness and delicacy, with masculine learning and genius," as William Wirt told his wife Elizabeth in 1810.[21]

Mothers and fathers displayed an equally strong commitment to the education of their daughters. Simultaneously, however, that commitment was inflected by gender. Mothers in the postrevolutionary decades looked on daughters as surrogates, investing their own aspirations in a generation that could claim the educational opportunities available at the newly established female academies. Antebellum mothers who themselves had benefited from schooling at one of the academies or seminaries anticipated that their daughters could become their intellectual companions.

Whether postrevolutionary or antebellum, nearly all these women registered the absence of daughters with a singular intensity. This sentiment, which is tangible in so many of their letters, was countered by the conviction that a daughter's education was well worth a mother's sacrifice.

Written in June 1823, Margaret Barr Brashear's letter to two of her daughters illustrates a typical resolution of these conflicting impulses. Telling Rebecca and Caroline, both of whom were enrolled in a school in Lexington, Kentucky, that they should immerse themselves in their studies, she reminded them that if they neglected "the means, and opportunities now offered for improvement, the time will arrive when you will lament and regret it." That their mother lamented and regretted the separation was apparent in Brashear's stark acknowledgment: "I suffer in the loss of [your] society." Still she assured them that the privations she experienced in their absence were less important than Rebecca's and Caroline's education. Other mothers made the same reckoning. In a letter dated June 13, 1833, that Sarah Clifton Wheeler marked "My Dear Mother's last letter," Sarah Wheeler told her daughter, then a student at a school in Wilmington, Delaware, that their separation was a daily trial. Wheeler took her solace from the same source as Brashears, her daughter's "advancement in y[ou]r studies." Williana Wilkinson Lacy acknowledged her desire "to have you at home on many accounts," as she said to her daughter, Bessie. But that weighed less in the balance than this mother's determination "to have a daughter well educated."[22]

In a circular tucked away in the 1839 annual report of Philadelphia's Literary and Missionary Association, Sarah Sleeper, who had celebrated Martha Hazeltine, called students and graduates at New Hampton Female Seminary to envision all that might be accomplished by women who claimed the mantle of learning. In addressing the seminary's alumnae, she expanded the school's social network beyond those currently enrolled. The vehicle that Sleeper chose was New Hampton's newly constituted literary society. She set forth two objectives, one of which was shared by virtually every literary society at a female academy or seminary. The Association of the New-Hampton Female Seminary for the Promotion of Literature and Missions had been established to benefit the members' intellectual and moral faculties, she told the alumnae. The cultivation of an individual's faculties was surely necessary, but it was only a prelude. Sleeper set for all the students a much larger objective—"the elevation of our sex universally." By improving on the knowledge they commanded, the interpretive skills they mastered, and the speaking and publishing they engaged in, women might well "secure, as ornaments of the coming age, a Joanna Bailey, a Sherwood and Edgeworth, a Sigourney and Hemans, a Hannah More and a Jane Taylor." With these predecessors as models, and with their contemporaries as companions in aspiration, Sleeper expected members of literary societies to dedicate themselves to more than personal enrichment. Calling on them to commit themselves to the transformation of the United States, she declared: "Were the ladies of our country to make appropriate efforts, the whole nation might be elevated in its physical and intellectual abilities, and its moral powers developed to an expansion and energy that would produce a more glorious revolution, than that which gave it existence." The confidence with which Sleeper rallied women to mount a second and still more radical American Revolution is striking. And she did not stop there. Sleeper asked them to commit as well to "laboring for the heathen," either as wives of missionaries or as missionaries themselves. In converting "our sex in pagan lands" to the tenets of evangelical Protestantism, they would establish a global network. And, as Sleeper confidently predicted, armed with the largest social network possible, they would mount the same revolution throughout the world.[23]

Many literary societies used the same strategy as Sarah Sleeper—building influence and connecting communities by increasing the numbers of women in their social networks. The roster of "acting members" published annually by the reading circle of the Townsend Female Seminary in West Townsend, Massachusetts, listed graduates who were making their way in the world as missionaries in India and Thailand and as teachers in Massachusetts, Pennsylvania, Vermont, Iowa, Connecticut, Virginia, Maryland, Alabama, Ohio, and Mississippi. Students at the female seminaries in New Hampton, New Hampshire, and Charlestown, Massachusetts, organized similar networks that linked current students with hundreds of women who had gone before them. The annual reports issued by all three of these literary societies illustrate the making of a national network. Although the majority of women who attended these seminaries continued to reside in New England, a significant number of those who counted themselves as members of these social networks had migrated beyond its borders—to Ohio, Virginia, New York, Indiana, North Carolina, Pennsylvania, Georgia, New Jersey, Illinois, Wisconsin, and Michigan. Like the letters that students exchanged after they had completed their schooling, the reports, which interleaved descriptions of students' enterprises with excerpts from graduates' letters, brought students and graduates together in ever-widening networks of shared resources and strategies.[24]

In reminding alumnae of the relationships they had forged at the intersection of female learning and female friendship, the reports secured and strengthened the social networks through the affective bonds of intimacy. As one woman who had attended Charlestown Female Seminary observed, graduates welcomed "the coming of the 'Report,' as I would that of a dear friend—for not only do I look on that as a friend in itself but as bringing tidings of a host of other friends." In electing honorary members, Townsend Female Seminary's literary society extended its membership beyond the school's graduates. Other societies invited influential makers of public opinion into their social networks. The Sigourney Club was the most notable in this regard, taking the name of one of antebellum America's most famous authors. Initially they offered honorary membership only to Lydia Sigourney, as did the students who established a literary society at Female College in Greensboro, North Carolina. Members of the Sigourney Club were still more ambitious, according the same privilege to three successive governors of South Carolina.[25]

The annual reports issued by the literary societies at Townsend, Charleston, and New Hampton seminaries read as if they were the records of a voluntary association dedicated to benevolence. The same militantly evangelical Protestantism is everywhere in evidence, as are the strategies that informed organized benevolence. Charleston's circle registered their affiliation in the titles they chose for their officers. Instead of the typical president and vice president, they listed their officers as first and second and directresses, the titles commonly employed for officers of benevolent societies. In committing themselves to the "promotion of literature and missions," students at New Hampton's seminary combined the collective pursuit of knowledge with the increasingly powerful missionary movement. Their commitment to evangelizing the West was manifest in the subjects they addressed: "The Cause of Missions" and "The Dignity of the Missionary Enterprise," as they titled their conversations. Those at Charlestown welcomed the quarterly report of one Reverend Herrick, a colporteur who relied on their donations to support his yearly visits to a thousand families in the West. Members of both societies read about the most recent successes in evangelism in reports such as "The Latest Missionary Intelligence." Whatever the specific topic they addressed, students embraced a religiously inflected nationalism that obligated Americans to bring the entire world into the evangelical fold. When they graduated from these schools and took their places in civil society, students had already identified America's republic as God's nation. It comes as no surprise that many of them attached the adjective "Christian" to the rights and obligations of American citizenship. "Christian" was actually a misnomer, as members of Charlestown's circle demonstrated. Setting aside an entire meeting in October 1846, they asked themselves, "Is it probable that enlightened America will ever submit to the servile yoke of Rome?" Certainly not, at least if any of those who went west had any say in the matter.[26]

The zeal displayed by these New Englanders was not an exclusively regional phenomenon, as some historians have presumed. As Bessie Lacy reported to her brother Horace, the students at Edgeworth Female Seminary in Greensboro, North Carolina, were also bent on conversion. Their objective was global, their means a student-initiated missionary society, which contributed thirty dollars to a missionary from India who visited the school in the late 1840s. "We are ladies of great business here," she declared with no little pride. The "business," as she called the task that reflected the increasing importance of the international dimension of the missionary movement, touched Lacy personally. Meeting the missionary and helping to fund the cause had filled her with the desire to "go to India and teach the poor heathen of Jesus Christ."[27]

Evangelically oriented literary societies displayed an equal concern with a host of secular issues that constituted the discourse of postrevolutionary and antebellum civil society. In their debates, the sectionalism that would culminate in the Civil War became more pronounced as the social and economic interests of northerners and southerners diverged. The surviving records of two of these literary societies, the Sigourney Club in South Carolina and the Social Circle in Charleston, Massachusetts, are a window through which we can glimpse the members' engagement in a common national discourse and an increasingly heated sectional debate. Both of these societies were committed to a familiar mandate, "the pursuit of intellectual and moral excellence," as the members of Charlestown's circle announced. The high school's club met weekly, the seminary's circle biweekly. The members of the Sigourney Club who presented essays and the "critics," as the club's constitution dubbed them, who interrogated the presentations opened the conversation at the society's weekly meetings. Biweekly meetings of the Social Circle followed the same agenda.[28]

Members of the club and the circle displayed no hesitation in confronting the most explosive issues with which Americans grappled in the decades between the American Revolution and the Civil War. The tensions that had begun to fracture the nation ideologically by the late 1840s were readily apparent in debates that focused on two of the most divisive issues confronting antebellum Americans —the national economy and race. In 1848 the Sigourney Club debated whether "the pursuit of agriculture is more conducive to moral and intellectual improvement than that of manufacture." For daughters of middling and elite planters who depended on the land and the labor of slaves, the matter required little debate. Agriculture surely had more merit. Not only was cultivating the land superior to capitalism as a mode of production, but its practice instilled the republican virtue that postrevolutionary Americans had made the foundation for the nation. In contrast to the supposed degeneracy spawned by northern capitalism, the pursuit of agriculture, white southerners claimed, produced the publicly spirited yeoman farmer who had taken his place in the pantheon of American heroes. As residents of a state at the leading edge of capitalist transformation, members of the circle would have disagreed. Like other residents of Massachusetts, they would likely have ranked manufacture at least equal to agriculture. They would also have claimed a second hero whom northerners had recently installed in the national pantheon—the white male who freely contracted his labor in exchange for wages. Able to fulfill his desire for economic independence and social advancement, he was also presented as the key contributor to the nation's growth.[29]

Members of both societies spoke directly to the subject of race. More than a decade after the Cherokee Removal had driven Indians from their land and opened millions of acres to the slave labor system, members of the Sigourney Club asked themselves if "white men were justified in taking possession of this country and driving the Indians from North America." We do not know what they decided in 1849. Perhaps they allied themselves with those southerners who had opposed removal, perhaps not. We can be more certain about the position taken by members of Charlestown's circle. In March 1847, they posed the same question—with a different inflection and a telling addition: "Which has the white man most injured, the Indian or African?" In both the inflection and the addition of African Americans, these students marked themselves as New Englanders.[30]

In a letter in which Lucy Stone recalled that she and Antoinette Brown Blackwell had "learned to stand and speak" as members of literary societies, she herself was speaking from the perspective of more than five decades of activism on behalf of women's rights. Stone, one of the movement's most influential leaders and a graduate of Mount Holyoke Seminary, understood the transformative potential of these societies and the schools that housed them. In cultivating reasoning and rhetorical faculties, modeling persuasive self-presentation, and disciplining the mind, literary societies reinforced the formal instruction provided in the classrooms of female academies and seminaries. We can be certain that Antoinette Brown Blackwell agreed with her friend. In an exchange of letters some forty years earlier, she told Stone about the impact of one such society. In the winter of 1847, the fifty members, including Brown, had organized themselves in typical fashion. In a weekly rotation, six submitted compositions for all to read and then led the debate at the meeting. "All take a deep interest in the exercises," Brown declared. Brown herself had "never before improved so rapidly in my life in the use of the tongue."[31]

Liberal learning and the aspirations that learning stimulated played a key role in the unprecedented entry of women into the nation's public life. That approximately the same number of women and men were enrolled in institutions of higher learning is striking in its own right. It also provides the key to understanding why many women educated at these academies and seminaries pressed the boundaries that limited a woman's engagement with the world beyond her household. Claiming membership in postrevolutionary and antebellum civil society, women educated at these schools entered public life as writers, educators, editors, and reformers. As its title indicates, *Notable American Women* recovers women "notable" in terms of social, intellectual, political, and cultural leadership. The three volumes of biographical entries show that the large majority of the leaders of postrevolutionary and antebellum America's organized benevolence and social reform attended a female academy or seminary. The same can be said for the educational reformers who not only attended women's schools but also became founders and teachers. The correlation between being educated at a female academy or seminary and becoming a member of the nation's community of letters is at least as strong for the writers and editors who came to maturity between 1790 and 1840. The combined privileges of skin color, social standing, and advanced education provided these women with an unparalleled opportunity to set the terms of women's engagement with public life. In elaborating and projecting an increasingly expansive role as makers of public opinion, they did exactly that.[32]

Notes

1. Sarah Pierce, "Address at the Close of School, October 29, 1818," in *Chronicles of a Pioneer School from 1792–1833, Being the History of Miss Sarah Pierce and Her Litchfield School*, ed. Elizabeth C. Barney Buel, comp. Emily Noyes Vanderpoel

(Cambridge, Mass., 1903), 177; Schools and Academies Collection, American Antiquarian Society, Worcester, Mass. See also Lynn Templeton Brickley, "Sarah Pierce's Litchfield Female Academy, 1792–1833" (Ph.D. diss., Harvard University Graduate School of Education, 1985), esp. 192–309. Litchfield's collegiate curriculum was installed after Pierce's nephew, a graduate of Williams College, began teaching with her. The texts that students read were the same as those Brace had been assigned at Williams. Portions of this essay have been drawn from *Learning to Stand and Speak: Women, Education, and Public Life in America's Republic* (Chapel Hill: University of North Carolina Press, 2006).

2. Maria Campbell to Mary Humes, September 21, 1819, Campbell Collection, Special Collections, Duke University, Durham, N.C. Wellesley, which was chartered as a seminary in 1870, was renamed Wellesley College in 1873. Antioch College and the University of Iowa began to admit women in 1852 and 1856 respectively. We would do well to observe Anne Firor Scott's caution about defining the content and character of higher education in pre–Civil War America: "The quality of difficulty of a curriculum was not necessarily revealed by the label placed upon it, and a wide variety of institutions were engaged in providing some part of what would eventually come to be defined as a collegiate education." Many in early nineteenth-century America used the term "seminary" as a designation for all institutions of higher education, including male colleges. See Anne Firor Scott, "'The Ever Widening Circle': The Diffusion of Feminist Values from the Troy Female Seminary, 1822–1872," *History of Education Quarterly* 19 (Spring 1979): 3, 7, 22.

3. See Pierce, *Chronicles of a Pioneer School*; Theodore Sizer et al., eds., *"To Ornament Their Minds": Sarah Pierce's Litchfield Female Academy, 1792–1833* (Litchfield, Conn.: Litchfield Historical Society, 1993), esp. 26–29; Scott, "The Ever Widening Circle," 5; Schools and Academies Collection, American Antiquarian Society, Worcester, Mass.; Thomas Woody, *A History of Women's Education*, 2 vols. (New York: Science Press, 1929), 1:380, 361, 343; David Allmendinger, "Mount Holyoke Students Encounter the Need for Life Planning, 1837–1850," *History of Education Quarterly* 19 (Spring 1979): 29.

4. *Annual Catalogue of Hartford Female Seminary, Together with an Account of the Internal Arrangements, Course of Study and Mode of Conducting the Same* (Hartford, Conn.: George F. Olmsted, 1831); Isabella Margaret Elizabeth Blandin, *History of Higher Education of Women in the South Prior to 1860* (Washington, D.C.: Zenger, 1909; reprint, Washington, D.C., 1975), 81, 245–46; Margaret A. Nash, "'A Salutary Rivalry': The Growth of Higher Education for Women in Oxford, Ohio, 1855–1867," in *The American College in the Nineteenth Century*, ed. Richard Geiger (Nashville: Vanderbilt University Press, 2000), 168–82; School and Academies Collection, American Antiquarian Society, Worcester, Mass. See also Kathryn Kish Sklar, *Catharine Beecher: A Study in American Domesticity* (New Haven: Yale University Press, 1973), esp. 59–104. The examples I have cited in these paragraphs were selected from a much larger number of female academies and seminaries with similar enrollments.

5. Catalog, Lafayette Female Academy, 1821; broadside, First Female School, 1829; "Statement of the Course of Study and Instruction," circular, Mount Vernon School, 1830; circular, Albany Female Academy, 1821; Knoxville Female Academy, 1831, Schools and Academies Collection, American Antiquarian Society, Worcester, Mass; petitions to the State Legislature, 1823, Mississippi State Archives, Jackson, Miss. The postrevolutionary female and coeducational academies are the subject of Kimberley Tolley's "'A Triumph of Reason': Female Education in Academies in the Early Republic," in *Chartered Schools: Two Hundred Years of Independent Academies in the United States, 1727–1925*, ed. Nancy Beadie and Kimberley Tolley (London: Routledge Falmer, 2002), 64–86.

6. Scott, "The Ever Widening Circle," 3–25.

7. South Carolina Female Collegiate Institute Collection, South Caroliniana Library, University of South Carolina, Columbia; Anne Bouknight Holladay, "More than Manners: A Study of Private Female Education in South Carolina from 1830 to 1880" (Ph.D. diss., University of South Carolina, 1996), 170–71; Kathryn Kish Sklar, "The Founding of Mount Holyoke College," in *Women and Power in American History: A Reader*, ed. Kathryn Kish Sklar and Thomas Dublin, 2 vols. (Englewood Cliffs, N.J.: Prentice Hall, 1991), 1:199–215; Susan Allen to Catherine Conover, May 17, [18]47, Mount Holyoke College Archives, South Hadley, Mass.

8. Holladay, "More than Manners," 167; Lucy Goodale to Mary Goodale, December 1841, Mount Holyoke College Archives and Special Collections, South Hadley, Mass.; Mary Lyon, "Mount Holyoke Female Seminary," South Hadley, Mass., September 1835, printed but not published for general circulation, Rare Books and Manuscripts, Huntington Library, San Marino, Calif., 2.

9. Journal of Caroline Chester, in "Sarah Pierce's Litchfield Female Academy," in Brickley, *To Ornament Their Minds*, 45.

10. Sarah Sleeper, *Memoir of the Late Martha Hazeltine Smith* (Boston, 1848), 1; diary of Sarah Porter, December 29, 1853; MSR, "Reading," in *Miss Porter's School: A History in Documents, 1847–1948*, 2 vols., ed. Louise L. Stevenson (New York: Garland, 1987), 1:43, 130–31, see also 40–43, 164, 166–68. The quotation from Isaac Bickerstaff that MSR paraphrased is as follows: "Reading is to the mind what exercise is to the body, as by one, health is preserved, strengthened, by the other virtue which is the health of the mind is kept alive, strengthened and confirmed." See "The Lucubrations of Isaac Bickerstaff Esq.," *Tatler*, no. 147 (March 18, 1710).

11. Harriet Hayne's *Mental Improvement* is deposited in the South Carolina Female Collegiate Institute Collection, South Caroliniana Library, University of South Carolina, Columbia.

12. Julia Hyde to Lucy Goodale, September 26, 1839, Julia Hyde Papers, Mount Holyoke College Archives and Special Collections, South Hadley, Mass.

13. Mary Virginia Early to Elizabeth Early, January 30, 1839, Early Brown Family Papers, Virginia Historical Society, Richmond, Va.

14. Maria Cowles to Henry Cowles, March 29, 1831, Ipswich Students, Alumnae, and Teachers, 1830–63, Correspondence, Mount Holyoke College Archives, South Hadley, Mass.

15. Laura W. Cone, "Advantages of Education," in *Miss Porter's School*, 1:124–25; "Some of the Characteristics of Ipswich Female Seminary, Communicated by the Senior Class," annual catalog,1829, Ipswich Female Seminary, Schools and Academies Collection, American Antiquarian Society, Worcester, Mass.

16. Virginia Terrell to Edward Graham, March, 12, 1812, Graham Family Papers, Special Collections, Duke University, Durham, N.C.

17. Josephine Downing Price to Isabella Downing Price, January 22, [1860], Charles Barrington Simrall Papers, Southern Historical Collection, University of North Carolina, Chapel Hill.

18. Lloyd Noland to Ella Noland, March 3, 1845, and Elizabeth Noland to Ella Noland, November, 14, 1849, Ella Noland Mackenzie Papers, Southern Historical Collection, University of North Carolina, Chapel Hill; John Springs to Mary Laura Springs, April 14, 1829, and April 4, 1831, Springs Family Collection, South Carolina Library, University of South Carolina, Columbia; William Kauffman Scarborough, *Masters of the Big House: Elite Slaveholders of the Mid-Nineteenth-Century South* (Baton Rouge: Louisiana State University Press, 2003), esp. 77–82.

19. Caroline Thayer, Report to Trustees of Elizabeth Academy, [1825], quoted in Blandin, *History of Higher Education*, 49.

20. R. Bentley to Sophia Bentley, September 3, 1858, Elijah Wetmore Papers, Special Collections, Duke University, Durham, N.C.

21. F. William Wirt to Elizabeth Wirt, September 9, 1810, quoted in Anja Jabour, "'Grown Girls, Highly Cultivated': Female Education in an Antebellum Southern Family," *Journal of Southern History* 64 (February 1998): 30.

22. Margaret Barr Brashear to Rebecca and Caroline Brashear, January 3, 1823, Brashear-Lawrence Papers; Sarah Wheeler to Sarah Clifton Wheeler, June 13, 1833, Southall and Bowen Papers; Williana Wilkinson Lacy to Bessie Lacy, August 23, 1845, Drury Lacy Papers; all in Southern Historical Collection, University of North Carolina, Chapel Hill.

23. Sarah Sleeper's circular was published in the *Literary and Missionary Association of the Philadelphia Collegiate Institution for Young Ladies Annual Report* (Philadelphia, April 1839), 34, 35. A copy of the report is deposited at the Library Company, Philadelphia.

24. Townsend Female Seminary Literary and Education Society Schools and Academies Collection, American Antiquarian Society, Worcester, Mass.; *Annual Report of the Whiting Association or Social Circle of the Charlestown Female Society, 1845–46, 1848–49, 1850–51, 1853–54*; *Annual Reports of the Young Ladies Association of the New-Hampton Female Seminary for the Promotion of Literature and Missions, 1846–53*, all published in Boston by Freeman and Bolles. Copies of the reports of both

of these seminaries are deposited at the American Antiquarian Society, Worcester, Mass. Nine yearly reports (from 1834–35 to 1842–43) of the New Hampton Female Seminary's literary society can be found at the Library Company, Philadelphia.

25. *Annual Report of the Whiting Association or Social Circle of the Charlestown Female Society*, 1845–46; Townsend Female Seminary Literary and Education Society, Schools and Academies Collection, American Antiquarian Society, Worcester, Mass.; Sigourney Club Records, Southern Historical Collection, University of North Carolina, Chapel Hill.

26. See Townsend Female Seminary, *Catalogues*, 1839, 1844–45, 1848, 1850, 1852; Whiting Association, *Annual Report*, 1845–46, 1848–49, 1850–51; Young Ladies Association of the New-Hampton Female Seminary, *Annual Reports*, 1846–53; Whiting Association, *Annual Report*, 1846, 10. Copies of these catalogs and reports are deposited at the American Antiquarian Society. See also Martin E. Marty, *Righteous Empire: The Protestant Experience in America* (New York: Dial, 1970); Candy Gunther Brown, *The Word in the World: Evangelical Writing, Publishing, and Reading in America, 1789–1880* (Chapel Hill: University of North Carolina Press, 2004); David Paul Nord, *Faith in Reading: Religious Publishing and the Birth of Mass Media in America* (New York: Oxford University Press, 2004).

27. Bessie Lacy to Horace Lacy, n.d., Drury Lacy Papers, Southern Historical Collection, University of North Carolina, Chapel Hill; Maria Cowles to Henry Cowles, March 29, 1831, Ipswich Students, Alumnae, and Teachers, 1830–60, Mount Holyoke College Archives and Special Collections, South Hadley, Mass.; Mary Lyon Collection, Memorabilia of Mary Lyon, presented by Amelia Woodward Truesdell, n.d., 17, Mount Holyoke College Archives and Special Collections. Although Lacy's letter is undated, internal evidence indicates it was written in the late 1840s.

28. The records of the Sigourney Club include bylaws, lists of honorary members, and minutes, noting the general business that members undertook and the topics they debated at the weekly meetings. The extant records that document the club begin with its founding in 1848 and stop in 1852, although there is no reason to believe that meetings of the club ended at that juncture. See Sigourney Club Records, Southern Historical Collection, University of North Carolina, Chapel Hill; catalog, 1851, Limestone Springs Female High School, Schools and Academies Collection, American Antiquarian Society, Worcester, Mass.; *Annual Report of the Whiting Association or Social Circle of the Charlestown Female Society, 1845–46* (Higham, 1847), 3.

29. Sigourney Club Records, Southern Historical Collection, University of North Carolina, Chapel Hill; Whiting Association, *Annual Report*, 1845–46, 1846–47, 12.

30. Whiting Association, *Annual Report*, 1846–47, 12.

31. Lucy Stone to Antoinette Brown Blackwell, May 5, 1892, Brown to Stone (winter 1847), both in Carol Lasser and Marlene Deahl Merrill, eds., *Friends and Sisters: Letters between Lucy Stone and Antoinette Brown Blackwell, 1846–93* (Urbana: University of Illinois Press, 1987), 20, 21, 263.

32. On the numbers of women and men enrolled in institutions of higher learning, see Schools and Academic Collection, American Antiquarian Society, Worcester, Mass.; and Colin B. Burke, *American Collegiate Populations: A Test of the Traditional View* (New York, 1982).

Down from the Pedestal

The Influence of Anne Scott's Southern Ladies

—LAURA F. EDWARDS

I first read Anne Scott's *The Southern Lady: From Pedestal to Politics* as an undergraduate at Northwestern University in the early 1980s, while writing a paper on the status of antebellum plantation mistresses for a course in U.S. social history. When I selected the topic at the beginning of the quarter, I had no idea what I was getting myself into. The only knowledge I had was what I had gleaned from popular culture. I knew the topic was not well studied, but that was why I wanted to do it. The challenge appealed to me. As an undergraduate, however, I relished the idea of the challenge while putting off the work until the end of the quarter. So it was too late to change my mind when I realized that my sense of intellectual adventure was misplaced, given the assignment, which was to write a synthetic paper based on secondary sources. There were even fewer books on southern women than I had anticipated. While other students in the course complained of having too much material, I spent my time on the hunt. I was only moderately successful, cobbling together a collection of readings on southern history (few of which featured women, white or black), women's history (few of which touched on the South), and an odd assortment of books on white southern women (not all of which were appropriate to the topic). I missed many things I should have read. But I did manage to find *The Southern Lady*.

Anne Scott's southern ladies were not the ones I expected to find. Instead of passive, self-absorbed belles, I found wives and mothers, thoughtful and articulate, hardworking and tough. They bristled with life, even when confined to their antebellum pedestals. More than that, they were interesting. The problematic elements of their lives—their support for slavery and racism—added to their allure, at least for me, by making them more challenging historical subjects. In fact, these women were so compelling that they made the book's argument irresistible. Given this formidable group of women, it made sense that only significant barriers, namely, the powerful patriarchal structures of the slave South, could keep them in subordination. It made even more sense that they would seize the opportunities available to them once the Civil War and emancipation upended that social structure.[1] Unable to imagine another narrative, I wrote a paper that took issue with *The Southern Lady* because I accepted the analysis so completely. The problem, I argued, was that the book placed too much emphasis on the changes resulting from the Civil War and emancipation. I substantiated that position by showing that white southern women were not as limited before the Civil War as the pedestal metaphor suggests. They participated in a wider world, reading, going to school, traveling, corresponding with friends and family, and maintaining a far-flung network of social contacts. My implication, although not particularly well stated, was that the route from pedestal to politics was explained as much in white women's antebellum past as it was in the social, economic, and political changes of the Civil War era. Even the structural constraints of the slave South could not have kept Anne Scott's southern ladies down. How could they?

It is painfully obvious now that my paper was based more on desire than on evidence. (I do not think it would have passed muster with Anne for that reason.) But my desire did have a basis in the scholarly literature. Before I read *The Southern Lady*, I assumed that white women in the slave South were historically marginal. Of any group of Americans in the past, they were the least likely to have influenced the course of U.S. history. I had to reconsider both that presumption and my view of history after I read the book. Once I realized that these women mattered, the past, present, and future also looked much different. Obviously there were possibilities that I had not yet considered—and, as a college student trying to find her own way in life, those possibilities were important. I needed to believe in Anne Scott's southern ladies. I needed that so badly that I even ignored the assignment, constructing my analysis not from other historians' findings but from information gleaned in their footnotes and in published primary material. I do not recall what grade I received. But I do remember everything about piecing together the ideas for this paper, because it took on much more meaning for me than most course assignments.

Looking back, I am surprised by how prescient this hurried, ill-formed paper was. Its basic spirit still infuses my scholarship on southern women, rich and poor, white and black. I still enter into my research with the conviction that all women in the South matter in history, that it is impossible to understand history without them, and that their presence will change the way we understand history. Looking back, I am also acutely aware of *The Southern Lady*'s influence, both on my own work and on the scholarship more generally. Before 1970, the field of southern history was not known for its emphasis on women, white or black. As I was scouring the library for books, a new generation of historians—many of whose work is included in this volume—had already taken up the challenge. As the scholarship on southern women developed, it first elaborated on the issues developed in *The Southern Lady* and then moved on. Yet even the work that ultimately parted ways from Anne Scott's southern ladies still owes a great deal to them. Like my own work, all these books are full of imposing women of historical consequence, who left their imprint on the South and whose legacy demands our attention.

The argument of this essay is similar to the one in my undergraduate paper, although the substance is very different. I argue that southern women participated more actively in the slave South's public culture than we have realized and that those experiences are crucial in understanding changes in women's roles after the Civil War. This position might seem at odds with Anne Scott's identification of the Civil War as a watershed for southern women. Yet I see my analysis as following directly from *The Southern Lady* in more important ways. At the center of my story are women—not just plantation mistresses but also enslaved women, free black women, and white women of poor to modest means—who were constrained, but not immobilized, by the patriarchal order. These women, I argue, were crucial in creating and regulating social relationships and customary norms that were central in governing the public order in the antebellum period. The expectation that women would participate in public matters contextualizes women's movement into social reform and party politics after the Civil War. These women entered new and different kinds of public arenas. But what they did should not obscure the actions of other women, many of whom did not participate actively in reform movements but nonetheless expected to participate in governance at the local level both before and after the Civil War.[2]

The sources for this essay—local court records from North and South Carolina—are very different from the ones Anne Scott used in *The Southern Lady*. The women are also different from those who appeared in that book's pages.[3] They are white and black women who, for the most part, were poorer and less literate than Anne Scott's ladies; these are the southern women who never made it up on the pedestal in the first place. My focus here ultimately narrows to white women, but the analysis is based on research that includes free black and enslaved women. These women—white and black, rich and poor, free and enslaved—did not all experience the slave South in the same way. Yet the larger claims about women's historical importance in the public realm apply to them all. I tell the story of these women in the spirit of Anne Scott's book: these are women to whom we should attend and who matter in our understanding of southern history.

To understand the influence of women on public issues in the slave South, it is first necessary to reconsider the institutional structures of law and government. Historians of southern women have accepted the existing scholarship and its portrayal of the region's profoundly hierarchical and rigidly exclusionary public order. It seemed clear that statutes and appellate decisions denied individual rights to all enslaved men and women and also restricted the civil and political rights of free black and poor white men as well as all free women. Given those legal restrictions, no southern woman, regardless of status, had direct access to the legal or political system. But we have relied too heavily on state-level sources and assumed too much about the terrain of law, government, and political culture in the South between the Revolution and the Civil War. Statutes and appellate decisions provide only a partial view, obscuring the presence of a highly localized system that rooted law and government in daily lives of ordinary southerners, women as well as men. Women, particularly white women from well-connected families, played key roles in this localized system.

During the Revolution, lawmakers in North Carolina and South Carolina decentralized the most important functions of government, drawing on Revolutionary ideology, established elements of Anglo-American law, and undercurrents of local political unrest. These changes dramatically altered the existing structures of imperial rule by placing government business in local venues that we identify with the legal system. The most visible of these venues were the circuit courts, which met on a regular schedule in county seats or court towns and held jury trials. Not only did circuit courts provide obvious symbols of government authority, but their grand juries also made recommendations for the enforcement and modification of laws at the local, state, and even national levels. Grand juries interpreted their authority broadly: they issued pronouncements on foreign policy, trade, and federal legislation; they advised legislatures to pass statutes on a range of issues, usually related to local concerns about slavery, transportation, crime, and family relations; they also dispatched local officials to investigate abused apprentices, unreported births, distributions to the deserving poor, unkempt roads, and other suspicious situations, such as "disorderly" houses, which usually involved some combination of noise, sex, liquor, violence, and gambling.[4]

But circuit courts were only the most conspicuous part of a system dominated by even more localized legal proceedings, including magistrates' hearings and trials, inquests, and other ad hoc legal forums. Magistrates not only screened cases and tried minor offenses but also kept tabs on the orphaned, ill, and poor, as well as matters involving markets, health, and morals. In most legal matters, the interested parties collected evidence, gathered witnesses, and represented themselves. If lawyers entered the picture, they did so in the final stages, in the unlikely event that a case went to a jury trial. Cases were decided by common law in its traditional sense as a flexible collection of principles rooted in local custom, established through social relationships in local communities. It was in all these informal, nominally legal arenas that North Carolinians did the business of "keeping the peace," a well-established concept in Anglo-American law that expressed the ideal order of the metaphorical public body, subordinating everyone (in varying ways) within a hierarchical system and emphasizing social order over individual rights.[5]

Localized law did not operate by the same rules as law and government at the state level. The system had no use for distinctions that would later become so important, particularly at the state level: it allowed local custom, politics, and law to mingle freely and blurred the demarcation between "local administration" and "state government." To modern eyes, those elements make localized law seem artless and ill formed. In the context of postrevolutionary government, however, local legal practice was not some quaint, folksy exception to a formalized, rational body of state law. Local decisions officially shared space with legislation and appellate decisions as central components of state law, precisely because state governments were relatively weak and delegated so much authority to local jurisdictions. In fact, the state level was largely dependent on local jurisdictions.[6]

Not all areas of law and government, however, were equally localized. Property law, as developed in equity and common law, had been claimed by lawyers even before the Revolution. In colonial economies that looked outward to the Atlantic world, knowledge of property law was crucial to economic success. By the time of the Revolution, links to international markets resulted in the development of relatively sophisticated financial structures to assist in property exchange, capital formation, and the management of credit and debt. That was true even in the North Carolina backcountry, which lagged behind coastal areas economically. The influence of professionalized law was pervasive enough that even ordinary economic transactions, such as the purchase of land, required the interposition of lawyers. Lawyers solidified their hold on property and commerce in the decades following the Revolution, given the unsettled state of the economy, the scarcity of cash and credit, and the uncertainty of land titles in the Carolinas. The trend continued into the nineteenth century, largely because of the widespread use of notes, mortgages, and other instruments of debt as the primary means of economic exchange and capital formation. Over time, property law became even more professionalized, with standardized rules used by lawyers throughout the state. As such, it was more easily organized into a coherent body of law and centralized at the state level, because the legal practice had already moved in that direction. Indeed, the preponderance of property cases—civil cases—in circuit courts and the appellate level registered the relative inaccessibility of this area of law.[7]

Local areas maintained authority over everything else—a broad, ambiguous area of public law, which included all crimes as well as a range of ill-defined offenses that disrupted the patriarchal order of the peace. In theory, the patriarchal order of the peace was hierarchical and inclusive. The concept was based in a long-standing, highly gendered construction of government authority, which subordinated everyone to a sovereign body, just as all individual dependents were subordinated to specific male heads of household. That metaphorical body was represented first through the king and then, after the Revolution, through "the people," via the agency of the state—although the state's form was still an open question in the postrevolutionary decades, a situation that made it possible to locate so much governing authority at the local level. The sovereign body, though, was always a patriarch, whatever its location or physical embodiment. That remained the same, whether sovereignty resided in local jurisdictions or centralized institutions or whether it took the form of a male king, a female queen, or a combination of men and women from different social ranks as "the people."[8]

The peace was inclusive only in the sense that it enclosed everyone in its patriarchal embrace, raising its collective interests over those of any given subject. This form of inclusion did not have anything to do with democracy. Keeping the peace meant keeping everyone—from the lowest to the highest—in their appropriate places, as defined in specific local contexts. The system's localized character did not mean that it was egalitarian.

The localized system was no more progressive than the community leaders who guided it—and the white southerners who controlled those communities were intent on maintaining the rigid inequalities of a slave society. This patriarchal system neither protected the interests nor recognized the rights of free women or slaves. Yet it still incorporated women, white and black, into its basic workings, because they were part of the social order that the legal process was charged with maintaining. They provided "information"—a legal term referring to evidence of disorder that was then investigated and could result in a formal criminal charge—to magistrates. Anyone, even enslaved women, could give information. Once charges were filed, women served as witnesses, giving depositions and sworn testimony. They also served as witnesses of the legal process, an important role, particularly in a system that sought to repair rifts in the social order. Women mattered because the localized system required their physical presence. It needed the information that women had about other community members, and it was charged with protecting a social order of which women were a recognized part.[9]

The patriarchal peace subsumed everything as well as everybody, including personal problems that we would expect to be private. Given the logic, it was possible for anyone's problems to emerge and assume public significance, given the right circumstances. In the localized system, people established and expressed the importance of their problems through the categories of "private" and "public." A means, rather than end, these concepts provided useful tools for establishing and ranking the seriousness of problems, determining how they would be treated within the legal process. Private issues either remained with those immediately involved or became civil matters, also called private matters in legal terminology, as conflicts that involved two discrete parties, not the larger public interest. Public matters, which affected the good order of the peace, had wider ramifications and merited collective intervention of some kind. Beyond that, the consensus broke down, because southerners invariably disagreed about what exactly should be private and public in any given situation. In local practice and common parlance, then, the terms did not refer to normative principles or specific categories of people (such as domestic dependents) or places (domestic spaces) that were inherently private or public. Any given matter could be either one or the other, depending on the circumstances. In the context of localized government, a domestic matter was not, by its nature, private. What made it private was the decision that the outside intervention of the peace was inappropriate or unnecessary. Those determinations were part of a dynamic process—the ongoing negotiations necessary in maintaining order within communities.[10]

Everyone was expected to participate in the maintenance of the peace. Even those without rights—including white women and slaves—had access to localized law in the sense that they were expected to provide information about community disorder. Inquests provide excellent examples. When a death occurred, the neighborhood gathered to pay their respects, to clean and dress the body, and to grieve. That process could also reveal evidence of wrongdoing. Sometimes the signs were easily spotted by those who first saw the body. Sometimes they were uncovered by the women whose job it was to ready the body for burial. And sometimes they emerged through the mourners' conversations as information was shared and the pieces began to form ominous patterns. When doubts acquired critical mass, the coroner—or someone designated to act as one—was called, if he was not already there. The gathering then reconstituted itself as a legal hearing: a jury was formed, often from among those in attendance, and mourners became witnesses. One by one, they offered their observations, repeating for the record what had already been said. And so law arrived at the wake, at the invitation of no one and everyone.[11]

Southerners also appealed to the peace to enforce their own notions of the public order, producing an endless stream of complaints to magistrates and grand juries about threats to community health, welfare, and order. They ran the gamut: from dilapidated fences and ill-kept roads to neighbors with a penchant for late nights, drinking, or pilfering to threats or actual instances of physical violence. Among the offenses that southerners considered worthy of legal intervention were domestic issues that historians often consider private and therefore exempt from public regulation. Masters filed charges against hired servants and slaves whom they could not control; white and free black wives filed charges against husbands; and free children informed on their parents. Free families brought their feuds to court for resolution, with wives, husbands, parents, children, siblings, aunts, uncles, and cousins all lining up to air their dirty laundry. Neighbors routinely involved legal officials in their quarrels, sometimes using the system in combination with insults, threats, and violence, as yet another weapon in an ongoing conflict. In all these instances, men and women marched off to magistrates, certain that they could mobilize the local legal system to resolve their personal problems.[12]

Judgments relied on the situated knowledge of observers in local communities, in which an individual's "credit," or reputation, was established through family and neighborly ties and continually assessed through gossip networks. Local officials and juries judged the reliability of testimony based on an individual's credit as well as on impersonal, prescriptive markers of status, such as gender, race, age, or class. In this system, the words of women, free and enslaved, could assume considerable legal authority, because they knew so much about their households and their communities. In the vagrancy case of James Woodruff, for example, the white men who testified only knew so much. They could speak about the work they hired Woodruff to do, what they paid him, what he obtained from them in trade, and what he grew on his own small patch of land. They suspected that Woodruff did not work enough to support his family, a key issue in South Carolina's capacious rendering of vagrancy. But the men could not speak to the conditions of Woodruff's family. They did not know whether Woodruff turned over any of his admittedly meager earnings to his family. They did not know the extent of his family's need. But their wives did, because they visited Woodruff's wife regularly. They knew what the family ate, how much, and how regularly. The way they spat out the fact that Woodruff's wife made bread from chaff underscored their distaste—and that was only the symbolic starting point in Woodruff's catalog of sins. The situation was so bad, according to one woman, that Woodruff's wife had begged her to go over her husband's head to her father, to contact him and let him know that she and her children "would starve if there was not something done." These women's voices shaped the entire case. They shifted the focus away from Woodruff's interactions with other men and defined the issues in terms of their own concerns with domestic order and their contact with his wife. The magistrates and freeholders of the jury not only allowed them to do so, but endorsed their view.[13]

Women used this kind of legal dynamic to turn the tables on the men who had authority over them. Vagrancy charges can often be traced back to the wives of the accused. That may have been the situation in James Woodruff's trial. It is more evident in the trial of Robert Mitchell, which was largely his wife's doing. She had pointedly complained about her husband's laziness and parsimony to others, turning niggling doubts about her husband's behavior into something more concrete. According to one witness, "Mitchell's wife complained that Mitchell allowed her to a pint of meal at a time and would quarrel with her for cutting much meat at once." Another "heard the wife of Mitchell say that Mitchell had not worked any of consequence for two or three weeks." Ultimately Mrs. Mitchell lost the battle but won the war, which was probably her goal all along. Although her husband was acquitted, she had successfully mobilized her neighbors, turning their attention to her problematic husband. Even after the trial, those eyes would remain on her husband, providing her with moral support that she did not have before.[14]

Enslaved women used similar tactics, publicizing their owners' bad behavior to protect themselves. When slaves fled to white neighbors' houses to evade beatings or to seek shelter afterward, they expected more than a temporary haven. Exhibiting the bloody results of their masters' brutality could prompt white neighbors to intervene or plant information that could be called on later. Even if no direct action was taken at the time, these appeals set the rumor mill in motion. Judy, a slave in Anderson District, made her grievances about her master public. She voiced specific complaints: her owners did not give her enough to eat, and they used force too freely. Her complaints worked their way through the church membership and ultimately arrived back on her owners' doorstep, where they provoked a confrontation between her and her master. After that, Judy's master, Brother Johnson, brought her up on charges at their church, for disobedience and lying. Worst of all, according to Brother Johnson, was Judy's assertion that she had "good backers in the church to do the Evel she had done, or Else she wood not have done it." The complaint did not go the way Brother Johnson expected, because Judy had prepared the congregation to doubt what he said. The "good backers" Judy counted on required Brother and Sister Johnson to apologize for their mistreatment of Judy. Ultimately Judy's recalcitrance got her excluded from the church, as well. But the Johnsons' anemic apology did not satisfy the congregation, either. Church members continued to investigate, subjecting the couple to continual scrutiny. Several months into the matter, Brother Johnson complained of the church "leving him behind and working over his head." The church conceded it had, and the issue cooled somewhat, but not completely. The cloud of suspicion that hung over the Johnsons remained.[15]

Women exercised influence in law without being able to change or even challenge their subordination within a patriarchal order. Most often, women supplied information about disorder that had nothing to do with them, as did the women at inquests or vagrancy trials. They initiated cases involving violence to someone else, a suspicious death, or other kinds of community disorders. In trials, they supplied background about the relationships and events surrounding a conflict. But even when women made complaints involving their own interests, local officials treated the cases as offenses against the peace, not against the women themselves. Local officials acted when they were convinced that women's injuries disrupted the social order. They righted specific wrongs done to the metaphorical public body without extending additional rights to women as a group. Acting on behalf of the peace, local officials followed up on the complaints of one wife or even one enslaved woman. They undercut the domestic authority of one husband or one master. But the interests of the peace drew boundaries around each case, at least in terms of its implications for the legal status of the women involved. Within this system, individual judgments did not translate into legal statements about all wives, all slaves, all husbands, or all masters in like conditions. These cases were about the peace, not the legal category "women."[16]

To the extent that women influenced public matters at all, it was because, not in spite of, their subordination within a patriarchal order. Women's subordination created the social connections that bound them to the peace, making them visible and influential within localized systems of governance that characterized the slave South. The extent of their influence depended on the fulfillment of their prescribed roles. But women also used their influence to protect customary arrangements that were important to them, and the customary arrangements that were central to women's visions of the peace often prevailed. Women's visions of the peace did not always match those of the white men in their communities. They leaned into the limits, working creatively within established customary practices, sometimes embroidering and embellishing them, sometimes turning them completely inside out and refashioning them to fit their own circumstances. Enslaved women, for instance, worked to maintain privileges they had worked out with their masters: to move off the plantation, to congregate with other slaves, to hire out their time, to work plots of land in their free time, to cultivate unused land, to trade what they produced, and to own property. Free women, who wielded more influence, used it to address a range of issues in their lives, from claims to property to the exercise of their husbands' patriarchal authority.

How specifically did free women seek to define the legal terms of household property in cases of divorce, separation, and domestic violence? Given the legal conventions of such cases, it is easy to see women as only victims. The fortunate ones were cast off like old clothes, left by ne'er-do-well husbands to make do on their own. The less fortunate were physically abused in the process, bruised and battered by the men who were supposed to love and protect them. These legal cases, however, also highlight the dynamics through which free women shaped the terms of patriarchy.

To see this dimension of the cases, it is necessary to view them from the perspective of localized law. Localized law's emphasis on the maintenance of order provided free women entry into the legal process. In their everyday lives, women established relationships and practices that, when accepted or even just tolerated over time, became local custom—a part of the peace that the localized legal process was supposed to protect. Women could then turn those customary practices into usable legal principles that defined the boundaries of patriarchal authority—the peace—within localized law. Free wives, in particular, pulled at the outer edges of the peace in ways that stretched legal discourse, including a much broader array of ideas within the practice of localized law than would otherwise have been the case. The results reinforced the patriarchal order, but in ways that also allowed women some say in the law's content and exercise. More than that, divorce, separation, and domestic violence cases suggest that free women expected to have some say about matters relating to the public peace. They were not just wives; they were also women who saw themselves as integral members of extended families and communities.[17]

When marriages went awry, the conflicts often played out through property. At first glance, wives' property claims seem odd, if not downright impossible, given the legal presumption that wives surrendered property rights to their husbands with marriage. Yet husbands' property *rights*, as established at the state level, existed alongside practices in localized law that recognized wives' property *claims*, which had legal standing in this part of the system, even though they were not the same thing as individual rights of ownership. While seemingly contradictory, wives' claims and their husbands' rights existed side by side, without negating their husbands' rights or patriarchal status, until conflict erupted within the marriage. When that happened, many wives expected legal support for their claims, precisely because they had been accommodated within marriage and recognized through customary practice. Within the practice of localized law, wives sustained a variety of claims to property: they established possession of property that they produced or acquired by marketing goods of their own making; they maintained control over articles that they brought into the marriage; they retained strong connections to property that their own families gave them, including slaves and land; they had recognized interests in their husbands' property and labor, because it was necessary to their support; and they refused to surrender their bodies completely to their husbands or other men. Even estranged husbands recognized the legitimacy of their wives' claims. As Edward Southwick informed the North Carolina legislature, his wife "took with her all the property that originally belonged to her and also a considerable part of his property."[18]

Wives' claims to property, however, can be difficult to see and interpret because they often appeared in legal contexts—particularly divorce and separation cases—that also transformed them. The established conventions of these legal matters, which had deep roots in professionalized property law, treated all property claims in terms of individual rights. Reflecting the emphasis on individual property rights in the statutory construction of divorce and separation, such matters were categorized as "private" and were handled as civil cases. That was true even at the local level, where many cases were decided, particularly after statutory changes that moved jurisdiction from the legislature to the local courts. Outside the legal rules of divorce and separation, however, marital disputes were never private matters. Nor did they center only on the conflicting property rights of those involved. Wives, in particular, underscored that point by bringing customary claims from localized law into these matters.

Some of the most contentious marital disputes involved resources brought into the marriage by wives. Property, particularly landed estates, symbolized women's ties to their own families. Those ties figured in the lives of husbands as well as wives, as the voluminous collections of letters in southern archives indicate. Wives were also daughters, sisters, cousins, nieces, aunts, and mothers, just as husbands were also sons, brothers, cousins, nephews, uncles, and fathers. While these networks incorporated friends and neighbors, extended family ties featured prominently. In most instances, marriage and parenthood strengthened these relationships for both men and women. As men and women took on new roles as husbands and wives, they also acquired new responsibilities for their own kindred. Wives balanced their familial obligations, keeping up with their own relatives while also tending to the needs of their new households. Some husbands, however, saw the continued presence and influence of their wives' families as a challenge to their own authority. In a range of cases, from divorce and separation to incidents that ended in violence and even murder, husbands blamed meddling in-laws for the breakdown of the marriage. Thomas Chandler's response to the divorce petition of his wife Sarah was typical. Sarah, who filed complaints of domestic abuse against her husband on two separate occasions before petitioning for divorce, charged her husband with repeated, particularly sadistic acts of violence. Chandler responded with denial, finding fault with her family instead. "The disquiet which has existed in his family," he insisted, "and the differences existing between [him and his wife] have been principally created by the mischievous and malicious interferences of his said wife's mother & her friends."[19]

Property fueled the flames. When parents gave property to their daughters, they usually did so with the expectation that the family patrimony would pass through them, thus extending the family line through the grandchildren. Many were unwilling to surrender it to their female relatives' husbands, who could take it out of the family of origin forever. Even when lineage restrictions were not outlined in formal legal instruments, they were still assumed. Husbands owned the property of their wives' families only as long as they used it for the benefit of that family's descendants—as determined by watchful relatives. One of the reasons Sarah Chandler's relatives interfered was because they did not want her husband to drink away their family's future. Concern for their family's property interests was inseparable from their concern for the welfare of Sarah and her children. Esther Preslar felt confident enough about that general principle to make the point directly to her husband. After drinking too much and working too little, he confronted her about an apparently long-standing grievance, insisting that "he wanted his land back." "He should have it," she spat back, "if he behaved himself." At that point in the argument, he resorted to violence, and she left to go to her father's house, an act that underscored the source of her leverage. If the land had been his, not just his to use, he would not have needed to argue about it. But since it was the legacy of his wife's family, he needed to fight to control it—and her.[20]

Augustus Converse fell afoul of his wife's family for similar reasons. The problem was the estate of his wife, Marion Singleton Deveaux, which she controlled, through her father's will, to pass on to her children. While Marion's first husband accepted those terms, Augustus Converse could not reconcile himself to the situation in which "all his rights as husband were subordinate to her claim." He tried everything from seduction to force to get it, but only succeeded in alienating both Marion and her relatives, whose support he needed to get around the terms of the will. Like Richard Singleton, the family patriarch, Marion and the rest of the family saw Singleton land as the Singleton legacy. Ultimately the situation deteriorated to the point where Marion filed for a separation in equity court, an action supported by her family. Opposing it, Augustus lodged charges against Marion's family for "unwarrantable interference in his domestic concerns." But he was unable to convince Marion of her "duty to him" and "the impolicy of allowing herself to be changed, and shifted in opinion by every suggestion of her relatives." What Augustus saw as a legitimate assertion of patriarchal authority, Marion and her family saw as incompetence, born of insecurity and imperiousness. In their eyes, his inability to accept Marion's responsibilities as a Singleton and his self-serving efforts to commandeer her family's property proved his failure. One of Marion's aunts referred to him as "that grasping bad evil Man."[21]

The patriarchal imperatives of wives' families confounded the construction of coverture on the professionalized side of property law, which turned family resources into the husband's private domain, defined in terms of his property rights. Marion's separation case was as much about the Singleton family's estate as it was about her welfare. In fact, the conflation of Marion's interests and those of her family was the point: she remained part of her family in a way that blunted her husband's property rights and his patriarchal authority. When Marion was isolated with Augustus Converse, she had no choice but to endure his psychological bullying and physical violence. Within the context of her family, though, it was Augustus who was vulnerable. Marion stayed for extended periods at the homes of her kin in New York, Philadelphia, and Virginia, as well as South Carolina. When the marriage fell apart, the entire Singleton clan rallied to Marion's side. They not only encouraged Marion to file for a separation but also crafted a legal settlement, in which August received a substantial settlement for relinquishing all claims on Singleton family property and leaving the state of South Carolina. That outcome depended on the aid of influential family friends. Marion even dropped "Converse" from her name, which is why she appears in the archival records as Marion Singleton Deveaux—Robert Deveaux was Marion's first husband.[22] No wonder so many wives dragged their feet or remained behind when their husbands moved west. Doing so removed wives from patriarchal networks in which they had recognized claims on family resources.[23]

Wives took a similar view of property that they accumulated through their own labor. While accepting the property rights that husbands acquired through coverture, wives tended to see them as a privilege contingent on the fulfillment of specific duties. Many wives assumed an ongoing role for themselves in this arrangement, allowing husbands the use of their property without surrendering all claims to it. When their husbands proved unworthy of that trust, wives expected to take the property back or, if it was gone, to be released from further obligations. That logic, which characterized many separation and divorce petitions, was particularly clear in Tabitha Fox's petition to obtain economic independence from her husband—a divorce from bed and board. Before her marriage,

Fox had worked as a weaver and ran her father's household. She "applied her earnings to the purchase and raising of stock and procuring articles of furniture and utensils for house keeping." By the time of her marriage, she had amassed an impressive amount of property, including "a valuable horse, bridle and saddle, 6 head of cattle, 10 head of Hogs, 20 head of sheep, 2 excellent beds & furniture, valuable case of drawers, tables, and a very good supply of Household and kitchen furniture." While married, Fox applied "her" property to the needs of the household, subsuming it within the property that her husband "owned," although she still maintained her own sense of possession over the items that she contributed to the household economy. Her willingness to do so ended when her husband abandoned his own marital obligations. Then his rights no longer applied to "her" property.[24]

Wives also saw labor, one of the most valuable forms of property, in more expansive terms, as a family resource that could never be reduced to a personal possession. By that logic, wives maintained interests in their husbands' labor as well as their own. Those assumptions framed wives' complaints about their husbands' indolence, one of the most common of their marital grievances, which ran through divorce petitions, vagrancy cases, domestic violence prosecutions, and a range of other matters. These complaints were more about husbands' waste of collective resources than their failure to provide. That was Tabitha Fox's point. Although her husband had already run through all the property she brought into the marriage, she carefully listed all those items. Why? In the context of her petition, the list was akin to double-entry bookkeeping, with her positive balance on the one side and her husband's negative account on the other, canceling out everything she had done. Fox carefully separated her labor from that of her husband while highlighting the relationship that should have tied them together: a marriage that established the collective interests of the family. Wives like Tabitha Fox expected to contribute to the household economy. They understood that their husbands would not always be able to contribute regularly. Even so, they accepted their husbands' authority to direct the family's labor for the benefit of the household. But they drew the line when husbands squandered that resource and the property they had accumulated. Esther Preslar captured the reasoning with stunning clarity: when husbands ceased to "behave," they lost access to family resources.[25]

Wives' views of labor were rooted in economic realities. It was impossible for most men to support their families through their labor alone, despite the rhetoric of male independence and the ideology that associated women with a domestic realm characterized by altruistic sentiment and then, later, as a separate sphere unto itself. The memoir of Edward Isham of North Carolina underscores the point, although from the perspective of a man who took women's labor for granted. Actually, like other men, he seems to have transformed the masculine prerogative to direct women's labor into the right of appropriation. Just before his execution for murder in the 1850s, Isham recounted his life to his lawyer, the young and completely enthralled David Schenck, who later became a prominent political leader in North Carolina. The story has all the hallmarks of a tall tale, tracing Isham's dramatic exploits in drinking, gambling, fighting, and womanizing across the Southeast, from North Carolina to Alabama. The one thing that does ring true, largely because neither Isham nor Schenk intended to highlight it, is Isham's reliance on women. There were many women in his life, both lovers who chose his company and relatives who did not. Some women followed him, perhaps with the mistaken impression that he would settle down and contribute to their support. They did not last long, because it was usually Isham who needed support. As a result, he followed women himself, seeking them out when he needed shelter and sustenance. Most of these women were barely hanging on, but they were the ones with houses, food, and resources—and none of that was because of Edward Isham.[26]

While embellished to the point of fiction, Isham's account does contain elements of economic truth. Cash and credit were scarce for decades following the Revolutionary War. Although prosperity followed the cotton boom in the early nineteenth century, land became scarce. Prices soared in settled areas, and speculators gobbled up large tracts in the West. The volatility of the economy added a new dimension of instability as hard-won gains disappeared into the dips of the business cycle. Even the prosperous were vulnerable. Young men without property had it worse, because they had few alternatives that did not require large initial capital outlays.[27]

Wives' contributions were crucial in this economic environment. Among wealthier southerners, women provided access to capital through their family networks. As the records of R. G. Dun and Co. indicate, kinship networks lay behind many a man who maintained the appearance of independence as a household head who provided for his family. Men may have managed the family resources, but the property belonged to their wives' families or their wives, who retained ownership through a trustee or other legal device. In some cases, the terms were dictated by the wives' families. In others, the property was in a wife's name to shield it from creditors.

Either way, the technicalities of ownership did not affect men's standing or credit in the daily life of local communities. But it did matter within the increasingly formalized rules of property law on the civil side: in that legal world, husbands had no credit if they did not own the property outright themselves. That was why R. G. Dun's locally based informers spent a lot of time, with ears to the ground, trying to discern the "real" owners.[28]

Women also provided crucial economic support through their labor. Domestic produce—textiles, linens, clothing, butter, eggs, poultry, fruits, and vegetables—kept families going in times of economic uncertainty. Consider the differences between Tabitha Fox and her husband. Fox described him as a "likely" man. But he had no property other than a "pretty good mare" at the time of their marriage. Landless and without the patronage of family, he had few options. By contrast, Fox could market her skills. After her husband went through all the family property and abandoned her, she gave up on farming, left the countryside, found work for her older children in a cotton mill, and "commenced weaving again" to support her family. By her own account, they were getting by on their own.[29]

Like so many wives, Tabitha Fox stepped up when her husband stumbled. She expected to do that, as most wives did. What she and other wives could not countenance was the assertion of their husbands' interests over those of their families. According to Fox, her husband spent everything he and his family earned on himself, as if he were not married at all. The phrase "wasted his substance" communicated all the elements of that situation. A husband squandered all the family's resources that he was supposed to manage, including land, movable goods, the labor of his wife and children, his own ability to labor, and even his good name. Tabitha ran out of patience when her husband reappeared, with the intent of living off her earnings, after she had established herself on her own. She might be able to contend with his demands, but not with those of his creditors. When dissolute husbands were distant memories, their property rights came back to haunt their wives through creditors. They arrived with lawyers and the considerable arsenal of property law, which included the force of the state, to seize wives' property in payment for their husbands' outstanding debts.[30]

The looming presence of creditors in wives' petitions indicates the pull of opposing legal trends at the state level that fought with the customary emphasis on localized law. Those legal developments gave husbands absolute rights in the labor of their household dependents. Fox, like other aggrieved wives, used the good order of the peace to check those developments and to constrain their husbands' rights. Husbands could direct the household's labor for the interests of the family, but they could not appropriate their own or their wives' labor for their sole benefit. The clearest articulation came in the context of legal cases where wives' claims were forced into the rubric of competing property rights. Even in this legal context, though, wives insisted on a view of labor as a communal resource, rather than private property. From that perspective, husbands' property rights in their wives' labor were always contingent, because they were based on their fulfillment of marital responsibilities in which absolute control of their wives' labor was never really a possibility.

Wives also limited their husbands' rights in their bodies. The most dramatic examples involve domestic violence, a particularly extreme expression of husbands' rights. To challenge abuse, wives leaned on neighbors and kin, acting on a view of marriage in which they, as wives, remained connected to the social order, not isolated within their husbands' households. In Spartanburg District, for instance, Mrs. Littlefield regularly sought shelter with her neighbors when her husband turned violent. Mrs. Watkins, of nearby Laurens District, did the same, spreading news in the neighborhood that her husband "whipt" her. In both instances, the women's information about their husbands featured prominently in their husbands' vagrancy trials. In these and other cases, community members had to pick up the pieces of broken domestic relations, whether they liked it or not. Churches mediated domestic disputes as part of their mission to promote harmony among all their congregants.[31] So did family members, as Westley Rhodes of North Carolina discovered. After he beat his wife "in a most cruel manner," she "fled to her father's house." Her mother came marching back to her son-in-law's house, where she "reprimanded him for his conduct" and "struck him with a tobacco stem which she had picked up on the road." As the actions of Westley Rhodes's wife indicate, intervention required a wife's active participation. She had to make her problems known before family and community members could do anything.[32]

It was a short step from informal community forums to the localized legal system. Domestic violence figured in a range of legal matters, including divorce and vagrancy, involving free women, white and black, from varied economic backgrounds. Domestic violence also appeared as a public legal matter in its own right. The prosecution of wife beating as a breach of the peace was routine at the magistrates' level. Magistrates issued peace warrants, an action that brought husbands under public scrutiny by forcing them to post bond to keep the peace toward their wives. Of course, peace warrants were not an ideal solution. It is difficult to imagine that arrest and posting bond did anything to improve a husband's temper. Still, peace warrants allowed wives a way out of the confines of domestic privacy by ensuring public monitoring of the situation and promising penalties for further abuse. With this process, wives legally transformed their husbands' violence from personal conflicts into illegal acts that endangered the public order. They also affirmed a view of marriage in which their husbands' patriarchal authority did not sever wives' ties to either the community or the public, juridical body represented by the peace.[33]

The legal implications of wives' claims emerged in sharp relief when local officials took the next step and prosecuted husbands for assaulting their wives. To do so, officials invoked the peace, construing wives' injuries as a threat to the social order and forcing husbands to account for their actions. Domestic violence, for instance, appeared on the court dockets as criminal matters in both North Carolina and South Carolina before the Civil War. Such cases made their way through the system with little fanfare or note, precisely because the notion that wives' injuries constituted an offense to the peace was well established within localized legal culture. They surfaced regularly, but not frequently; it is impossible to be more exact than that, because of the incomplete nature of the records. Records exist for cases that were heard by grand juries or went to trial at the district or superior court level. At this level, courts dealt with domestic violence cases anywhere from once a year to once a decade, depending on the county. But the existing records underestimate the number of such complaints, since many of the cases that magistrates fielded went unrecorded.[34] In many instances, the fact that the conflict had reached the district or superior court indicated that the tide of public opinion had already turned against defendants. Not surprisingly, a significant portion of defendants pled guilty. The courts took these cases seriously, issuing convictions and sentences that ranged from the symbolic to the severe. In Kershaw District, South Carolina, for instance, Christopher Cain was fined one dollar in 1803; Henry Butler was imprisoned for twelve months in 1824; and David Jamison was fined twenty dollars and imprisoned for three months in 1836.[35]

That domestic violence cases appeared on court dockets may seem surprising, given the legal and cultural impediments to prosecuting husbands. Those impediments—which took the form of long-standing patriarchal principles that gave husbands the authority to discipline their wives and that discounted the credibility of wives' testimony—remained in place despite the prosecution of domestic violence. When domestic violence was prosecuted in localized law, the presumption was that husbands could use physical force against their wives. So the crime was the injury to the public body, which placed the legal emphasis on the severity of the husbands' physical acts: the question was whether the violence rose to the level of a public disturbance, not whether the wives' rights had been violated. As a result, explanations about the cause of the conflict—which established whether the victim had done something to justify the violence—rarely made it into the record. Usually the documents contain only generic language indicating that the wife experienced violence that breached the peace. Typical were the case documents of Mary Jamison, which stated that her husband "did assault & beat the deponent & that he has frequently at other times beaten her & threatened her with great violence." Further explanation was unnecessary, since physical evidence of abuse usually corroborated the complaint.[36]

When officials did elaborate, they specified the weapons used, the length of the ordeal, and the severity of the blows, presumably to buttress the case. Kershaw District officials were meticulous in this regard, blazing a grisly trail through the underside of marriage. In 1807 Mary McAdams claimed that her husband assaulted her "by aiming at her hand a dutch oven, which had she not warded it off by receiving the blow on her left arm, must have taken her life." He "did also some time before beat her in a cruel manner with a pair of fir tongs to the danger of her life." In 1818 Mary Parker listed three incidents of violence, substantiated by her neighbors. The first time, her husband "beat hir . . . with his fist & kicked her in the most violent manner." The second time "was with a hickery stick over the hips & loins while he held hir with hir head between his knees." The third "was with his fist, and by butting her & forcing her head against the wall with the appearant intention of braking her scull." That time, her husband also drew "his knife and swore that he would cut [her] throat, & forced her to drink ardent spirits." In 1824 Sarah Butler claimed that her husband "did shoot at the body of her the said Sarah and that she has reason to believe and does believe that it was with a premeditated intention to murder her the said Sarah." These allegations played crucial legal roles in cases that depended on establishing the severity of the violence wives had experienced. Brutality had to reach beyond the discretionary authority that all husbands could exercise; it had to upset the good order of the community at large.[37]

Wives' desperation is painfully audible in the documents. They begged local officials to act, corroborating their complaints with the physical evidence of their bruised and bloody bodies. But their desperation also carried a strong undertone of confidence: not the self-possession of women standing up for themselves to challenge existing norms, but the certainty of women who were deeply embedded within their communities, intimately familiar with local customs, and entitled to support, given their particular circumstances. As these women saw it, they had experienced forms of physical violence that fell outside their husbands' patriarchal prerogatives, and they were certain that existing social networks should do something about the situation. Yet they also knew that support would not materialize without effort. They had to generate it, mobilizing their own connections to neighbors and kin and pushing them to acknowledge the situation as a problem. Wives talked. They displayed their injuries. They appeared on doorsteps, sometimes with angry husbands on their heels. They even posted notices in newspapers, advertising their husbands' bad behavior. When wives failed to create allies, they nonetheless turned reluctant bystanders into material witnesses. Those networks amplified their voices and extended the scope of the problem, transforming a marital conflict between husband and wife into a larger community concern.[38]

Wives struggled to make their voices heard in domestic violence cases, but they did so within a system where the logic of their subordination neither isolated them within private households nor exempted their husbands from public scrutiny. By contrast, wives ran into trouble when individual rights replaced the collective interests of the peace in the legal system. The new logic made it nearly impossible to prosecute husbands; wives' injuries could not qualify as a violation of their rights, since they were not legally recognized individuals who could claim the full array of rights in their own names. The rubric of rights also turned the cases toward the reasons for the conflict, with husbands defending their actions in terms of a violation of their rights. They made claims to their wives' services: food preparation, housekeeping, sex, child care, and emotional support, as well as financial assistance in the household economy, when required. Then they stretched these expectations, turning services that wives provided within the context of a marital relationship into individual rights. When wives denied them those rights, they could retaliate, however they saw fit, to secure what was theirs. Husbands also insisted on domestic privacy, arguing that their rights as husbands turned the marriage into a private relationship. Husbands in the late eighteenth century and the early nineteenth construed their wives' domestic services and the marital relationship in similar terms. Many may have seen themselves as "disciplining" wives who had not provided adequate domestic services, which were the men's due as husbands—at least as they saw it. But such views did not carry the legal weight that they later would: husbands' claims and, especially, their use of violence to enforce them did not always comport with the peace.[39]

The standard of rights, operative today, still foils the prosecution of domestic violence. Given the pervasiveness of that standard and its attendant difficulties, it is no wonder that historians have assumed that wives in the nineteenth century, who had far fewer rights than wives in the twentieth, had no legal recourse against domestic violence. Yet they did, because rights were not the means for mounting criminal charges against husbands; the maintenance of "quiet," orderly households was central to the community, so husbands who beat their wives could be charged with disrupting the peace.[40]

Wives' domestic violence cases shared important elements with other cases of assault against women. Women—married and unmarried—were frequent targets of violence, usually at the hands of male neighbors or kin, although women also attacked other women. Some of these acts had nothing to do with the fact that the victims were women: in a society where violence was commonplace, women were not exempt. As women, though, they were also particularly vulnerable. Some men expanded patriarchal principles that established husbands' authority over their wives to make broad claims of masculine authority over all women. Women's subordinate status also lowered their credit, opening them up to scorn and abuse from men and other women. Regardless of the reasons for violence, women fought back, using the same strategies that wives employed in domestic violence cases. If the victim was married, her husband was usually listed as the prosecutor. Not only was his presence legally necessary, but it also lent credibility to his wife's claims. But husbands often played supporting roles, particularly if the incident occurred in their absence. Their wives were the ones who initiated the process and provided all the details necessary for the case to go forward in the courts. Unmarried women prosecuted their claims themselves, bringing in neighbors and kin to provide statements and to testify to their good credit. Women found it easier to prosecute cases against men who were not their husbands. Even so, they still required support to amplify their voices. Through that process, though, they made important legal points, placing limits on the meaning of their subordination within the patriarchal order. Their position as women did not make them equally subordinate to all men; nor did it mean that they were so degraded and isolated as to have no recourse against such abuse when it did happen.[41]

Not all women, however, could transform violence into a violation of the peace. Their ability to do so depended on credit, the assumed, unstated context that made explanations of domestic conflicts unnecessary. In 1818, for instance, fourteen men submitted a petition affirming the credit of Mary Parker, who filed charges against her husband for domestic abuse. "We the subscribers," they wrote, "do hereby certify that since Mrs. Parker . . . has lived in our neighbourhood, we have never seen any thing in her conduct, & deportment but what was fair & becoming." Because she had credit, her complaint had validity. That her husband's credit was poor made her more believable. He noted as much in his own statement. "Some of those persons who signed Mrs. Parkers good character," he admitted, "did it from principles of charity & goodness." "Others," however, "did it for the purposes of gratifying their envious and malicious designs . . . to sink him in public esteem."[42]

Consider the difference between Sarah Chandler and Mary Meadows, both of whom lived in Granville County, North Carolina. In 1824, Sarah Chandler swore out two complaints against her husband. The first time, the magistrate issued a peace warrant. The second time, he charged her husband with assault and battery. One year later, the Granville County Superior Court granted her a divorce in a case that featured evidence of her husband's abuse.[43] In their depositions, neighbors and kin emphasized the ways that Thomas Chandler's behavior negatively affected the larger community. The severity of the abuse clearly transgressed community norms. He neglected his duties, as a neighbor as well as a husband. He fought constantly, introducing unnecessary conflict into the community and threatening vital social networks. He drank to excess and neglected to work his property as he should, failing to support his family and to fulfill his part in the economic web that knit rural communities together. He squandered the property that Sarah had brought into the marriage, threatening the patrimony of her family and their efforts to provide for their heirs, Sarah's children. The effects of Thomas Chandler's domestic abuse spun outward, affecting everyone in the community in direct, tangible ways. That was the basis of the criminal actions against him. That logic also figured into the divorce. When Sarah Chandler petitioned for divorce in 1826, cruelty was grounds only for a separation, not a divorce. Yet the evidence of domestic abuse, established through the legal guise of the peace, buttressed her cause in a localized system where a jury decided her case.[44]

Evaluations of Thomas Chandler's credit dominate the records. Yet in this case and others, the wives' credit was equally determinative. That

Sarah Chandler was able to proceed with her legal suits indicates her credit's weight, which prompted the outpouring of community support. But the value of women's credit, which solidified their connections in their communities and established their place within the peace, is most apparent in cases where women had none. Mary Meadows's husband was as disreputable as Thomas Chandler. But so was Mary Meadows. Loud and opinionated, she was particularly vocal on the subject of her husband. As one witness later testified, Mary Meadows vowed that she "intended to have him [her husband] fixed at . . . court, so that he should not be scandalizing her." To that end, she complained about him repeatedly in the neighborhood, displaying a decided lack of skill in bringing her neighbors over to her side. Once, while grinding corn at her neighbors', the Duncans, with several other women, she offered to work for the Duncan family for one year without pay if John Duncan would kill her husband. Susannah Duncan overheard a conversation between Mary Meadows and Thomas Murray, who had his own quarrel with her husband and had gone so far as to load a gun to shoot him, before deciding against it. Mary Meadows reportedly said that "she wished that Murry had . . . blowed that load through him." She made a similar statement to Samuel Jackson, rebuking him for not "knock[ing]" her husband's "brains out" when the two men had fought earlier. When no aid was forthcoming, she felt compelled to take matters into her own hands. She told James Hobgood that she intended to have her husband beaten, boasting that he "would be the worst whiped man he [Hobgood] ever saw." The beating would be so severe, she claimed, that "his hide would not hold shucks." One week later, her husband was found murdered and emasculated, his severed testicles stuffed in his mouth. Mary Meadows and a slave named George were arrested for his murder. The documents do not divulge all the gossip that obviously surrounded this notorious case. Some of the statements suggest that Mary Meadows and George were involved in an illicit relationship, although the records do not establish that as a fact. Just as problematic, though, was the obvious distaste for Mary Meadows that had accumulated more slowly and less dramatically through daily interactions with her neighbors. Because of her own dismal credit, Mary Meadows's marital disputes became part of the peace only when she was accused of her husband's murder.[45]

The concepts that wives articulated in these cases acquired legal resonance, even when they lost their suits. More to the point, women made the arguments that they did because they knew which points already had legitimacy within their local communities. Success in localized law generally depended on aligning one's cause with well-established customary arrangements, not departing from them. Yet women also played crucial roles in creating the customary foundation that shaped the dynamics of localized law. Their claims then percolated through the system, where they shaped matters in the localized system and occasionally lodged in statute or appellate law. Take, for instance, the definition of cruelty in North Carolina statute law. In the statute framed after the Revolution, cruelty covered any situation whereby a "person shall either abandon his family or maliciously turn his wife out of doors, or by cruel or barbarous treatment endanger her life, or offer such indignities to her person as to render her condition intolerable or life burthensome." Evaluating the evidence in context, where it was impossible to separate the people involved from legal abstractions, the local courts saw cruelty—and other causes for separation and divorce—more frequently than did the legislature. In 1828, the North Carolina legislature acknowledged this altered legal landscape and expanded the statutes to include situations where "a man shall become an habitual drunkard or spendthrift, wasting his substance to the impoverishment of his family."[46] The phrase "wasted his substance" also captured complaints that wives frequently made, not just in the context of divorce, about their husbands' appropriation of family resources. The "substance" that had been "wasted" included a man's labor, health, guidance, and social standing, as well as property, all of which should have gone for the good of the family, as wives saw it. The phrase carried legal meaning because it expressed long-standing assumptions about marital relations, maintained within the terms of the peace, largely through the efforts of women. The 1828 statute distilled those values in stylized form, importing custom to modify a realm of law that mediated marital conflicts through the model of competing property rights.

None of the women in this chapter demanded civil or political rights, certainly not before the Civil War and probably not afterward, either. Yet all assumed their centrality to the social order, though they recognized and accepted their subordination within it. And all insisted—at some level—on having some say about the dynamics of their own lives and those of their communities. That legacy is crucial in understanding southern women's changing relationship to law and politics during and after the Civil War.

First, it expands our vision of politics so that we can see women's *various* claims, even when they did not involve what we now think of as women's issues. Specifically, it allows us to see poor white and African American women's political claims. During the Civil War, when slavery was crumbling but emancipation was still uncertain, African Americans used the law in new ways, initiating cases and trying to mobilize the system to pursue social justice for themselves, their families, and their communities. These efforts, which are well documented in the primary records and secondary literature, included African American women. They began during the Civil War, with refugees and black soldiers firing off letters and complaints to federal officers and agencies. They continued after the Civil War, before the passage of the Fourteenth Amendment and under the notorious state Black Codes, which limited African Americans' individual rights and barred them from using local and state courts in most instances. Freedpeople nonetheless brought complaints to federal Freedmen's Bureau officials, turning them into legal intermediaries. After the passage of the Fourteenth Amendment and the democratic restructuring of southern state governments, freedpeople made valiant efforts to use all the new legal arenas open to them, at the local, state, and federal levels. As recent scholarship suggests, African Americans made substantive claims about the postemancipation social order in these legal arenas that went beyond their individual rights: they made powerful statements about economic justice, racial equality, and political democracy.[47] Freedpeople turned to the legal system because of the dramatic policy changes of the era, which not only granted them individual rights that allowed new kinds of access, but also encouraged them to think that the system could now be a more reliable ally. As important as those changes were, however, they constitute only part of the story. African Americans' past experiences also encouraged them to look to the legal system. Like other southerners, they were familiar with the system's workings. More than that, they had experienced law as a system designed to protect community order. After emancipation, African Americans had every reason to think that they could assume more active roles in defining the public order, even when their claims to individual rights were tenuous.

Those expectations are particularly pronounced in the actions of freedwomen, who did not acquire the full range of rights that freedmen did. In fact, African American women shed the legal bonds of slavery only to acquire all the legal disabilities of other free women. In fact, few of these women used the legal system to claim civil and political rights for themselves as women. Rather, they acted on the expectation that they, as women, could use the legal system to participate in the governance of their communities. This time, however, they could create an order that reflected their interests and concerns. They used the legal system, for instance, to address a range of domestic issues that directly affected their lives: they filed for divorce, brought charges against their husbands for neglect and abuse, informed on annoying neighbors, testified in cases involving community conflicts, and prosecuted neighbors and even family members on behalf of their children. These uses of the legal system were strikingly similar to those of white southern women of poor to modest means, who had expected the legal system to resolve such problems before the Civil War and continued to bring such cases afterward.[48] The actions of African American women are strikingly similar to those of many white women who approached the legal system with the same expectations, although with very different notions of what the peace should look like. They too used the legal system to regulate social relations and to insert their own visions of order into the process of local governance.

This perspective, then, roots Anne Scott's southern ladies not only in the antebellum past but also within a political culture that always involved women, although not always in the same way or working toward the same ends. Anne's ladies took the leap and demanded the vote and a place in party politics. But their actions were connected to those of other southern women, before and after the Civil War, who also expected that they should have a say in community governance, particularly at the local level. That expectation—and that expectation only—is what links these different groups of women together. From there, they diverged, pursuing political goals that went in radically different, often conflicting directions. Yet we do southern women a disservice if we evaluate their political activities by one standard—the pursuit of civil and political rights for women. We miss the diversity that characterized southern women, for good and for bad, and we miss their full importance in shaping the trajectory of southern history.

Finally, the southern women I found in the local records remind me a little of Anne Scott herself. They are formidable women, like Anne. They saw themselves as part of southern society, and they, like Anne, proceeded with the assumption that they should have a say in what was happening around them. And they shaped the terrain on which others worked, just as Anne Scott's work has shaped the terrain on which we all, as southern women's historians, work.

Notes

1. Anne Firor Scott, *The Southern Lady: From Pedestal to Politics, 1830–1930* (Chicago: University of Chicago Press, 1970).

2. This chapter draws on material from Laura F. Edwards, "Status without Rights: African Americans and the Tangled History of Law and Governance in the Nineteenth-Century U.S. South," *American Historical Review* 112 (April 2007): 365–393; "Enslaved Women and the Law: The Paradoxes of Subordination in the Post-Revolutionary Carolinas," *Slavery and Abolition* 26 (August 2005): 305–23; and *The People and Their Peace: Governance and Authority in the Post-Revolutionary South* (Chapel Hill: University of North Carolina Press, 2009), esp. chaps. 3 and 5.

3. This chapter is based on legal records and a range of other sources from both the local and state levels, 1787 to 1840. Materials from the local level are from Orange, Granville, and Chowan Counties in North Carolina and Kershaw, Anderson-Pendleton, and Spartanburg Districts in South Carolina. The research includes extensive runs of court documents from those areas. Unlike sampling, which abstracts cases from context, this intensive approach reveals information that is essential in understanding the underlying conflicts and their resolutions. Such an approach also allows insight into the ways that people defined law, on the ground, in the years following the Revolution. That perspective is particularly important, since so many areas of law were left to local discretion in this period. The research then extends outward to other counties to include divorce, apprenticeship, poorhouse, and church records. At the state level, the materials cover statutes, appellate decisions, and various published legal sources; state government documents such as governors' correspondence, legislative committee reports, pardons, and petitions; newspapers; and the diaries and letter collections of various leaders in state law and politics. Although I focus on particular examples from these source groups, my analysis is representative of larger patterns within the research more generally.

4. Edwards, *The People and Their Peace*, chap. 2.

5. Ibid.

6. Ibid. New trends in legal and political history have emphasized the importance of localism throughout the United States, suggesting that the South was not so distinctive. See esp. William H. Novak, *The People's Welfare: Law and Regulation in Nineteenth-Century America* (Chapel Hill: University of North Carolina Press, 1996).

7. Edwards, *The People and Their Peace*, chap. 2. Property matters on the civil side of the law constituted the great bulk of court business in most southern jurisdictions. In *Vengeance and Justice: Crime and Punishment in the Nineteenth-Century American South* (New York: Oxford University Press, 1984), Edward Ayers estimated that there were about three or four civil cases for every criminal case in a typical southern court (32). See also Ariela Gross, *Double Character: Slavery and Mastery in the Antebellum Southern Courtroom* (Princeton: Princeton University Press, 2000), 23. Those patterns also characterized the courts in Granville County, Orange County, and Chowan

County. At that time, civil suits over financial and property transactions predominated throughout the United States.

8. Edwards, *The People and Their Peace*, chap. 4. This discussion draws on the scholarship that uses gender to illuminate women's status and their relation to government in the early modern period and the Age of Revolution. See, e.g., Susan Dwyer Amussen, *An Ordered Society: Gender and Class in Early Modern England* (Oxford: Blackwell, 1988); Kathleen M. Brown, *Good Wives, "Nasty Wenches," and Anxious Patriarchs: Gender, Race, and Power in Colonial Virginia* (Chapel Hill: University of North Carolina Press, 1996); Nancy Fraser and Linda Gordon, "A Genealogy of Dependency: Tracing a Keyword of the U.S. Welfare State," *Signs* 19 (Winter 1994): 309–36; Carol Karlsen, *The Devil in the Shape of a Woman: Witchcraft in Colonial New England* (New York: Oxford University Press, 1987); Linda K. Kerber, *Women of the Republic: Intellect and Ideology in Revolutionary America* (Chapel Hill: University of North Carolina Press, 1980); Joan B. Landes, *Women and the Public Sphere in the Age of the French Revolution* (Ithaca: Cornell University Press, 1988).

9. Edwards, "Status without Rights," "Enslaved Women and the Law," and *The People and Their Peace*, chaps. 3 and 4.

10. Ibid.

11. The patterns in inquests are drawn primarily from Court of General Sessions, Coroner's Inquisitions, Kershaw District; Court of General Sessions, Coroner's Inquisitions, Pendleton District; Court of General Sessions, Coroner's Inquisitions, Anderson District; all in South Carolina Department of Archives and History (SCDAH). In North Carolina, coroners' reports are not filed separately but are sometimes attached to murder cases.

12. Edwards, *The People and Their Peace*, chap. 3.

13. *State v. James Woodruff*, 1834, Spartanburg County, Magistrates and Freeholders Court, SCDAH. These issues are discussed in more detail in Edwards, *The People and Their Peace*, chaps. 3 and 4.

14. *State v. Robert Mitchell*, 1844, Vagrancy Trials, Magistrates and Freeholders Court, Spartanburg District, SCDAH. These issues are discussed in more detail in Edwards, *The People and Their Peace*, chaps. 3 and 4.

15. For the dispute between Brother Johnson and Judy, see September 10, 16, and 17 and October 4, 1824, and January 5, 1827, Big Creek Baptist Church, Anderson District, South Caroliniana Library (SCL). For a similar analysis of African Americans' use of church disciplinary hearings, see Betty Wood, "'For Their Satisfaction or Redress': African Americans and Church Discipline in the Early South," in *The Devil's Lane: Sex and Race in the Early South*, ed. Catherine Clinton and Michele Gillespie (New York: Oxford University Press, 1997), 109–23. These issues are discussed in more detail in Edwards, *The People and Their Peace*, chaps. 3 and 4.

16. Edwards, "Status without Rights," "Enslaved Women and the Law," and *The People and Their Peace*, chaps. 3 and 4.

17. This section is based on *The People and Their Peace*, chap. 6.

18. Mary Southwick, 1810, Petitions, General Assembly, Sessions Records, North Carolina Department of Archives and History (NCDAH). Edward Southwick submitted a competing petition, which is attached to his wife's petition.

19. *Sarah Chandler v. Thomas Chandler*, 1826, Divorce Papers, Granville County, NCDAH.

20. Ibid. *State v. Alvin Preslar*, 1856, no. 5626, Supreme Court Original Cases, NCDAH. Sometimes women made direct claims to their husbands' property, usually in the context of alimony, indicating that they saw it as a family possession.

21. Quotes from Answer of Augustus L. Converse in *Marion Converse v. Augustus L. Converse*, Sumter District Equity Court Records, roll 227, 1854, SCDAH; Illegible [probably her mother's sister, Betty Coles] to Marion Deveaux Converse, Charlottesville, January 11, 1858, Singleton-Deveaux Family Papers, SCL.

22. Marion's petition in the separation suit reveals how she involved her family during her marriage. *Marion Converse v. Augustus L. Converse*, Sumter District Equity Court Records, roll 227, 1854. See also Marion Converse to Matt Singleton, December 20, 1853; Marion Converse to Matt Singleton, December 25, 1853, Singleton Family Papers, SCL. For the extended family's and friends' responses, see, e.g., Betty Coles to Marion Deveaux, February 19, 1854; Betty Coles to Marion Deveaux, April 1, 1854; Betty Coles to Marion Deveaux, April 11, 1854; Betty Coles to Marion Deveaux, May 16, 1854; Betty Coles to Marion Deveaux, July 31, 1854; Betty Coles to Marion Deveaux, January 15, 1855; Betty Coles to Marion Deveaux, June 5, 1856; Betty Coles to Marion Deveaux, June 28, 1856; Betty Coles to Marion Deveaux, September 17, 1856; Betty Coles to Marion Deveaux, January 11, 1857; Sally W. Taylor to Marion Converse, March 11, [1850–55]; Singleton Family Papers, Library of Congress (LC); J. Hamilton to Marion Converse, November 22, 1853; Illegible to Marion Deveaux Converse, Charlottesville, January 11, 1858; Singleton-Deveaux Family Papers, SCL. For the final cash settlement with Augustus Converse, see Agreement, February 20, 1857, Singleton-Deveaux Family Papers, SCL. The rest of the family correspondence, particularly the Singleton-Deveaux Family Papers, SCL, and the Singleton Family Papers, LC, indicates that Marion lived as if the marriage had never happened. Marion Deveaux to Sissie [Marion Deveaux], February 8, 1858; V. M. Deveaux to Sissie [Marion Deveaux], April 3, 1858; John B. Moore to Marion Deveaux, August 6, 1858; in Singleton-Deveaux Family Papers, SCL. One family history, which indicates that Marion was unsuccessful in her suit, may be referring to the fact that the Singletons were unable to get some of the property back and had to pay Augustus Converse a sizable settlement. Cassie Nicholes Papers, SCL.

23. Joan Cashin, *Family Venture: Men and Women on the Southern Frontier* (New York: Oxford University Press, 1991), 44–49; Edward E. Baptist, *Creating an Old South: Middle Florida's Plantation Frontier before the Civil War* (Chapel Hill: University of North Carolina Press, 2002), 25–26.

24. *Tabitha Fox v. John Fox*, 1840, Divorce Records, Randolph County, NCDAH. For petitions in which women or other deponents refer to "their" property, either

property that women produced or property they brought into the marriage, see *Mary W. Green v. Joseph Green*, 1847; *Hannah Mitchell v. Robert B. Mitchell*, 1831; *Eli Ann Royster v. William Royster*, 1853; *Patty Scott v. Harvey Scott*, 1824; *Susan Yarborough v. Thomas Yarborough*, 1832; Divorce Records, Granville County, NCDAH. *Andrew Arwick v. Susannah Arwick*, 1850; *Elizabeth Brower v. Christian Brower*, 1833; *Lydia Hussey v. Jesse Hussey*, 1854; *Sally Jackson v. George Jackson*, 1819; *Susannah Lamb v. Nathan Lamb*, 1850; *Mary Moffitt v. Samuel Moffitt*, 1841; *Susannah Presnell v. Randal Presnell*, 1855; *Bethany York v. Seymore York*, [1844]; *Tabitha York v. Jabez York*, 1837; Divorce Records, Randolph County, NCDAH. Elizabeth Sumner, 1801; Drusella Byars, 1808; Mary Gregory, 1808; Hanna Gunter, 1808; Lucy Crockett, 1808; Rebecca Kinster, 1809; Frances Murden, 1809; Mary Warren, 1809; Bond V. Brown, 1809; Mary Scott, 1809; Mary Southwick, 1810; Margaret Jackson, 1825–26; Mary Turner, 1826–27; Elizabeth Dare, 1826–27; Frances H. Dilliard, 1828–29; Petitions, General Assembly, Sessions Records, NCDAH.

25. *Tabitha Fox v. John Fox*, 1840, Divorce Records, Randolph County, NCDAH. *State v. Alvin Preslar*, 1856, no. 5626, Supreme Court Original Cases, NCDAH. Women's divorce petitions often contain formulaic language about their husbands' refusal of support to establish abandonment, one of the statutory grounds for divorce. In some petitions, however, women elaborated, revealing a clear sense of labor—their own, their children's, and their husbands'—as a family resource. See, e.g., *Martha Meacham v. Samuel Meacham*, 1839; *Lucy Minor v. John Minor*, 1834; *Eli Ann Royster v. William Royster*, 1853; *Susan A. Satterwhite v. James A. Satterwhite*, 1859; *Mary Stanfield v. John A. Stanfield*, 1839; *Amanda Walker v. William Walker*, 1847 (she is also referring to his appropriation of slaves' labor); *Elizabeth Wheeler v. Moses Wheeler*, 1831; Divorce Records, Granville County, NCDAH. *Jane Hicks v. Willis Hicks*, 1834; *Susannah Lamb v. Nathan Lamb*, 1850; *Nancy Pugh v. Jesse E. Pugh*, 1836; *Hannah Ridge v. Meredith Ridge*, 1849; Divorce Records, Randolph County, NCDAH. Elizabeth Stevens, 1808; Sally Hampton, 1823–24; Jane Welborn, 1823–24; Petitions, General Assembly, Sessions Records, NCDAH.

26. Biography of Edward Isham, alias Hardaway Bone, Notebook of David Schenck, David Schenck Papers, NCDAH. See also the transcription of his narrative and interpretive essays in Charles C. Bolton and Scott P. Culclasure, eds., *The Confessions of Edward Isham: A Poor White Life of the Old South* (Athens: University of Georgia Press, 1998). While Isham turned his life into a tall tale, the economic dynamics were not unusual in this period. See Paul E. Johnson, "The Modernization of Mayo Greenleaf Patch: Land, Family, and Marginality in New England, 1766–1816," *New England Quarterly* 55 (December 1982): 488–516.

27. For the difficulties presented by economic change in this period, see in particular Edward J. Balleisen, *Navigating Failure: Bankruptcy and Commercial Society in Antebellum America* (Chapel Hill: University of North Carolina Press, 2001); Scott A. Sandage, *Born Losers: A History of Failure in America* (Cambridge: Harvard University Press, 2005). Concerns about economic volatility are apparent in much

of the scholarship on the South in the period between 1787 and 1860. See Charles C. Bolton, *Poor Whites of the Antebellum South: Tenants and Laborers in Central North Carolina and Northeast Mississippi* (Durham, N.C.: Duke University Press, 1994); Peter Coclanis, *The Shadow of a Dream: Economic Life and Death in the South Carolina Low Country, 1670–1920* (New York: Oxford University Press, 1989); Paul D. Escott, *Many Excellent People: Power and Privilege in North Carolina, 1850–1900* (Chapel Hill: University of North Carolina Press, 1985).

28. See, e.g., William I. Leary, North Carolina, vol. 5, p. 237; James D. Williams, North Carolina, vol. 5, p. 234A; Dr. W. I. McKain, South Carolina, vol. 11, p. 42; in R. G. Dun and Co. Collection, Baker Library, Harvard Business School.

29. Women supporting themselves was unusual, but not uncommon; the same skills that women contributed to the household economy also had value outside it. Guion Griffis Johnson, *Ante-bellum North Carolina: A Social History* (Chapel Hill: University of North Carolina Press, 1937), 245–50. Recent scholarship has stressed the value of women's labor on the market. Whereas most of that work focuses on the North, the same trends were evident, although to a lesser degree, in the South. See Jeanne Boydston, *Home and Work: Housework, Wages, and the Ideology of Labor in the Early Republic* (New York: Oxford University Press, 1990); Christopher Clark, *The Roots of Rural Capitalism: Western Massachusetts, 1780–1860* (New York: Cornell University Press, 1990); Thomas Dublin, *Women at Work: The Transformation of Work and Community in Lowell, Massachusetts, 1826–1860* (New York: Columbia University Press, 1979); Johnson, "Modernization of Mayo Greenleaf Patch."

30. For petitions that identify husbands' debts and creditors as the reason for obtaining a divorce or separation, see *Susan Yarborough v. Thomas Yarborough*, 1832, Divorce Records, Granville County, NCDAH. *Christiana Deving v. Thomas Deving*, 1821; *Susannah Lamb v. Nathan Lamb*, 1850; *Even Lane v. John Lane*, 1829; *Mary Moffitt v. Samuel Moffitt*, 1841; *Susannah Presnell v. Randal Presnell*, 1855; *Nancy Pugh v. Jesse E. Pugh*, 1836; *Hannah Ridge v. Meredith Ridge*, 1849; *Eltha Vuncannon v. John Vuncannon*, 1841; *Tabitha York v. Jabez York*, 1837; Divorce Records, Randolph County, NCDAH. Susannah Query, 1801; Mildred Wills, 1801; A. E. Barbara Elrod, 1803; Elizabeth Davis, 1808; Lucy Crockett, 1808; Jane O'Briant, 1808; Catherine Oel, 1809; Mary Warren, 1809; Nancy Johnson, 1809; Phebe McKaughan, 1810; Susan P. Davis, 1821–22; Levice Pennington, 1821–22; Jane Welborn, 1823–24; Margaret Jackson, 1825–26; Sarah McCully, 1825–26; Mildred McLilley, 1826–27; Elizabeth Dare, 1826–27; Nancy McKinney, 1826–27; Petitions, General Assembly, Sessions Records, NCDAH.

31. Churches regularly mediated domestic conflicts. For records where such cases were particularly prominent, see Abbott's Creek Primitive Baptist Church, Minutes, 1783–1879, Davidson County; Bush Arbor Primitive Baptist Church, Church Minutes, 1806–1919, Anderson Township, Caswell County and Bush Arbor Primitive Baptist Church, Anderson Township, Caswell County, Minutes, 1807–1960; Red Banks Primitive Baptist Church, Minutes, 1791–1904, Pitt County; Three Forks Baptist Church, minutes, 1790–1895, Wilkes County, N.C.; Wheeley's Primitive

Baptist Church, Roxboro, Session Minutes and Roll Book, 1790–1898, Person County, N.C.; all in NCDAH. Methodist Church, Horry County, Waccamaw Circuit and Conwayborough Circuit; Bethabara Baptist Church, Laurens County; Thomas Memorial Baptist Church, Marlboro County; Church Book, Bethesda Baptist Church (Primitive), 1823–1905, Kershaw District, S.C.; all in SCL. Fall Creek Baptist Church Records, 1819–90, Chatham County, no. 4418, SHC. See also Lacy K. Ford Jr., *Origins of Southern Radicalism: The South Carolina Upcountry, 1800–1860* (New York: Oxford University Press, 1988), 33–36; Jean E. Friedman, *The Enclosed Garden: Women and Community in the Evangelical South, 1830–1900* (Chapel Hill: University of North Carolina Press, 1985), esp. 14–20.

32. *State v. Marvel Littlefield*, 1841; Vagrancy Trials, Court of Magistrates and Freeholders, Spartanburg District. *State v. Thomas Watkins*, 1819; Vagrancy Trials, Court of Magistrates and Freeholders, Laurens District. The account of Westley Rhodes appears in Bill Cecil-Fronsman, *Common Whites: Class and Culture in Antebellum North Carolina* (Lexington: University of Kentucky Press, 1992), 133; see also 156–64. Women often mention fleeing to the houses of neighbors or relatives in divorce petitions that allege physical abuse. See also Laura F. Edwards, "Law, Domestic Violence, and the Limits of Patriarchal Authority in the Antebellum South," *Journal of Southern History* 65 (November 1999): 733–70.

33. Manuals for justices of the peace dating from the early part of the century clearly stated that wives could swear out peace warrants against their husbands. In law, the offense acquired the status of a public crime because it was a breach of the public peace. There was no clear legal line between peace warrants and other crimes involving violence. By this logic, local officials could charge abusive husbands with the crime of assault either in addition to or as a component of the peace warrant. See John Haywood, *The Duty and Office of Justices of the Peace, Sheriffs, Coroners, Constables, &c. According to the Laws of the State of North Carolina* (Raleigh, 1808), 6–7, 15–16, 28–32, 191; John Faucheraud Grimké, *The South Carolina Justice of the Peace* (Philadelphia, 1788), 7–9, 23–32, 450–68. Between 1800 and 1840, for instance, there are twenty-five peace warrants that were saved in the Granville County Criminal Action Papers, NCDAH; but that figure does not represent all the peace warrants, let alone all the complaints, since not all the magistrates' papers were saved. The peace bonds for Anderson District and Pendleton District in South Carolina are separated from the other court records, unsorted, and extremely voluminous. A sampling of these records indicates that magistrates routinely swore out bonds against husbands on complaints of their wives and daughters. See Peace Bonds, 1828–1905, Court of General Sessions, Anderson County, SCDAH. For similar patterns, see Stephanie Cole, "Keeping the Peace: Domestic Assault and Private Prosecution in Antebellum Baltimore," in *Over the Threshold: Intimate Violence in Early America*, ed. Christine Daniels and Michael V. Kennedy (New York: Routledge, 1999), 148–69.

34. There were twelve recorded assault cases in Granville County between 1800 and 1840. Criminal Action Papers, Granville County, NCDAH. At least fourteen

assault cases were recorded in Kershaw between 1795 and 1840. Indictments, Court of General Sessions, Kershaw District, SCDAH. Only one assault case was recorded in Anderson District. *State v. Andrew Oliver*, Spring Term 1839, no. 6, Indictments, Court of General Sessions, Anderson District, SCDAH. For similar patterns, see Cole, "Keeping the Peace."

35. *State v. Christopher Cain*, 1803, Indictments; *State v. Henry L. Butler*, 1824, Journal and Indictments; *State v. David Jamison*, 1836, Indictments; all in Court of General Sessions, Kershaw District, SCDAH.

36. *State v. David Jamison*, 1836, Indictments, Court of General Sessions, Kershaw District, SCDAH.

37. *State v. Joseph McAdams*, 1807; *State v. John Parker*, 1818; *State v. Henry L. Butler*, 1824; all in Indictments, Court of General Sessions, Kershaw District, SCDAH.

38. The cases from Kershaw District are particularly revealing of wives' strategies in mobilizing community support.

39. After the Civil War, the records were more likely to include husbands' explanations, which emphasized wives' failure to provide domestic services as a violation of their rights; see Edwards, "Women and the Law." In the late eighteenth century and the early nineteenth, by contrast, the records tended to omit such explanations, largely because they were irrelevant to the proceedings. When they were included, husbands usually cited their wives' alienation of affection or adultery as the reasons for their violence.

40. Existing scholarship in southern history focuses on the courts' refusal to deal with domestic violence: Peter Bardaglio, *Reconstructing the Household* (Chapel Hill: University of North Carolina Press, 1998), 33–34; Victoria E. Bynum, *Unruly Women: The Politics of Social and Sexual Control in the Old South* (Chapel Hill: University of North Carolina Press, 1992), 70–72; Edwards, "Women and the Law." Studies of violence by husbands against wives in the nineteenth century generally also tend to emphasize community controls over legal ones, affirming the idea that the issue remained outside official structures of governance. See David Peterson del Mar, *What Trouble I Have Seen: A History of Violence against Wives* (Cambridge: Harvard University Press, 1996); Linda Gordon, *Heroes of Their Own Lives: The Politics and History of Family Violence* (New York: Viking, 1988); Pamela Haag, "The 'Ill-Use of a Wife': Patterns of Working-Class Violence in Domestic and Public New York City, 1860–1880," *Journal of Social History* 25 (Spring 1992): 447–77; Jerome Nadelhaft, "Wife Torture: A Known Phenomenon in Nineteenth-Century America," *Journal of American Culture* 10 (Fall 1987): 39–59; Elizabeth Pleck, *Domestic Tyranny: The Making of Social Policy against Family Violence from Colonial Times to the Present* (New York: Oxford University Press, 1987); Christine Stansell, *City of Women: Sex and Class in New York, 1789–1860* (Urbana: University of Illinois Press, 1987), 78–83.

41. Assaults against women and prosecuted by women—or women and their husbands or fathers—were common in the local court records. See Edwards, "Law, Domestic Violence, and the Limits of Patriarchal Authority."

42. *State v. John Parker*, 1818, Indictments, Court of General Sessions, Kershaw District, SCDAH.

43. *State v. Thomas Chandler*, 1825, Criminal Action Papers, Granville County, NCDAH. *Sarah Chandler v. Thomas Chandler*, 1826, Divorce Papers, Granville County, NCDAH.

44. Thomas Chandler had a history of violence that continued after his separation from Sarah. *State v. Thomas Chandler*, 1825 (for the assault of Henry Yancey); *State v. Thomas Chandler and Polly Cutts*, 1829 (for fornication and adultery); both in Granville County, Criminal Action Papers. In 1823 he was pardoned for the maiming of Henry Yancey; Gabriel Holmes, Pardon of Thomas Chandler, September 11, 1823, vol. 25, p. 111, Governors' Letters Books (GLB), NCDAH.

45. *State v. George and Mary Meadows*, 1847, Criminal Actions concerning Slaves and Free Persons of Color, Granville County, NCDAH. For a more detailed discussion of this case, see Laura F. Edwards, "Law, Domestic Violence, and the Limits of Patriarchal Authority"; see also Bynum, *Unruly Women*, 85–87.

46. Johnson, *Ante-bellum North Carolina: A Social History* (Chapel Hill: University of North Carolina Press, 1937), 217–23.

47. African Americans' use of law—at all levels—is a common theme in the secondary literature on the Civil War and Reconstruction.

48. Ira Berlin, Stephen F. Miller, and Leslie S. Rowland, "Afro-American Families in the Transition from Slavery to Freedom," *Radical History Review* 42 (1988): 89–121; Nancy D. Bercaw, *Gendered Freedoms: Race, Rights, and the Politics of Household in the Delta, 1861–1875* (Gainesville: University Press of Florida, 2003); Victoria Bynum, "Reshaping the Bonds of Womanhood: Divorce in Reconstruction North Carolina," in *Divided Houses: Gender and the Civil War*, ed. Catherine Clinton and Nina Silber (New York: Oxford University Press, 1992), 320–33; Laura F. Edwards, *Gendered Strife and Confusion: The Political Culture of Reconstruction* (Urbana: University of Illinois Press, 1997); Noralee Frankel, *Freedom's Women: Black Women and Families in Civil War Era Mississippi* (Bloomington: Indiana University Press, 1999); Susan E. O'Donovan, *Becoming Free in the Cotton South* (Cambridge: Harvard University Press, 2007); Hannah Rosen, "'Not That Sort of Women': Race, Gender, and Sexual Violence during the Memphis Riot of 1866," in *Sex, Love, Race: Crossing Boundaries in North American History*, ed. Martha Hodes (New York, 1999), 267–93; Leslie A. Schwalm, *A Hard Fight for We: Women's Transition from Slavery to Freedom in South Carolina* (Urbana: University of Illinois Press, 1997), 147–268; Karin L. Zipf, *Labor of Innocents: Forced Apprenticeship in North Carolina, 1715–1919* (Baton Rouge, 2005).

"How are the daughters of Eve punished?"

Rape during the Civil War

—CRYSTAL N. FEIMSTER

Anne Firor Scott's publication in 1970 of The Southern Lady *has proved invaluable to anyone interested in understanding the lives of women in the American South. Scott described her purpose as "fourfold: to describe the culturally defined image of the lady; to trace the effect this definition had on women's behavior; to describe the realities of women's lives which were often at odds with this image; to describe and characterize the struggle of women to free themselves from the confines of cultural expectation and find a way to self-determination." Indeed, it has been with similar intentions that I examine the wartime experience of black and white women in the South.*

> Scarlett's breath came back to her as suddenly and painfully as after a blow in the stomach. A Yankee, a Yankee with a long pistol on his hip! And she was alone in the house with three sick girls and the babies! As he lounged up the walk, hand on holster, beady little eyes glancing to right and left, a kaleidoscope of jumbled pictures spun in her mind, stories Aunt Pittypat had whispered of attacks on unprotected women, throat cuttings, houses burned over the heads of dying women, children bayoneted because they cried, all of the unspeakable horrors that lay bound up in the name of "Yankee."
> —MARGARET MITCHELL, *Gone with the Wind*

As a young girl growing up in the South, I was forced to watch *Gone with the Wind* throughout my primary and secondary education. As May dwindled into June, teachers grew weary of lecturing on multiplication tables or constitutional history and resorted to showing "historical films" to pass the time, with *Gone with the Wind* at the top of the list. I hated the movie at every age—and not because I wanted to crawl under my desk and die of humiliation every time a black person came on-screen. Rather, the film's violent content, specifically its sexual undertones, gave me nightmares. In one instance, Scarlett, confronted by a Yankee soldier, shoves a pistol in his face and pulls the trigger. The viewer understands Scarlett's motivation: that implicit in the "unspeakable horrors that lay bound up in the name of 'Yankee'" is the threat of rape.

Few scholars have addressed the sexual threat captured in this confrontation between Scarlett and the Union solider. In fact, historians have accepted without question the idea that Union soldiers rarely raped southern women, black or white, and have argued that sexual violence was rare during the Civil War. Yet Mitchell's fictional account of one woman's wartime experience makes clear that a perceived threat of rape during the Civil War was all too real for southern women.

Wartime rape is an issue both ancient and contemporary, evident more recently in reports of mass rapes in the Yugoslavian wars of secession and the genocidal massacres in Rwanda, but equally present in accounts from the Torah, the Bible, Homer, Anglo-Saxon chronicles, and in mythological events like the rape of the Sabine women. Indeed, much historical evidence seems to suggest that whenever and wherever men go to war, rape and the threat of sexual violence against women are inevitable, even strategic components of warfare.

Many years after the Civil War, Rebecca Latimer Felton blamed Confederate officers for failing to protect southern women from the horrors of invasion. In her 1919 memoir, she complained, "In the hour of her [Georgia's] deepest humiliation the commander-in-chief of Georgia's reserves had nothing, not a man to offer to stand between her innocent women and what an invading army might inflict upon them."[2] Southern men, especially the planter elite, Felton argued, had put "the profit of slavery" before the protection of southern womanhood.[3] Left to defend themselves, she held, southern women had proved that they were capable of participating in their own protection. Mary Chestnut, a plantation mistress in South Carolina, complained in her wartime diary, "I think these times make all women feel their humiliation in the affairs of the world. With men it is on to the field—glory, honour, praise & power. Women can only stay at home—& every paper reminds us that women are to be violated—ravished & all manner of humiliation. How are the daughters of Eve punished?"

Chestnut's words, like Felton's, capture the vulnerability and fear that women experienced during the Civil War and reveal her frustration and anger over white men's failure to protect women against sexual violence. While their husbands and fathers sought "glory, honour, praise & power" on the battlefield, elite southern white women were for the first time left unprotected and vulnerable to rape. Whether they lived on huge plantations or on isolated farms, many white women found themselves without male protection. The combined threat of slave revolts and the harsh realities of Yankee invasion forced elite southern white women for the first time to make public demands for protection and to participate in their own defense. Their acts of public protest and aggressive self-defense not only served as a political challenge to the image of the dependent and fragile southern belle but also called into question southern manhood and white men's ability to protect southern women. During the Civil War, elite white women feared sexual assault by both white and black men and openly acknowledged sexual violence as a component of war. For the first time, elite white women felt the need to make public demands for protection and to openly acknowledge sexual violence against black women. Most importantly, they challenged traditional notions of southern womanhood, not only in their public demands for protection but in their efforts to defend themselves. They understood the problem of rape in gender, rather than racial, terms.

Despite scholarly claims that the Civil War was a low-rape war, the fact that many women feared sexual assault and that hundreds and perhaps thousands of women suffered rape cannot be ignored. Not only did men and women write about sexual assaults and the fear of rape in their diaries and letters, but women, black and white, free and enslaved, pressed charges against their alleged rapists. At least 250 Union soldiers were court-martialed for the crime of rape. We cannot fully understand the postbellum rape hysteria without taking seriously the sexual vulnerability and violation that women have experienced in all wars, which the Civil War, in particular, marked for southern women.

Like many of the residents of Cass County, Felton disapproved when Georgia broke from the Union. Despite her initial dismay, she supported and remained loyal to the Confederacy. Many years later she explained, "There never was a more loyal woman in the South after we were forced by our political leaders to go to battle to defend our rights in ownership of African slaves, but they called it 'State's Right,' and all I owned was invested in slaves and my people were loyal and I stood by them to the end."[4]

White southern women, whatever their opinions of secession, quickly rallied to war and formed a solid block of moral and material support.[5] Eager to fulfill the duties required of southern womanhood and convinced that southern white men would do their part to defend home and hearth, Felton too made the sacrifices demanded by the Confederacy. "Upon nobody," explained Felton, "did the storm [war] fall more dreadful and unexpectedly than upon the women of the South." Although her children were too young to fight and her husband was physically unfit for service, she found ways of supporting the war effort. She organized and became the first president of the local Ladies Aid Society. She attended the sick, made military shirts from treasured dresses and blankets from expensive carpets, knitted socks from a dwindling supply of wool, found substitutes for coffee, tea, and sugar, and boiled the earth of her smokehouse for salt.[6] When food was short, the Feltons cultivated their farm to raise corn for the Confederate armies.

Dr. Felton, Rebecca's husband, used his medical and religious training to attend the sick at a nearby military camp. He spent many nights away from the farm, and his absence forced her to manage the plantation. As the Confederacy became more dependent on female labor and communities were stripped of able-bodied men, many women had to take charge of their plantations and assume active public roles.[7] To discard long-held beliefs of female frailty and dependence proved difficult, but Felton, like many southern women, embraced the challenge of running a plantation. She argued that "the fortitude of women of the Confederacy" had kept southern homes and families intact.[8]

For every plantation mistress who embraced her new independence, there was one who was overwhelmed and found managing slaves extremely difficult, if not impossible. Unprepared or unwilling to take on the responsibilities of running a plantation and managing slaves full-time, some women sold their slaves and abandoned their plantations. Others persevered but complained nonetheless.[9] In South Carolina, Emily Harrison confided in her diary, "I shall never get used to being left as the head of the affairs at home. I am constituted so as to crave a guide and protector. I am not an independent woman nor ever shall be." In a letter written to the Confederate secretary of war, Amanda Walker of Georgia declared that she was not "a fit and proper person" to supervise slaves. The *Macon Daily Telegraph* agreed: "Is it possible that Congress thinks . . . our women can control the slaves and oversee the farms? Do they suppose that our patriotic mothers, sisters and daughters can assume and discharge the active duties and drudgery of an overseer?"[10] Congress concurred and passed the much-contested "Twenty-Nigger Law" that exempted from service one white man on each plantation of twenty or more slaves. In the end, however, most women had little choice; they either rose to the challenge or failed miserably.

Women's anxieties about managing slaves had as much to do with their ideas about women's proper roles as with fears of slave insurrections. John Brown's raid on Harper's Ferry in 1859 had made it difficult for slaveholding women to maintain the pretense that their "servants" were happy and content with the system.[11] As far away as Florida, Susan Bradford sighed, "We feel that we can trust none of the dear black folk. I am afraid to say a word for fear it will prove to be just what should have been left unsaid."[12] Recounting the fear on her plantation in 1860, when rumors spread that slaves were planning an insurrection in Cartersville, Rebecca Felton focused on what Southerners considered a "fate worse than death," the rape of white women by black men. Reports came in during a Methodist revival held on the Felton plantation. The men, she explained, sat under the revival tent "armed to the teeth" so that immediately following the last sermon they could "go out quietly to suppress the 'rising.'" The mere suggestion of a slave rebellion exposed white men's worst fears, that they would be unable to protect their wives and daughters from sexual violence. "The terror of these risings," wrote Felton, "made Southern fathers and husbands desperate as to remedies. It is the secret of lynching instead of a legal remedy. It was 'born in the blood and bred in the bone,' and a resultant of domestic slavery in the Southern States."[13] Felton reasoned that lynching by southern white men was a natural response to the unspoken crime of rape. Writing after the war, Felton linked lynching to slave insurrections and reasoned that the threat of black rape, like lynching, was rooted in slavery.

The combined threat of slave revolts and Yankee invasion left many southern women paralyzed with fear. In 1861 a widow moaned in a letter to her sister, "Can we cope with an enemy abroad & one at home—negroes are fully alive to the state of things & are much more sensible than one would suppose. . . . I can imagine all sorts of noise at night and sometime think they are right at my door."[14] Whether southern women imagined slaves or Union soldiers outside their bedroom doors, they feared the worst: rape. It hardly mattered that slaves rarely sexually assaulted their mistresses. For white women living on isolated farms and plantations without male protection, the threat of slave violence seemed all too real.

Stories of planned insurrections and accounts of slaves turning on their mistresses spread like wildfire. In the summer of 1864, Georgia newspapers reported the lynching of two African American men accused of raping white women. Felton received a letter from her mother in which she worried, "I am the only white person on the place tonight."[15] After learning that slaves had murdered her cousin Betsy Witherspoon in her sleep, Mary Chestnut confessed in her diary, "Hitherto I have never thought of being afraid of negroes. I had never injured any of them. Why should they want to hurt me?" Giving in to her fears, Chestnut wrote, "I feel that the ground is cut away from under my feet," and she asked, "Why should they treat me any better than they have done Cousin Betsy?"[16] Undoubtedly, slaveholding women all over the South asked themselves the same question.

Yet, like Chestnut, many mistresses fought against their worst fears and hoped that their slaves would remain loyal and offer protection against invading Yankees. In the postwar period, many southern white women, despite their wartime fears, remembered their slaves as loyal and faithful, and few, if any, slaves had in fact raped their mistresses. Felton argued that the "fidelity and general excellence" of colored women "scattered all over the Southland" had prevented slaves from turning on their masters. Southerners, she explained, "owed the security of Confederate homes" to their faithful slaves.[17] In Fayetteville, North Carolina, Mrs. Anne K. Kyle agreed: "But for the kindness of my servants I don't know what would have become of me. They were very faithful. One walked up and down the passage all night and the other stayed on the back porch. Still I was afraid to close my eyes."[18] As for the question of rape, Felton explained, "When the majority of white men were in the army and plantations were crowded with slaves large and small there were fewer disturbances than occurred before or since the Civil War."[19] Elizabeth Saxon of Alabama shared her opinion: "Able-bodied white men all gone, the women and children were under their care; their willing hands labored, and by their sweat and toil our coarse fare was provided. Not an outrage was perpetrated, no house was burned. Afar off on lonely farms women with little children slept at peace, guarded by a sable crowd, whom they perfectly trusted."[20] Regardless of how southern white women remembered their wartime fears, it is clear that many of them had imagined the worst and would continue to do so long after the Civil War ended.

As the war progressed and federal troops began occupying southern territory, some women's fears seemed to shift from their slaves to Yankee troops. Rumors spread that northern soldiers planned to rape their way through the South, and refugees and local newspapers reported "outrages against women" and other atrocities allegedly committed by Union soldiers.[21] Although the U.S. military defined rape as a crime worthy of court-martial and execution, Union officers used rape and the threat of sexual violence as weapons of warfare against southern women, black and white. Some Union officers tolerated and even encouraged rape as part of a campaign of terror. For example, in New Orleans as early as 1862, General Benjamin Butler tacitly sanctioned the use of sexual violence to subdue and punish Confederate women who insulted or offended federal troops. In charge of forces garrisoning the city, General Butler issued his infamous General Order No. 28: "As the officers and soldiers of the United States have been subjected to repeated insults from the women (calling themselves ladies) of New Orleans," he declared, "it is ordered that hereafter when any female shall . . . insult or show contempt for any officer or soldier of the United States, she shall be regarded and held liable to be treated as a woman of the town plying her avocation."[22] General Butler reduced southern "ladies" who resisted federal occupation to the status of common prostitutes, thus making them unworthy of protection. White women who refused to behave in accordance with traditional notions of womanhood invited sexual overtures, wanted or unwanted. If they were raped, they would be responsible for their own victimization.

In a letter to the editor of the *New York Times*, Goldwin Smith criticized Butler's order as "coarse" and "highly reprehensible," but he also agreed with the general that southern white women were "unsexing themselves" and "provoking a dangerous collision between the citizens and the garrison, by their actions." Smith not only blamed southern women for provoking General Butler but also argued that "in spite of all the 'tenderness' and 'grace' ascribed to them by their admirers," southern women were not above "sending their female servants to a public flogging house to be flogged naked by the hands of men."[23] In his opinion, this was yet another reason why southern women should expect little mercy at the hands of federal troops.

Outraged Southerners agreed with Mayor John T. Monroe of New Orleans, who said that General Butler had given federal troops "license . . . to commit outrages . . . upon defenseless women."[24] President Jefferson Davis characterized Butler's order as an invitation to soldiers "to insult and outrage the wives, the mothers, and the sisters of our citizens," and he declared Butler "a felon, deserving of capital punishment."[25] The "Woman's Order" was criticized throughout the Confederacy as an affront to southern womanhood, and it confirmed white women's growing fears that northern men were brutes intent on waging war on "defenseless" women.[26] All over the South, women vented their rage. "I cannot express to you the indignation this thing awakened," fumed Clara Solomon of New Orleans in her diary. "I hear that the men were perfectly exasperated for you know the insult offered to us is also to them."[27] In South Carolina, both Mary Chestnut and Emma Edward Holmes wrote in their diaries that Butler's orders confirmed that Yankee soldiers were "fiends" and "beasts" determined to dishonor southern women.[28]

At the same time that southern women expressed their fear and outrage at Butler's threat, they also revealed that, in fact, they were not completely defenseless. Before federal troops ever arrived in Louisiana, Sarah Morgan of Baton Rouge confided in her journal that she had a "pistol and carving knife ready." After learning of Butler's order, she wrote, "Come to my bosom, O my discarded carving-knife, laid aside under the impression that these men were gentlemen." Julia LeGrand of New Orleans recorded in her diary that "Mrs. Norton has a hatchet, a tomahawk, and a vial of some kind of spirits with which she intends to blind all invaders."[29] Women all over the South armed themselves. On Oakland, her family plantation eight miles north of Holly Springs, Mississippi, nineteen-year-old Cordelia Lewis Scales wrote to a dear friend, "I wish you could see me now with my hair parted on the side with my black velvet zouave on & pistol by my side & riding my fine colt, Beula. I know you would take me for a Guerilla. I never ride now or walk without my pistol. Quite warlike, you see."[30] In a letter to her husband, Julia Pope Stanley of Georgia wrote, "Oh that I had more faith. But when I hear of how our women are insulted by the Yankees, my heart almost faints within me." In the end, however, she concluded that "every woman ought to be armed with a dagger to defend herself."[31] Even Jefferson Davis made sure his wife Varina had a pistol for her protection. While he made a point to show her how to use it, he suggested, "You can at least, if reduced to the last extremity, force your assailants to kill you."[32] If death represented the only alternative to rape, then it is not surprising that southern white women went to extremes to protect themselves.

Whether or not Union soldiers and officers read Butler's order as a free pass to rape, a few officers followed his example and used the threat of sexual violence to subdue Confederate women. Union major Thomas J. Jordan told women in Sparta, Tennessee, that if they refused to cook for his troops, he would be forced to "turn his men loose upon them and he would not be responsible for anything they might do," and in Selina he advised, "They had better sew up the bottoms of their petticoats" if they were unwilling to serve his troops. In Rome, Georgia, after stripping and spanking a group of young women who had emptied their chamber pots onto passing soldiers, Union troops aware of Butler's declaration justified their actions: "No one but an abandoned woman would do a thing like that. Abandoned women had no rights that anyone was bound to respect."[33]

In the fall of 1863, the W&A railroad tracks that ran by the Felton farm brought the harsh realities of war to Rebecca Felton's doorstep. Trains carried wounded soldiers and supplies through Cartersville, and as early as September, battles on the outskirts of town sent residents further south seeking refuge. Every day brought news that Union soldiers waged war against citizens, liberated and armed slaves, burned homes, and raped women.

In December the Confederate Congress intensified white women's fears when it declared, "The conduct of the enemy has been destitute of that forbearance and magnanimity which civilization and Christianity have introduced.... Houses are pillaged and burned, churches are defaced, towns are ransacked, clothing of women and infants is stripped from their persons.... Helpless women have been exposed to the most cruel outrages and to that dishonor which is infinitely worse than death."[34] Congress encouraged women to flee for their protection, and Felton pleaded with her husband to find safer quarters for the family. Not until March 1864 (two months before Union troops invaded and occupied Cartersville) did the Feltons, along with their three children and "fifteen colored slaves in charge," abandon their home for a small farmhouse in a pine forest three miles outside Macon.[35] Three months later, Felton woke to find Dr. Felton on the porch talking to a Union officer. "When day light came," she discovered that "the face of the earth was covered with 'blue coats' mounted cavalry."[36] She watched in terror as federal troops raided her smokehouse and chicken coop and invaded the slaves' quarters.[37]

With Dr. Felton by her side, Rebecca could expect Yankee soldiers to treat her with some respect, but her female slaves could not count on the same courtesy. It comes as no surprise that most southern accounts of Yankee rape were of black women. Ironically, it was in the context of war that southern whites for the first time were willing to acknowledge the rape of black women and suggest that they were worthy of protection. In the spring of 1863, John N. Williams of the Seventh Tennessee Regiment wrote in his diary, "Heard from home. The Yankees has been through there. Seem to be their object to commit rape on every Negro woman they can find."[38] In Columbia, South Carolina, Dr. Daniel Heyward Trezevant recounted how seven Yankees raped and murdered "Mr. Shane's old Negro woman."[39] When federal soldiers raped black women, they often did so in the presence of white women. B. E. Harrison of Leesburg, Virginia, wrote a letter to President Abraham Lincoln complaining that federal troops had raped his "servant girl" in the presence of his wife, and General William Dwight reported, "Negro women were ravished in the presence of white women and children."[40]

Such public acts of sexual violence served to demonstrate power over black women, threaten white women, and mark southern defeat. Just as the rape of white women implied that southern men were unable to protect their mothers, wives, and daughters, so the rape of slave women meant they could no longer protect their property. In Sperryville, Virginia, Mrs. Swindler witnessed the rape of her "Negro servant" Polly Walker by three men of the First New York Light Artillery.[41] In Sandtown, Georgia, Mrs. Campbell and her mother witnessed the rape of their slave Sylvia Campbell when three men of the Second Kentucky Cavalry (Union) broke into their home. Sylvia testified that the sergeant held a gun to her head and raped her four times before another man dragged her into the woods. The unsympathetic senior Mrs. Campbell testified, "Yes, they dragged the nigger into the woods. She has not been able to do a lick of work since, but lies around useless. Her mistress has to wash all her own clothes." The sergeant was sentenced to two years' hard labor.[42]

Because so many Northerners viewed themselves as liberators of slaves, federal officials certainly did not openly condone the rape of slave women. While no federal soldiers were executed for raping black women, some were court-martialed and convicted. In the summer of 1864, Lieutenant Andrew J. Smith was sentenced to ten years of hard labor for "committing a rape on the person of a colored woman." In reviewing the sentence of the court-martial, the infamous General Butler supported the commanding general's guilty verdict. Summarizing the case, he explained, "A female negro child quits Slavery, and comes into the protection of the federal government, and upon first reaching the limits of the federal lines, receives the brutal treatment from an officer, himself a husband and a father, of violation of her person." Unwilling to entertain pleas for mercy on Smith's behalf, Butler defended the sentence and declared the officer lucky to walk away with his life. Noting how race informed military punishment, he explained, "A day or two since a negro man was hung, in the presence of the army, for the attempted violation of the person of a white woman," he argued, "equal and exact justice would have taken this officer's life; but imprisonment in the Penitentiary for a long term of years, his loss of rank and position—if that imprisonment be without hope of pardon, as it should be—would be almost an equal example."[43] Although Butler had subtly threatened the rape of white New Orleans women, he had little sympathy for "an officer of the United States Army" who raped a female slave. He believed that slave women deserved and expected military protection.

The summer raid on Rebecca Felton's farm marked only the beginning of her wartime suffering. After federal soldiers captured Atlanta, an epidemic of measles struck the Felton farm. Five-year-old Willie Felton and six slaves died.[44] When General William T. Sherman began his infamous march to the sea, destroying and burning all in his path, Felton was besieged by Confederate commissary officers, embittered deserters, and liberated slaves, all desperate for food and anything else they could get their hands on. In the spring of 1865 when Macon surrendered, Rebecca Felton again found herself directly caught up in the military struggle. When troops arrived at the Felton farm, "they took whatever we had that they wanted, and trampled down our crops," recalled Felton. Without Dr. Felton to offer protection, Rebecca must have feared the worst. She recounted how one soldier "rummaged" through her bedroom.[45]

Southern white women felt the threat of sexual violence most when soldiers invaded their private spaces to search for contraband or to plunder. In her postwar account, Clara D. MacLean of North Carolina described her terror when a soldier forced his way into her home: "Before I was aware of his intention, he had locked the door. I rose and walked toward it. 'Come,' I said, 'and I will show you the trunks in the other room, as there is nothing here, you see, in the way of arms.' But he had stationed himself in front of the door, his back toward it. For a moment, nay, a long minute—centuries it seemed to me—we stood thus." She claimed that she was eventually able to maneuver out of the room and the soldier's clutches.[46] In Covington, Georgia, Sarah Dutton Graves complained, "How awful we felt when the wretches were prying into every sacred thing in the house. . . . If I live a thousand years I shall never forget the enemies of our country."[47] In Virginia, Judith McGuire raged, "It makes my blood boil when I remember that our private rooms, our chambers, our very inner sanctums, are thrown open to a ruthless soldiery."[48]

If rebellious slaves and federal troops were not enough to worry about, southern women also had to worry about guerrilla fighters, Confederate deserters, camp followers, and southern men who had no problem taking advantage of women. Black and white men roamed the countryside, and it was often difficult for elite white women accustomed to acknowledging only men they knew to avoid contact with strange men. As women fled to safer accommodations, they found themselves more vulnerable than ever. Elizabeth Saxon recounted "a night of terror" during her trek from Alabama to Arkansas. Twenty-three miles outside Memphis, she was forced to rent a room in a small cottage in the woods from "a mean-looking, ferret-faced man." After eating dinner prepared by "a small black woman, who disappeared as soon as she cooked it," Elizabeth purchased candles from a man in a tiny shed off the portico, and with her two small children she retired for the evening. She had planned to ask the "negro woman" to stay in the room with her, but she was long gone. Upon returning to her room, she realized that the sliding bolt had been removed from the inside of the door, the lock was broken, and there was "no security whatever." She was terrified. "In those terrible times life was so cheap," she explained, "and the loneliness of our situation so great, the fact of the sum of gold I had about me and the looks of the man I had met in the shop outside, all conspired to arouse my fears."[49]

While her children slept, Elizabeth Saxon wrote letters to her friends. She had been writing for some time when she heard a soft step outside her door. Whoever lurked outside might not have imagined that she carried a pistol in her dress pocket. "No man could send a bullet straighter to its mark than I," she explained. She flung the door wide open and found the man who had rented her the room standing outside in his stocking feet. "I thought I heard you," she said, "I am glad you are here. I want to ask you some questions. Come in." She backed into the room. When they sat down, she drew the pistol from her pocket. "This is a very lonely place," she began, "and in troublous times like these it seems a poor place to sleep in with neither lock nor bolt on the door. How am I to fast it?" He scoffed, "Nobody is going to hurt you. I only came to ask you what time you wanted to be called in the morning. What are you doing with that pistol?" Saxon said, "I am only holding it in my hand now and I expect to be up all night. I have much writing to do. I have carried this pistol in my pocket since I left home; it is heavy and I am tired. I have not had any use for it, and it is not likely that I shall, but if there should be any need to use it, I shall most certainly do it." As the man rose to leave the room, he challenged, "I'll bet you couldn't hit the side of a house if you did shoot."[50] He was not, however, willing to test his theory.

In hopes of avoiding situations like Saxon's, many women of the planter class went to federal troops for protection. Rebecca Felton was no exception. She recalled, "A trooper named Dowling, a youth from Cincinnati, was billeted in my house.... There were stragglers and camp followers roaming the country, and he left a loaded musket for my protection when he was not around."[51] In Camden, Arkansas, Virginia McCollum Stinson managed not only to get a Yankee guard but also took in a federal officer to board for extra protection. She explained, "After the guard came and the federal officer, I had no more serious trouble." When it came time for the officer to leave, she recalled, "Woman like I burst in tears and said 'Oh!! Capt. Rohadaback what will become of me and my little children, when you are gone.' He tried to comfort me and said 'I don't think my men will molest you at all.'"[52]

As the war dragged on, Union officers became less likely to respond to white women's pleas for protection. Determined to bring the South to its knees by terrorizing and depriving civilians of the means of maintaining and supporting the Confederacy, General Sherman and his men showed little sympathy for women they believed were responsible for keeping the war going.[53] Josephine Bryan Worth recounted that when Sherman raided Fayetteville, North Carolina, her aunt's plea for a guard was rejected: "You'll git no protection. That's played out long ago."[54] Taking to heart Sherman's declaration to "make Georgia howl," Union soldiers not only deprived women of guards but robbed them of food, livestock, and anything else of value they could find. Property that could not be carried away was often burned. As destruction and violence escalated, women waited in terror and despair for the Yankees to arrive. More hated than Butler, Sherman and his troops represented southern white women's worst nightmares. In fearful anticipation of Sherman's march through South Carolina, Emma Holmes wrote, "The progress has been like the commencement—all the barbarities of savage warfare followed in Sherman's wake. Fire, desolation, destruction of all property unremovable—all provisions, cattle & negroes carried away—the rape and consequent death or insanity of many ladies of the best families. Alas what pen can portray the sufferings inflicted by that army of demons, white and black."[55]

If Sherman was guilty of waging war against "defenseless women and children," then Confederate soldiers were guilty of failing to protect them. Confederate officers and soldiers notoriously abandoned cities and towns as federal troops advanced. Time and time again, as southern men fled for their lives, they left southern white women at the mercy of their enemies. In May 1863, Mary Ann Loughborough, who had followed her husband's regiment from Jackson to Vicksburg, Mississippi, recorded how the women of the city greeted Confederate soldiers who confessed they were "running" from federal troops. "Why don't you stand your ground?" "Shame on you all!" "We are disappointed in you! Who shall we look to now for protection?" cried the women.[56] In a letter to her husband, Julia Davidson complained, "The men of Atlanta have brought an everlasting stain on their name. Instead of remaining to defend their homes, they have run off and left Atlanta to be defended by an army of women and children." She concluded, "God help us for there is no help in man."[57] In Virginia a group of women declared the Confederate army incompetent and suggested the formation of a ladies' regiment in the Army of the Shenandoah.[58] As far as they were concerned, southern women were entitled to protection against sexual violence, and for the first time they were willing to demand it publicly. Even as elite white women clung to traditional notions of manhood in their demands for protection, their actions challenged images of frail and defenseless womanhood.

While it is difficult to know how many women suffered a "fate worse than death" during the war, it is clear that federal officers and soldiers used the threat of sexual violence to subdue and demoralize southern women and that, in fact, white women did suffer rape. For example, in North Carolina during the spring of 1865, Private James Preble "attempted to rape" both "Mrs. Rebecca Drake and Miss Louis Bedard" and "did by physical force and violence commit rape upon the person of one Miss Letitia Craft."[59] Preble was one of twenty-two Union soldiers who were court-martialed, convicted, and executed for rape.[60] While all the victims were white, African American men made up half the twenty-two men executed, which suggests that race played a key factor in the military decision to court-martial and execute the men. Many more soldiers, however, were court-martialed and given lesser punishments for rape or attempted rape.

Because rape was considered worse than death, and southern culture discouraged women from discussing sex, most incidences of rape on lonely farms, like Felton's, likely went unreported. Moreover, in a society where a woman's virtue represented her most valuable commodity, a sexual assault was a theft from which few could recover. Thus elite white women had much to lose from reporting rape. At the same time, Union officers probably ignored rapes, especially those reported by black and poor white women. Finally, rape symbolized the failure of southern manhood. Southern men would have been loath to let neighbors know they had been unable to protect their wives and daughters.

The battle over slavery cost Rebecca Felton and most women of her class all that they held dear. For many the initial sense of grief and helplessness following military defeat faded into angry determination never again to depend solely on the protection of men. For women born and reared in the plantation South, however, the promise of protection was too powerful to discard completely. Thus, from the destruction of the Civil War, Rebecca Felton, like many other women of her class, sought to salvage the pedestal that elevated southern womanhood and guaranteed protection against sexual assault.

Notes

Parts of this essay appear in "General Benjamin Butler and the Threat of Sexual Violence during the American Civil War," *Daedalus* (Spring 2009), and *Southern Horrors: Women and the Politics of Rape and Lynching* (Cambridge: Harvard University Press, 2009).

1. Anne Firor Scott, *The Southern Lady: From Pedestal to Politics, 1820–1920* (Chicago: University of Chicago Press, 1970), x.

2. Felton, *Country Life in Georgia in the Days of My Youth* (reprint, New York: Arno Press, 1980), 91.

3. Ibid., 92–94.

4. Ibid., 86.

5. Drew Gilpin Faust, *Mothers of Invention: Women of the Slaveholding South in the American Civil War* (New York: Vintage Books, 1997); George C. Rable, *Civil Wars: Women and the Crisis of Southern Nationalism* (Urbana and Chicago: University of Illinois Press, 1991); Catherine Clinton and Nina Silber, eds., *Divided Houses: Gender and the Civil War* (Oxford: Oxford University Press, 1992); Edward D. C. Campbell Jr. and Kym S. Rice, eds., *A Woman's War: Southern Women, Civil War, and the Confederate Legacy* (Charlottesville: University of Virginia Press, 1996).

6. Felton, *Country Life*, 88–89, 101–2.

7. Drew Faust, "Altars of Sacrifice: Confederate Women and the Narratives of War," in Clinton and Silber, *Divided House*, 171–99.

8. Felton, *Country Life*, 105.

9. Faust, *Mothers of Invention*, 55–62.

10. "Emily Harris Diary, November 7, 1863," "Letter from Amanda Walker to the Confederate Secretary of War," and *Macon Daily Telegraph*, September 1, 1862, quoted in Faust, *Mothers of Invention*, 121–22, 55–57.

11. Faust, "Altars of Sacrifice," 182–83.

12. Susan Eppes, *Through Some Eventful Years* (Gainesville: University Press of Florida, 1968), 119.

13. Felton, *Country Life*, 87.

14. Catherine Clinton, *Tara Revisited: Women, War, and the Plantation Legend* (New York: Abbeville Press, 1995), 118.

15. John E. Talmadge, *Rebecca Latimer Felton: Nine Stormy Decades* (Athens: University of Georgia Press, 1960), 18.

16. C. Vann Woodward, ed., *Mary Chestnut's Civil War* (New Haven: Yale University Press, 1981), 198–99.

17. Felton, *Country Life*, 98–99.

18. United Daughters of the Confederacy, *War Days in Fayetteville, North Carolina: Reminiscences of 1861 to 1865* (Fayetteville, N.C.: Judge Print. Co., 1910), 44.

19. Felton, *Country Life*, 98.

20. Elizabeth Lyle Saxon, *A Southern Woman's War Time Reminiscence* (Memphis: Pilcher, 1905), 33.

21. Lee Kennett, *Marching through Georgia: The Story of Soldiers and Civilians during Sherman's Campaign* (New York: Harper Collins, 1995), 84.

22. Benjamin F. Butler, *Autobiography and Personal Reminiscences of Major-General Benjamin F. Butler: Butler's Book* (Boston: Thayer, 1892), 418. On Butler and the women of New Orleans, see Faust, *Mothers of Invention*, 207–14; Mary Ryan, *Women in Public: Between Banners and Ballots, 1825–1880* (Baltimore: John Hopkins University Press, 1990), 130–71; George Rable, "'Missing in Action': Women of the Confederacy," in Clinton and Silber, *Divided Houses*, 134–46; Hans L. Trefousse, *Ben Butler: The South Called Him Beast!* (New York: Twayne, 1957), 107–21; and Gerald M. Capers, *Occupied City: New Orleans under the Federals, 1862–1865* (Lexington: University Press of Kentucky, 1965).

23. Goldwin Smith, "The Alleged Federal Atrocities," *New York Times*, August 10, 1864.

24. John T. Monroe, "Letter to Major General Benjamin F. Butler (May 16, 1862)," in *Private and Official Correspondence of Gen. Benjamin F. Butler during the Period of the Civil War*, vol. 1 (Norwood, Mass.: Plimpton Press, 1917), 497–98.

25. Jefferson Davis, "A Proclamation," in *The War of Rebellion: A Compilation of the Official Records of the Union and Confederate Armies*, ed. Bvt. Lieut. Col. Robert N. Scott, ser. 2, vol. 5 (Washington: Government Printing Office, 1880–1901), 795–97.

26. See *Civil War Diary of Sarah Morgan*, ed. Charles East (Athens: University of Georgia Press, 1991), 76–77; *The Diary of Miss Emma Holmes, 1861–1866*, ed. John F. Marszalek (Baton Rouge: Louisiana State University Press, 1979), 165, 191; Woodward, *Mary Chestnut's Civil War*, 343; *The Civil War Diary of Clara Solomon: Growing Up in New Orleans, 1861–1862*, ed. Elliott Ashkenazi (Baton Rouge: Louisiana State University Press, 1995), 367–70; *The Secret Eye: The Journal of Ella Gertrude Clanton Thomas, 1848–1889*, ed. Virginia Ingraham Burr (Chapel Hill: University of North

Carolina Press, 1990); and *Brokenburn: The Journal of Kate Stone, 1861–1868*, ed. John Q. Anderson (Baton Rouge: Louisiana State University Press, 1955), 111.

27. *Civil War Diary of Clara Solomon*, 367–70.

28. *Mary Chestnut's Civil War Diary*, 343; *Diary of Miss Emma Holmes*, 165.

29. Julia LeGrand, "New Orleans Is Full of Rumors, December 20, 1862," in *Heroines of Dixie: Confederate Women Tell Their Story of War*, ed. Katharine M. Jones (New York: Bobbs-Merrill, 1955), 193–95.

30. Cordelia Lewis, "I Never Walk or Ride without My Pistol, October 29, 1862," in Jones, *Heroines of Dixie*, 179–82.

31. "Julia Pope Stanley," quoted in Kennett, *Marching through Georgia*, 146.

32. Varina Howell Davis, *Jefferson Davis, Ex-President of the Confederate States of America: A Memoir by His Wife* (New York: Belford, 1890), 2:577.

33. Reid Mitchell, *The Vacant Chair: The Northern Soldier Leaves Home* (New York: Oxford University Press, 1993), 102–3.

34. Clinton, *Tara Revisited*, 111.

35. Felton, *Country Life*, 88–89.

36. Ibid., 89.

37. Talmadge, *Rebecca Latimer Felton*, 22.

38. "John N. Williams," quoted in Thomas P. Lowry, *The Story the Soldiers Wouldn't Tell: Sex in the Civil War* (Mechanicsburg, Pa.: Stackpole Books, 1994), 84.

39. "Dr. Daniel Heyward Trezevant," quoted in Clinton, *Tara Revisited*, 129–30.

40. "B. E. Harrison," quoted in Mitchell, *Vacant Chair*, 107.

41. Lowry, *Sexual Misbehaviors*, 123.

42. Ibid., 147.

43. "Punishment of a Military Criminal," *New York Times*, August 2, 1864.

44. Talmadge, *Rebecca Latimer Felton*, 22.

45. Rebecca L. Felton, *The Romantic Story of Georgia's Women* (Atlanta: Atlanta Georgian and Sunday American, 1930), 22.

46. "Clara D. MacLean," quoted in Clinton, *Tara Revisited*, 30.

47. "Sarah Dutton Graves," quoted in Stephen V. Ash, *When the Yankees Came: Conflict and Chaos in the Occupied South, 1861–1865* (Chapel Hill: University of North Carolina Press, 1995), 40.

48. Judith McGuire, *Diary of a Southern Refugee: By a Lady of Virginia* (University of Nebraska Press, 1995), 21–22, quoted in Rable, *Civil Wars*, 158.

49. Saxon, *Southern Woman's War Time Reminiscences*, 54–55.

50. Ibid., 55–57.

51. Felton, *Romantic Story of Georgia's Women*, 22.

52. Virginia McCollum Stinson, "Yankee in Camden, Arkansas," in Jones, *Heroines of Dixie*, 283.

53. Lowry, *Story the Soldiers Wouldn't Tell*; Ash, *When the Yankees Came*.

54. "Josephine Bryan Worth," quoted in United Daughters of the Confederacy, *War Days in Fayetteville, North Carolina: Reminiscences of 1861 to 1865* (Fayetteville, N.C.: Judge Print. Co., 1910), 50.

55. Marszalek, *Diary of Miss Emma Holmes*, 384, 388.

56. Mary Ann Loughborough, "In the Cave at Vicksburg," in Jones, *Heroines of Dixie*, 225–26.

57. "Julia Davidson to John M. Davidson, July 19, 21, 26, 1864," quoted in Rable, *Civil Wars*, 171.

58. Jean V. Berlin, "Did Confederate Women Lose the War? Deprivation, Destruction, and Despair on the Home Front," in *The Collapse of the Confederacy*, ed. Mark Grimsley and Brooks D. Simpson (Lincoln: University of Nebraska Press, 2001), 179.

59. Robert I. Alotta, *Civil War Justice: Union Army Executions under Lincoln* (Shippensburg, Pa.: White Mane, 1989), 165.

60. Ibid., 30–32.

"A Quilt unlike Any Other"

Rediscovering the Work of Harriet Powers

—LAUREL THATCHER ULRICH

In an essay published in *Ms.* magazine in 1974, Alice Walker wrote of "a quilt unlike any other in the world" that she had seen on exhibit at the Smithsonian: "It is considered rare, beyond price. Though it follows no known pattern of quilt-making, and though it is made of bits and pieces of worthless rags, it is obviously the work of a person of powerful imagination and deep spiritual feeling." Walker thought that the quilt had been made by "an anonymous Black woman in Alabama, a hundred years ago." This woman, she thought, was "one of our grandmothers—an artist who left her mark in the only materials she could afford."[1]

The maker was not from Alabama, nor was she entirely anonymous. Although Walker seems to have forgotten it, the label beside the quilt read:

Made by Harriet
An Ex-slave
Athens, Georgia

Still, the mystery remained. The folklorist Gladys-Marie Fry was so moved by the quilt that for a while she returned every Saturday afternoon to sit on the bench in front of it and meditate. "Who was Harriet?" she asked. "What was her history?"[2]

Harriet's quilt reminded the art historian Robert Farris Thompson of the appliquéd banners of Dahomey, a kingdom in West Africa that is now the modern-day state of Benin. He quickly added a discussion of the quilt to his essay "African Influence on the Art of the United States."[3] When Adolph Cavallo, a curator at Boston's Museum of Fine Arts, saw the quilt, he immediately recognized its relationship to one that had recently arrived at his own institution. He quickly sent the Smithsonian a photograph of the Boston quilt and the full name of its maker, "Mrs. Harriet Powers."[4]

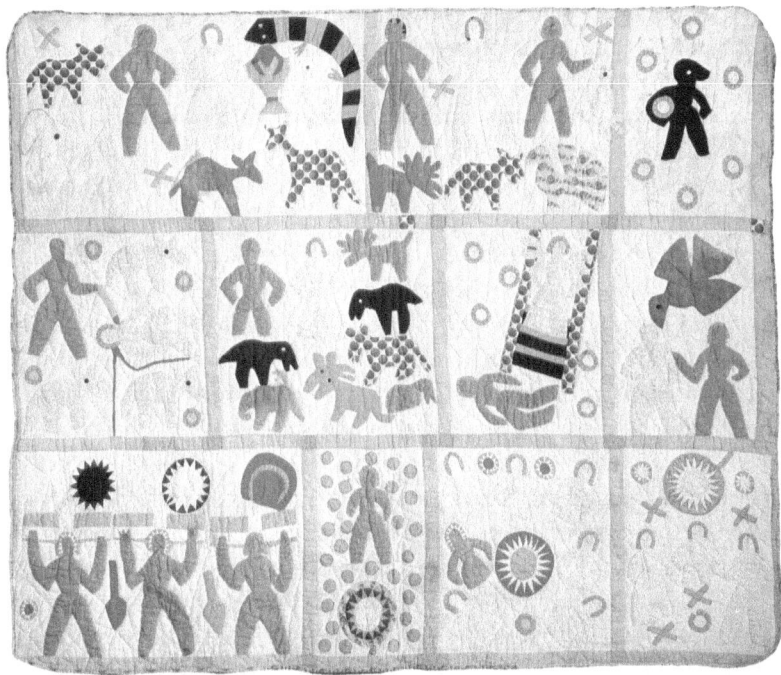

1. Harriet Powers, appliquéd quilt, 1885–86. Smithsonian National Museum of American History.

2. Harriet Powers, pictorial quilt, Athens, Ga., before 1895. Museum of Fine Arts, Boston.

That discovery sent Gladys Fry to Boston, where a curator took her to the storage area in the museum's lower level. "There I watched as she removed the quilt from a box and from its acid-free paper. I am not sure I was breathing. . . . My thoughts tumbled over each other. Harriet Powers's hands had touched this fabric, composed this square. The connection I felt with her at that moment was mystical. . . . My mind was in a daze. 'There are two of them! There are two of them!'"[5] In the fall of 1974, Fry presented a paper on Harriet Powers to the Folklore Society of America and then, with support from the Georgia Council for the Arts dug into Georgia records to see what else she could learn. The essay that Fry prepared for a 1976 exhibit on Georgia folklife was the first detailed account of the quilts and for many years the only serious attempt to recover Powers's history.[6]

The discovery of Harriet Powers's quilts stimulated a broader interest among art historians, folklorists, anthropologists, novelists, collectors, and quilters themselves.[7] Some joined Thompson's search for the African roots of American culture. Others were inspired by Cuesta Benberry's effort to record an African American presence in American quilting.[8] As museums began to display the new discoveries, folklorists worked to recover their stories. Beginning in the 1970s, the documentary photographer Roland Freeman interviewed hundreds of African American quilters, some of them unknown, a few of them famous. In San Francisco in 1992, Alice Walker showed Freeman her quilts and told him how piecing one of them had helped her to write *The Color Purple*. At the Boston Museum of Fine Arts in 1996, he photographed five of Harriet Powers's descendants in front of their ancestor's quilt. Research begun in the 1970s is still bearing fruit today, in landmark exhibits like those featuring the quilts of Gee's Bend, Alabama, or in the establishment of community-based projects like the quilting collective at Tutwiler, Mississippi.[9] But Harriet's quilts remain an essential part of the story.

When the Smithsonian contracted with an American company in 1991 to have historic quilts in their collection reproduced in China, otherwise well-behaved women wrapped themselves in their own quilts and picketed the National Museum of American History. Freeman believes that the inclusion of Powers's Bible quilt solidified the opposition: "To many quilters it was unthinkable and downright sacrilegious to replicate it."[10] Harriet's Bible quilt has become an American icon. The Smithsonian recently displayed it in an exhibit of "American treasures" alongside Thomas Jefferson's writing desk, Thomas Edison's lightbulb, and Dorothy's slippers from *The Wizard of Oz*.[11] The Boston quilt has also achieved iconic status, though of a somewhat different kind. Curators at the Museum of Fine Arts give the quilt the kind of care typically reserved for a rare drawing by Rembrandt or ancient Chinese silk. Concerned about light degradation, conservators allow the quilt to be displayed only once every five years, but the museum has attempted to satisfy public interest by placing detailed, high-quality digital images on the Internet.[12]

Yet despite all this attention, the interpretation of Harriet's quilts remains locked in the frameworks of the 1970s. Most writers still treat Powers as a singular figure, a humble genius emerging from the nightmare of slavery or a silent carrier of deeply repressed African traditions. In fact, she was an artist firmly grounded in her own time and place. Her quilts and her life make an excellent entry point for understanding contradictory ideas about race, gender, and modernity in the late nineteenth century and for exploring the place of African Americans in the twentieth-century quilt revival. That Powers lived and worked in Athens, Georgia, Anne Scott's hometown, makes a study of her contributions especially appropriate for this volume.

I begin with accounts left by Powers's contemporaries. I then turn to the scholarship that developed in the 1970s, showing how arguments about African origins eventually gave way to a renewed interest today in Powers's biography. I conclude with a brief exploration of the relationship of the quilts to Anne Scott's core topic: the organizational life of American women. The history of Harriet's quilts calls attention to a curious collaboration between the "new Negroes" who mounted exhibits at the Atlanta Exposition of 1895 and a handful of aspiring white women who saw themselves as "natural allies" to enterprising former slaves like Harriet.

Turn-of-the-Century Interpretations of Powers's Quilts

Thanks to the work of Gladys Fry and others, the rough outlines of Harriet Powers's life are now well known. Harriet and her husband Armstead spent the Civil War on their masters' farms near Athens and after emancipation acquired a few acres of their own. In 1886, Harriet exhibited the quilt now at the Smithsonian at a cotton fair in Athens. Jennie Smith, who taught art at the Lucy Cobb Institute, an elite school for white girls, saw the quilt there and offered to buy it, but "it was not for sale at any price." In a handwritten account now at the Smithsonian, Smith explained that Powers eventually changed her mind:

3. Stereoview from the Cotton States and International Exposition, Atlanta, Ga., 1895. Littleton Public Library, Littleton, N.H.

She arrived one afternoon in front of my door in an ox-cart, with the precious burden in her lap encased in a clean flour sack, which was still further enveloped in a crocus sack. She offered it for ten dollars, but I only had five to give. After going out and consulting her husband she returned and said—"owin ter de hardness of de times, my ole man lows I'd better tack hit," and not being a new woman, she obeyed. After giving me a full description of each scene with great earnestness and deep piety she departed, but has been back several times to visit the darling offspring of her brain. She was only in a measure consoled for its loss when I promised to save her all my scraps.[13]

In 1895, Smith arranged to exhibit the quilt in the Negro Building at the Cotton States and International Exposition in Atlanta. Two photographs from that exhibit survive. The first is the stereoview pictured here, which shows the quilt with several others, including one made in Liberia.[14]

A copy of a second photograph, now at the Smithsonian, has a handwritten label on the back from Lorine Curtis Diver of Keokuk, Iowa. Diver said she tried taking a picture with her own equipment but failed "because of the shadows," so she arranged for a professional photographer to do it, and recorded her own description of the quilt on the back.[15] In 1914, Lucine Finch, a writer and musician from Birmingham, Alabama, published what appears to be a copy of the same photograph alongside an essay based on a purported interview with the "aged Negro woman" who made the quilt. Finch did not give Powers's name, nor did she say when she interviewed her or where she got the photograph.[16]

Taken together, the accounts by Smith, Diver, and Finch offer an astonishingly rich body of material. All three accounts identify the figures on the quilt. It was indeed a Bible quilt, with scenes depicting the drama of redemption from Adam and Eve to Jesus. Just as important for those seeking to understand the quilt in its original condition are their comments on the quilt's colors. Smith stated flatly, "I regret exceeding that it is impossible to describe the gorgeous coloring of this work." She noted that the "ground-work," or background fabric, was "watermelon pink with green bars to frame each scene" but lamented that "all word painting would sound pale and faded compared with the original."[17] Fortunately Finch included color in her descriptions of most squares, reporting, for example, that in the scene depicting Jacob's ladder, the wings of the angel are rose colored, or in the scene of the Holy Family, the "little Jesus is in white, Mary in pale blue, and Joseph in speckled calico."[18]

Diver was also fascinated by the colors, though she may actually have been happier with the muted tones that exist today. Noting the purple and yellow polka-dot animals, the black-and-white striped peacock, and the red calico blood stitched onto the bright pink background, she concluded, "This colored woman was evidently 'color blind' or used only material at hand." Diver nevertheless admired the quilt and attempted to buy it, but she learned, presumably from Smith, that "it was too valuable as an exhibit at fairs."[19]

Although all three women admired the quilt, none of them knew what to make of it. They vaguely recognized the Bible stories to which it alluded, but seemed baffled by details they had never encountered in the progressive churches they attended or in the young ladies' academies in which they were educated. All three seemed surprised that the brightly striped serpent in the Garden of Eden had feet, Smith quipping that "the only animal represented with feet is the only animal that has no feet." But Powers was a careful student of the Bible. She presented the serpent as he existed in Eden, before the fall of man and before God cursed him to crawl on his belly. As she told Finch, "He 'blige ter have foots and han's an' all his features in *dem* days, ter git aroun' man, chile!"[20]

Smith and Finch both offered extensive quotations from Powers in dialect, a device that allowed them to admire the quilt while keeping their distance from the quilter's presumably "childlike" or "primitive" vision of God. Their interpretations differ, however, in tone. Smith was amused by a composition that Powers called "Satan amidst the seven stars," claiming to have no idea what that meant. The dark figure in the center of the square "is not as I first thought, a football player," Smith wrote, adding, "I am sure I have never seen a jauntier devil." In contrast, Finch wrote: "There may be a certain primitive and unconscious occultism in this strange symbol. It is sinister in its effect, positively diabolical in its feeling. The evil figure of Satan is black, with a pink eye (he is shown in profile. 'De yuther eye is behin', she said, 'an' wusser 'n dis one!')."[21] Where Smith discovered unintentional humor in Powers's compositions, Finch found mystery.

Where Finch alluded to the "strange mysticism" in Powers's portrayal of the Crucifixion, Smith found whimsy. She wrote that the three spheres Harriet used to describe phases in the darkening sun as being "attached to the crosses like balloons by a string." Both writers identified square 9 as Judas with his thirty pieces of silver, but where Smith noted simply that the "silver is done in green calico," French highlighted Powers's explanation of their number: "Missy Coomby counted 'em for me 'cos I kin count 'em backward same as I kin count 'em forwards, an' dat ain' no way to count!" Finch surely knew that in African American folklore counting backward was a form of conjuring, a way of bringing evil into the world, as Judas did when he accepted the silver.[22]

Finch, Diver, and Smith all acknowledged the religious grounding of Powers's quilt, but they appear not to have understood it. Apparently following Powers's own lead, Finch titled her essay "A Sermon in Patchwork." Diver, too, acknowledged that Powers's intent was to "preach the gospel" in patchwork and to show "Where Sin Originated." Among the hundreds of stories available to her, Harriet chose those that focused on a cosmic struggle between darkness and light, a drama that could be discovered not only in scripture but also in the skies. She splashed more than two dozen radiating spheres—suns and stars—across the bright pink ground of her quilt, alluding to biblical passages, especially in the book of Revelation, that were probably seldom mentioned in the genteel white world that Smith, Diver, and Finch inhabited.

Stars predominate as well in the second of Harriet's known quilts, the one now at the Boston Museum of Fine Arts. According to the museum's records, this second quilt was exhibited at the "Nashville Exposition," then bought by the "faculty ladies of Atlanta University" and presented in 1898 to the Reverend Charles Cuthbert Hall, a trustee of the university. It came to the MFA in 1964 from the estate of Maxim Karolik, a folk art collector, with a neatly written key in the handwriting of Hall's son, Basil. The museum also received a small photograph of Harriet wearing an apron appliquéd with motifs similar to those on her quilts.[23]

Unlike Smith and French, Hall avoided dialect in reporting Harriet's descriptions, but in many ways the account he preserved reveals a view of the world even richer and more complex than in the foregoing descriptions. Once again biblical themes dominate. We see the Fall and the redemption, and the stories of Jonah and Job, but these ancient stories are joined with miraculous events closer to home. Here is how Hall recorded them:

2. The dark day of May 19, 1780. The seven stars were seen 12. N. in the day. The cattle all went to bed, chickens to roost and the trumpet was blown. The sun went off to a small spot and then to darkness.

8. The falling of the stars on November 13, 1833. The people were fright and thought that the end of time had come. God's hand staid the stars. The varmints rushed out of their beds.

11. Cold Thursday, 10 of Feb. 1895. A woman frozen while at prayer. A woman frozen at a gateway. A mule with a sack of meal frozen. Icicles formed from the breath of a mule. All blue birds killed. A man frozen at his jug of liquor.

13. Rich people who were taught nothing of God. Bob and Kate Bell of VA. They told their parents to stop the clock at one and tomorrow it would strike one and so it did. This was the signal that they entered everlasting punishment. The independent hog that ran 500 miles from GA to VA. Her name was Betts.[24]

The "dark day" and the "falling stars" refer to events well known to scholars, a weather inversion in 1780 that in combination with massive forest fires in the Midwest did result in the darkening of the sun in parts of the eastern United States, and the Leonid meteor shower of 1833. For Harriet, and for many Christians even today, these fulfilled prophecies in both the Old and New Testaments predicting manifestations preceding the Second Coming of Christ.[25] As far as I know, the other stories have so far eluded researchers, though they too may have passed, by word of mouth or through now lost religious newspapers, from one part of the country to another. In a larger sense, one does not need a translator to understand that in the theology of the quilt, worldly power is transient and God's judgments unrelenting. People who now seem on top of the world will someday be called to account.

Obviously, a serious interpretation of Powers's quilts requires a deep knowledge of the religious culture that sustained her. It also requires some sense of the power dynamics that shaped her relationship with Jennie Smith and others who purchased and interpreted her quilts. In a poem written in 1984, Jane Wilson Joyce captured both themes in a narrative that melded Jennie Smith's anecdote about the first quilt with Hall's descriptions of the second, so that "the joyful animals" of the Creation are somehow joined to an amazing hog named Betts. Joyce helps us comprehend a vision that blended folklore with scripture, that found comfort in the notion that God's unblinking eye comprehended all his creations, and that still saw a "merciful hand" outstretched to help those who sought it. Unlike her nineteenth-century predecessors, Joyce acknowledges the suffering and the peril in the life of a woman who existed on the margins of white hegemony.

The poem concludes with a retelling of the moment when Powers gave up her quilt to Jennie Smith:

Owing
to the hardness of the times,
Harriet Powers
asked ten dollars for that quilt.

Owing
to the hardness of the times,
she took
five.

Handed it over
to Jennie Smith
wrapped in two sacks
like a baby; like a mother,
a slave mother,
Harriet slipped away to visit
her quilt. She was
"only in some measure consoled"
by the white woman's promise of
scraps.[26]

The poem captures both the poetry and the pathos of Powers's story. It also suggests the perpetuation of old patterns of bondage in the relationship between the African American quilter and the white collector.

Quilting Scholarship from the 1970s to the Present

In the 1970s, folklorists and art historians added new layers of meaning to Powers's quilts by building on Robert Ferris Thompson's suggestions about African influence. In an essay published in 1978, John Michael Vlach left no doubt about the political importance of this argument. Conventional quilts made by African Americans were "examples of cultural surrender," he wrote, while those that displayed African influence were "statements of cultural survival." He concluded that Powers's quilts were among the latter, despite their Christian symbolism.

Vlach built his case by visual analogy, displaying details from Powers's quilts alongside those in the appliquéd banners of Ghana and Benin. Although he admitted that most slaves imported into Georgia did not come from West Africa, he was nevertheless certain that some African textile traditions survived the Atlantic crossing. He was especially impressed with the whales and large standing birds that appeared in both sets of textiles. His argument rested in part on the limited knowledge available at the time on American quilts. Powers's quilts must have derived from West African examples, he argued, because Powers, like West African artists, worked with symbols. "Euro-American folk artists . . . tended not to use the appliquéd quilt in such a manner."[27]

Despite a note of caution from the anthropologist Monni Adams, who noted that the differences with Dahomean textiles were just as striking as the similarities, most commentators on Powers's quilts simply assumed that the case had been proved.[28] The Dahomean interpretation is now a staple even in elementary schools. In a book designed for schoolchildren, Mary E. Lyons explained that Powers "did not choose to make the floral designs that were so common in her day. Nor did she follow the geometric forms used by the American Indians. Instead, she cut out figures, animals, sunbursts, stars, and crosses that appear to come from Africa." She speculated that Harriet may have learned these techniques from "her mother, an aunt, or a grandfather."[29] The art historian Regenia Perry went further, finding correspondences between Powers's images and a host of pan-African images, including those in Robert Temple's *The Sirius Mystery*, which claimed that the Dogon of Mali had knowledge of ancient astronomy. Here, Perry concluded, was "yet another example of an inexplicable 'Africanism' in African American art."[30]

In 1980 Maude Wahlman completed a dissertation at Yale under Thompson's direction, using his methods to compare thousands of patchwork quilts with the woven textiles of West Africa.[31] The argument was no longer about Harriet alone. At stake was an entire universe of American quilting. In the catalog for a San Francisco exhibit in 1987, Thompson himself blew the trumpet:

> World enough and time eventually will empower us. We shall one day document and explain a massive body of African-American quilt-tops across the United States. Assume 800,000 quilts out there. This probably conservative figure refers to heirlooms and modern works. The finest of these quilts define the light as it falls from windows or the doors upon the bed, transforming that light into music, bluesy backhome warmth, resonating in the strips and blocks.[32]

Quilts were blues. They were jazz. They were Kongo "heat in the blood," pygmy percussion, and San-like hooting.[33]

The intensity of Thompson's assertions provoked an equally intense reaction until, as Freeman observes, "reputations, careers, and friendships" were harmed. "What should be said about all those quilts made by African Americans that don't fit the defined categories of African textile design?" people asked.[34] In Harriet's case, the argument for Dahomean influence was particularly weak. The geography was wrong. So was the chronology. The banners that supposedly influenced Harriet developed long after her people arrived in America; they depended on imports of European cloth and may even have been inspired by flags used in colonial commerce.[35]

A larger problem was that at the time when Harriet's quilts were discovered, there had been relatively little detailed examination of American quilts, especially those outside major museums. Since then, multitudes of quilts have been documented, among them over 9,000 quilts from Georgia, 1,300 of which were made before 1900.[36] A brief look at two Georgia quilts helps us to see the importance of making local as well as international comparisons. A remarkable pieced quilt by Mary Bryan of Elbert County, Georgia, displays a fascination with sunbursts and starbursts that was shared by thousands of American quilt makers in the nineteenth century, including Harriet Powers. A close look at the sunbursts in Powers's quilts shows that the technique she used in creating them was identical to that used by Bryan.

Unlike Bryan, however, Powers set her pieced suns and stars into a quilt that was primarily created by appliqué rather than piecework. Whereas Bryan's quilt was entirely geometric, Powers's was representational, built on stories understood by her audience. In that respect, her work is more like that of Mary Sorrels, a quilter who valued whimsy over technical precision. Sorrels's quilt honored her husband, a possum hunter. Her possums, pictured alive or splayed, inhabit the same universe, though not the same symbolic space, as Powers's "varmints."[37]

There is a paradox here. Harriet's quilts are unlike any others not because they are unrelated to work being done around her but because she, like many other women of her generation, treasured innovation. As Janet Berlo has pointed out, a focus on the almost mathematical replication of precise geometric patterns or the meticulous floral appliqué in some nineteenth-century quilts has obscured the many quilts that deliberately deviated from prescribed patterns. Harriet was one among many quilters who insisted on doing things her own way.[38] She was not alone in using quilts to interpret the Bible.[39] Nor was she the only nineteenth-century quilter inspired by astronomical wonders.[40] Her work was unique, but unique in ways that were grounded in nineteenth-century American culture.

The quilt historian Cuesta Benberry cautioned against leaping to conclusions about African influence without exploring other, more immediate possibilities, such as the influence of "black fraternal orders, lodges and benevolent associations."[41] In the 1990s, a research team at the University of Maryland, College Park, followed that lead. Working with local records,

4. Mary Bryan, pieced quilt, Elbert County, Ga., ca. 1840. Photograph courtesy Atlanta History Center.

they discovered that Harriet and Armstead Powers were members not only of the New Grove Baptist Church near Athens but of a fraternal society associated with it. In the light of this affiliation, images of suns, moon, stars, an all-seeing eye, and even the shape of the images in Harriet's portrayal of Jonah and the whale took on new significance.[42]

Under the leadership of William Gilcher, the Maryland team pushed forward other lines of interpretation, even managing to connect some of

5. Mary Elizabeth Moore Sorrels, "Possum Quilt," Pocataligo, Ga., ca. 1885. Photograph courtesy Atlanta History Center.

Powers's descendants with quilts they had never seen.[43] Although their project ran out of funding, residents of Athens are continuing the research. Catherine Holmes, a graduate student at the University of Georgia, found Harriet's grave and is now working on a full biography.[44] Al Hester, a retired journalism professor at the university, located a Works Project Administration interview with a black preacher who was almost certainly Harriet's son. Although Alonzo Powers did not mention his mother's quilts, he said that during slavery his mother and grandmother spun cotton raised on their master's farm. Alonzo also described walking to a country church where slaves and whites sat separately, but where his uncle was a deacon.[45] Unfortunately much of this work, which is ongoing, is as yet unpublished or known only in local sources.

The most ambitious recent work has come from a quilt maker and amateur historian, Kyra Hicks, who recently published an impressive compilation of primary research. Her most important find is a copy, apparently in Lorene Diver's hand, of a short autobiography written and signed by Powers shortly after she visited the Cotton States Exposition in Atlanta. In it, she offered the dates of her birth (1837) and marriage (1855), the number of her children ("6 dead and 3 living"), and explained how and when she learned to read and write: "I commenced to learn at 11 years old and the white children learn me by sound on a poplar lea." She explained that after she became a member of the Mount Zion Baptist Church in 1882, she "attended Sunday school and read the Bible more than ever." The federal census takers who in 1840 and 1880 marked her as illiterate may simply have been wrong, but it is also possible that Harriet built on whatever she had learned as a child through a postemancipation literacy program organized through her church.[46]

But the real focus of her statement was her quilts. She described four. The first, made in 1872, consisted of "4 thousand and 50 diamonds." The second, a "star quilt," took the premium in the Colored Fair in Athens in 1887. The third, which she did not date, was inspired by the intense Bible reading she began after joining the Mount Zion Baptist Church. It portrayed "the Lord's Supper from the New Testament" and included "2 thousand and 500 hundred diamonds." The fourth, which she made in 1888, and "afterward sold to Miss Jennie Smith," portrayed "Adam and Eve in the Garden of Eden." Although the dates don't quite line up—Smith said she first saw Powers's quilt in 1886—the general narrative is familiar. But it is Harriet's self-consciousness about her work that matters most.[47]

Thanks to Hicks's discovery, we now know that Powers could read and write, that she made more than the two known quilts, that she won a prize at an Athens Colored Fair, and that her scriptural quilts were inspired by her affiliation with a Baptist church. That she described the quilt she sold to Smith in relation to only one scene—"Adam and Eve in the Garden of Eden"—suggests that the other scriptural quilt, the one she said depicted "the Lord's Supper," may also have had multiple figures. Her comment that this quilt contained 2,500 "diamonds" introduces a mystery. In her discussion of southern quilting, Jennie Smith distinguished between familiar geometric quilt patterns she had known, like "Double Irish Chain," "Flying Geese," or "Lone Star of Texas," and Harriet's representational quilts. "I have spent my whole life in the south, and am perfectly familiar with thirty-six patterns of quilts," she wrote, "but I have never seen an original design and never a living creature portrayed in patchwork until the year 1886."[48] Was Harriet's first scripture quilt both geometric and representational, composed of thousands of tiny diamond-shaped pieces. Or did she mean something else?

Technically a quilt is a sandwich made from two pieces of fabric stuffed with something soft. The stitching, or quilting, that holds the whole thing together is the final step in the project. When done well, it gives the finished object a three-dimensional quality lost in most photographs. Diver, who was a quilter herself, understood the process. "The effect of these people & animals all punctured over with the most beautiful quilting was queer," she wrote.[49] "Queer" in this case meant she had never seen anything like it. A less imaginative quilter might simply have stitched around the outlines of each figure. In addition, Harriet covered the entire surface between figures with a free-form geometry that violated conventional practice but enhanced the dynamic quality of her composition. Her "diamonds" may have been tiny pieces of fabric patched together, but they could also have been the shapes she created in the final quilting.

Thinking about Powers's quilts in relation to the technology of quilting raises another question. Although early American women's heavily quilted petticoats were sometimes referred to as "quilts," the vast majority of quilts in the nineteenth century were bedcoverings. In a bedcovering, the purpose of the filling sandwiched between the two layers was to keep someone warm. Harriet's Bible quilt is big enough to have covered a bed and does have a filling, but its orientation betrays its true purpose. It was, as Powers told Finch, a "Sermon in Patchwork." Conventional bedcoverings were oriented with the short end at the top so that the design could be read while facing the bed. Harriet's quilt was obviously meant to be hung on a wall, like a map or a painting. The Boston quilt makes no pretense to being a bedcovering. It has a lining, but no filling, and therefore no quilting. The pictures march across the fabric like leaves in a book.

The most curious thing about the Boston quilt is the band of fabric splotched with brownish stain that runs between the top two right-hand squares and the images to their left. It looks at first as if Harriet simply ran out of the polka-dot fabric she used to border her squares, or perhaps needed to fill in a space so that the end squares would all line up. But if so, why did she choose this fabric? And why did she use smaller pieces of the same stained fabric in other squares? More than one person, looking at the quilt, has suggested that the stain looks like blood. If so, the illusion may have been intentional. The square just to the right of the largest stain depicts "the angels of wrath and the seven vials" and "the blood of fornications." Just below is the scene of crucifixion, with "blood and water" running from Jesus's side.[50] Perhaps someday, the Museum of Fine Arts will find a way to test the stain on Harriet's fabric, though to understand its meaning will require even closer attention to the religious culture that produced it.

Harriet Powers's quilts offer a seemingly endless stream of questions. Some of these relate to a core theme in the work of Anne Firor Scott: women's voluntary societies.

Race, Gender, and the Atlantic Exposition

In a startling passage from her presidential address to the Organization of American Historians in 1984, Scott listed some of the things that American women's organizations accomplished in the late nineteenth century and the early twentieth. The list consumed most of a page in the published version of her talk and included everything from building public playgrounds to tackling "the noxious convict lease system." Women did all of this through voluntary associations that had mostly been overlooked by historians.[51] Six years later, in her presidential address to the Southern Historical Association, she extended her argument. If white women's voluntary associations had suffered from lack of attention, black women's associations were the "most invisible of all." Although white women and black women were often involved in similar projects, "only occasionally was there any overlap or cooperation.... For the most part the two groups went separate ways."[52]

The biographies of Jennie Smith, Lorine Diver, and Lucine Finch fit well within the history of white women of the Progressive Era. The stories also reinforce the invisibility of black women's organizations in accounts of the discovery and preservation of Harriet Powers's quilts.

Smith, the well-educated daughter of a prosperous cotton merchant, devoted her life to promoting female education among other good causes. She was an active member of the Athens Women's Club and a cofounder of the Athens Art Association.[53] Although she is remembered today for her association with Powers, there is no hint of that in the contemporary sources that lauded her work in promoting the art of white women. In 1895 she mounted a lavish display in the white-only Women's Building at the Atlanta Exposition. The room featured hand-painted china, Indian silk draperies, frescoes by a Boston artist, and carpets in harmonizing colors of olive green and rose. The *Atlanta Constitution* predicted it would become a "pleasant retreat" for Lucy Cobb alumnae. There was nary a hint that on the other edge of the fairgrounds was a quilt that Smith had purchased from a former slave.[54]

According to a sketch in *The Blue Book of Iowa Women*, Lorene Curtis Diver belonged to virtually every voluntary society in her town: the Book Cub, the Woman's Club, the Audubon Society, the local chapter of the Daughters of the American Revolution, the Benevolent Union, the Monday Music Club, the Wednesday Reading Club, the Country Club, the Humane Society, the Sunshine Society, and the Civil League. She was also a devoted birdwatcher and a devout member of the Methodist Church. That she had any interest in the artworks of a former slave would have surprised those who read the biography published shortly after her death. Although she and her husband once traveled to India and China (where his father had been a medical missionary), her eulogist concluded that after spending a year "among the dark races of the far east," Diver enjoyed being in "the White Man's Country—England." The one hint of an interest in the "dark races" was her involvement in a DAR project to erect a statue to Chief Keokuk, the Sauk leader for whom her town was named.[55]

At first glance, Finch's career seems far removed from the genteel contributions of Smith and Diver. Younger than the others, Finch was more adventurous and without question a "new woman," as Smith might have put it. Yet her theatrical and literary work is a tip-off to the cultural movement that shaped the responses of all three women to the work of Harriet Powers.

Raised in New Orleans and Birmingham, Finch was a writer, musician, and dramatist who made her name performing "Negro tales" collected from family servants. A poet as well as a writer of local-color tales, she published alongside Lincoln Steffen and other Progressives in the *American Magazine*, gave readings at the same summer Chautauqua series where Jane Addams and Charles Cuthbert Hall gave speeches, and contributed plays, poems, and sketches to anthologies used by women's clubs and by teachers of oral expression. An alumna of the University of Chicago, she performed not only on the popular stage but in Carnegie Hall and at elite colleges like Princeton and Wellesley. In the 1920s she settled in Greenwich, Connecticut, where she taught drama, performed at posh soirees, did an occasional radio show, and kept an antique store with her companion, Clare Hamilton.[56]

The late nineteenth century was an era of nostalgia for a vanishing past, not only among southerners but among educated people all over the United States. It is not accidental that the Georgia fair where Smith first saw the Bible quilt also featured a Wild West show, or that Lorine Diver's monument to Keokuk, a "friendly Indian" who sided with the United States in the Black Hawk War, was also the first in a series of pioneer trail markers across Iowa.[57] In the South, nostalgia focused on an idealized but lost world of supposed racial harmony symbolized by the self-sacrificing and loyal "black mammy."

The Lucy Cobb Institute was founded in 1858 by a pro-slavery theorist, T. R. R. Cobb, and was managed for many years by his niece, Mildred Rutherford, a passionate supporter of the South's "lost cause." As historian of the United Daughters of the Confederacy, she collected stories about "faithful slaves" who remained loyal to their masters during the Civil War. Her sister, Mary Ann Lipscomb, a founder of the Athens Women's Club and later president of the Georgia Federation of Women's Clubs, succeeded her as president of the institute.[58] The symbol of "mammy" at the school was Rutherford's and Lipscomb's childhood nurse, "Aunt Dot," who served as a housekeeper and cook at the school. She was known to alumnae as an "old-time Negro" who knew her place and liked it. After her death, admirers commissioned a portrait of her to hang in the chapel.[59]

Rutherford and Lipscomb celebrated the mammy not only to counter northern charges that slavery was a brutal and repressive system but to model appropriate behavior for the contemporary women who cooked dinners, washed clothes, mended clothing, and cared for children in turn-of-the-century Athens. To accomplish that goal, they were not averse to working with African American women—and men—who were concerned about the moral uplift of their community. That becomes clear when we look more deeply at one of the rare examples Anne Scott found of cooperation between black women and white women.[60]

In 1907 the New York periodical the *Independent* published a story originally sent to the white Athens newspaper by Mary Lipscomb. It explained that when a "colored seamstress, Martha Holsey . . . could find no home where three colored orphans could be placed . . . she talked it over with her own people, and then, timidly, she asked the counsel of several white women for whom she had sewed." Together Holsey and her women's club worked with the white women's club to rent a "nice, clean cottage" where "a competent colored woman" not only cared for the orphans but ran a day-care center where working mothers (no doubt the maids, washerwomen, and seamstresses employed by Athens Club members) could leave their children. "The mothers will pay a small sum monthly, and this will be supplemented by the Athens Woman's Club."[61]

What is striking here is not the beneficence of the white women but the evidence of a black women's organization in Athens. It is symptomatic of the delicate line such groups had to walk that Lipscomb emphasized Holsey's timidity. It is also interesting—and very much in line with Scott's discussion of black women's organizations—that the project won the support of the African American community when Holsey and representatives of the white women's club met with them at "the colored Baptist Church" on a Sunday afternoon to explain their plan. Which church, we wonder. Could it have been one that Harriet Powers attended? The article concluded: "It is a simple story and touchingly sweet and Christian. How much better as a solution of the so-called race problem than grandfather clauses and disfranchisement, which only stir race hatred on both sides. May the movement grow!" Whether this not-so-subtle criticism of southern law came from Lipscomb or from the editor of the *Independent*, we do not know. That the encounter between the two women's clubs occurred is, however, confirmed in the surviving minutes of the white Athens Women's Club.[62]

This story has an intriguing postscript. In 1910, S. F. Harris, a black educator in Athens, joined a group of white businessmen to propose a "Black Mammy Memorial." This was to be not a statue but a school. "The work that is to receive special emphasis is the training of young women in DOMESTIC ART," the promotional pamphlet announced, adding that the "women who fill the places that the 'OLD BLACK MAMMY' filled with credit . . . should have the opportunities for preparation and moral fitness." As if this paean to slavery was not clear enough, it continued, "The Black mammy was trained in a school that passed with the institutions of her day. Where shall those who received her mantle be fitted for the places that were dignified by the industry, purity and fidelity of those distinctively Southern characters whom the South loved and will ever hold in tender memory?" Significantly, the one woman on the proposed institute advisory board was Mary Ann Lipscomb.[63]

Harriet Powers died on January 1, 1910, just as the idea for the new institute was emerging. She was not a mammy. Nor was she a household servant. She may have been a seamstress, like Holsey, but if so, she didn't claim that occupation on any known document. On the federal census form, she, like millions of other American women, identified her occupation as "keeping house." For a woman who had once been a slave, that was a major achievement. It is also remarkable that three days after her death, her town's white newspaper published the following notice: "Harriet Powers, an aged Negro woman who held the esteem of many Athens people, died from pneumonia Jan. 1st. Her remains were carried to her old home near the city for interment Sunday."[64]

This was not the first time Powers's achievements had been acknowledged in print. Fifteen years before, her Bible quilt had attracted the attention of at least one reporter whose dispatches from Atlanta were reprinted in Boston and Chicago. Understanding where Harriet Powers fit in the racial lineup at the fair offers another angle on her story. The Atlanta Cotton States and International Exposition was not just any fair. Nor was it merely the site of a famous speech by Booker T. Washington, trading civil rights for the goodwill of southern whites. As Theda Purdue has written, "The Cotton States Exposition took place at the midpoint of a crucial decade in the history of the South and the nation. In the 1890s the final 'battle' of the Indian wars took place at Wounded Knee, the census confirmed the closing of the frontier, southern states rewrote constitutions disfranchising African Americans, the Supreme Court decided that racial segregation was constitutional, and the United States embarked on overseas expansion in the Spanish American War." She concluded, "These events reflected a construction of race that few white Americans would have seen as anything other than scientifically rational, morally justifiable, imminently practical, and even divinely ordained."[65]

That construction rested on the idea of an evolutionary ascension from savagery to civilization. For most reporters, savagery was represented by the Dahomean display on the midway that featured real-life "Canibals" and "Amazon Warriors." As early as 1725, Europeans had reported the existence of women warriors in the kingdom of Dahomey. After the subjugation of the kingdom by France in the nineteenth century, exhibitors took the supposed Amazons on the road. Between 1890 and 1924, they appeared in most of the capitals of Europe, as well as at the World's Columbian Exposition in Chicago. Their presence in Atlanta gave the organizers a living demonstration of their key argument. The American South was a site of racial progress. As one African American newspaper reported, "The village representing the lowest savage life of darkest Africa, with its

6. Women at the Dahomey Village. Fred L. Howe Cotton States and International Exposition Photographs, 1895. Kenan Research Center at the Atlanta History Center.

7. Exterior of the Dahomey Village. Fred L. Howe Cotton States and International Exposition Photographs, 1895. Kenan Research Center at the Atlanta History Center.

half-clothed, unkempt natives, proves a wonderful contrast with the surrounding evidence of culture and refinement of the American negroes."[66]

The Negro Building at Atlanta was second only to the Women's Building in popularity. Although some national leaders of the African American community boycotted the fair, believing that black visitors would be ill treated in Atlanta and that the whole affair was intended to distract the nation from the loss of civil rights in the South, others saw it as an opportunity to demonstrate their worth. The building itself followed the evolutionary theme, emphasizing the distance that African Americans had traveled since slavery. At the pinnacle were the works of scientists, scholars, and European-trained artists like Edmonia Lewis. Powers's Bible quilt was displayed in a corner of the Georgia exhibit "reserved mostly for the work of the older ones who have been slaves," wrote Clara R. Jemison, an Alabama writer whose dispatches to the *Boston Evening Transcript* were picked up by the *Chicago Daily Tribune*. Although Jemison described the quilt in some detail and acknowledged the enthusiasm of the guide who pointed it out, she nevertheless assumed that it had been made by "a poor, ignorant slave, who could not read, and whose knowledge of the Bible was from the stories told her by others." She continued, "Each square represents one of these stories, and it is not only curious, but amusing, to see the impressions these stories made upon the mind of one who could not understand them."[67] Poor. Ignorant. Amusing. These are in fact the very descriptions attached to Harriet by Smith, Diver, and Finch.

For Susie Revels, the daughter of the famous black senator from Mississippi, the evidence of progress in the Negro Building was based on the achievements of educated male leaders: "Journalists, lawyers, physicians, and business men of various callings in life are represented, while in the construction and finishing arrangements of the Negroes' edifice, himself the mechanic, the artisan and the painter will display their exhibits. These stand to the well wishers, a decided encouragement; to the doubtful, a settled assurance."[68]

Alice Bacon, a teacher at the Hampton Institute, reflected similar ideas. She was thrilled with the speech of Booker T. Washington and his "policy of always taking thankfully what was given freely" and "of making no grievances and few direct issues." She provided a complete transcript of Washington's speech, including an important passage near the beginning where he traced the development of African Americans since slavery, reminding his listeners that they had started "thirty years ago with ownership here and there in a few quilts and pumpkins and chickens (gathered from miscellaneous sources)" and that it was a considerable achievement that they could now display "agricultural implements, buggies, steam engines, newspapers, books, statuary, carvings, paintings."[69]

So how might Harriet Powers have responded to all this progress? The autobiography recently discovered by Kyra Hicks offers one answer. Powers's quilts and the photograph preserved with them suggest another.

The autobiography suggests that she wanted to set the record straight, that there were rumors about her flying around that she wanted to squelch. She wanted her readers to know that she had attended the exposition herself on December 26, 1896 (the actual year was 1895).

> After leaving Atlanta it was said I was dead—it was not so, for I was at the Exposition because I present the Governor of the colored department a watermelon Christmas Gift. I am enjoying good health in Athens, Ga.

In a period when so-called coon songs parodied African Americans for their love of watermelons, Harriet unselfconsciously alluded to her Christmas gift. There is no way of knowing what it was she gave the official—a fresh watermelon saved from her own crop or some sort of watermelon pickles or preserves—but there is no question that she wanted to be known as alive and thriving and had personally given her gift to the man who was in charge of the "colored department." She also wanted people to know that she could read and write. Nor did she shrink from acknowledging the prizes she had won or the number of pieces she had stitched into her quilts. She signed her autobiography, "This I accomplish Harriet A. Powers." If there was going to be a parade of progress at the fair, she wanted to be part of it.[70]

The day Powers attended the fair was designated as Negro Day. One would like to think that she remained in Atlanta for the black Congress of Women that met the next day. "Of all the events sponsored by the Negro Building," Theda Purdue writes, "this was the most militant." Female leaders from eighteen states gathered to condemn segregated railcars and the convict lease system as well as alcohol abuse, obscene literature, and unkempt houses. They also asked for better-trained teachers in black schools and challenged African American women's groups to found orphanages and other social welfare institutions. There are few causes listed in Anne Scott's list of female achievements that were not on the agenda at this meeting. Since faculty, students, and alumnae of the

8. Harriet Powers. Undated photograph. Museum of Fine Arts, Boston.

South's black colleges were among the organizers, it seems likely that the still anonymous "women of Atlanta University," the group who purchased Harriet Powers's second quilt, were present. Without question, the women's meeting encouraged an already developing national network of black women's voluntary societies.[71]

Harriet Powers may or may not have been there. Her quilts do not convey a political agenda; they speak with a prophetic voice. She read the signs of Christ's coming in the heavens and of God's judgment in the common things of the earth, like the ticking cloth in the house of Bob and Kate Bell of Virginia, "people who were taught nothing of God." The very first square in her Bible quilt, the square picturing Adam and Eve with a brightly striped serpent who has not yet lost his feet, contains a curious

9. Lucy Stanton, "Aunt Liza's Porch," 1921. Special Collections and Archives, Robert W. Woodruff Library, Emory University. Photograph courtesy Georgia Museum of Art.

object. Some later commentators speculated that it might be an African drum, but Harriet told Lorine Diver it was a woman's dressmaker's form, for her a symbol of "Original Sin or Forbidden Fruit." She told Lucine Finch the same thing. "The trimming around the neck even is most carefully worked out in its significance. 'To ketch de eye, honey!' she said. 'To ketch de eye er mortal man. *Yas, suh!*'"[72]

Viewing Harriet's work in relation to other figurative quilts of the period reinforces this interpretation. She was surely not alone in portraying human figures in simplified form. What is striking about her quilts is not the use of stylized human figures but her lack of interest in clothing. She conveys the nature of her characters with props and gestures. Other quilters, working in a tradition of American needlework extending far back in time, lavished most of their attention on clothes, sometimes replicating current fashions in astonishingly accurate detail.[73] Harriet disdained that sort of display and perhaps in the process dismissed the trappings of civilization that her neighbors may have interpreted as "progress." If her objective was to identify the origins of evil, she found it not only in disobedience to God but in pride, ostentation, and material display.

For her own photograph, she wore a neat but unassuming dark dress and a light-colored apron. The apron is significant. Photographs, paintings, and cartoons of African American women in this period, including those eulogized as "mammy," almost invariably show them in long white aprons that reach almost to the hem of their skirts. Jennie Smith's neighbor and fellow artist Lucy Stanton created many portraits, some full-size, some miniatures on ivory, of the female servants in her family and neighborhood. Although her portraits conform in a general way to the mammy stereotype—these are obviously well-behaved and loyal servants—she was respectful of their individuality and sensitive to the dynamics that defined them as a group. One miniature, about the size of a three-by-five-inch card, portrays a group of women on "Aunt Liza's Porch." Their aprons form a sequence of white wedges stretching across the porch like a massive railing separating them from the street. On the far corner of the porch, a single black man wearing a top hat rocks on a spindly chair.[74] What is powerful about this picture is its invocation of a community of women in a world that too often portrayed women like Harriet as solitary figures sustained only by white patrons.

Harriet's apron was surely a badge of respectability, but it was not a marker of subservience. Around the hem were emblems like those on her quilts, radiating suns. The meanings of those emblems were probably available only to those who fully understood her symbolic system, but even without an explanation, they connoted a woman ready to proclaim her dignity and her faith.

Harriet Powers believed in God. She also believed in accomplishment. Although untrained, she was a self-conscious artist. She did not hide her quilts in a trunk or under a spread. When others admired her quilts, she insisted on explaining their meaning. Her quilts survived not only because they are remarkable works of art but because she spoke about them to anyone who would listen. Because she insisted on speaking for herself, she exposed an invisible network that brought a few white women and one visionary black woman together in common interest and mutual misunderstanding. Through their problematic but productive interaction, Harriet's quilt survives to puzzle and instruct later generations.

Notes

1. Alice Walker, "In Search of Our Mothers' Gardens," *Ms.* magazine, May 1974, reprinted in Walker, *In Search of Our Mothers' Gardens* (San Diego: Harcourt Brace Jovanovich, 1983), 239. This is clearly Harriet Powers's quilt, though Walker either misread or misremembered the label.

2. Gladys-Marie Fry, "'A Sermon in Patchwork': New Light on Harriet Powers," in *Singular Women: Writing the Artist*, ed. Kirsten Frederickson and Sarah E. Webb (Berkeley: University of California Press, 2003), 92. The Smithsonian did not yet have Harriet's full name. There is some question about the spelling of her name. On her gravestone it appears as "Harriett," explaining why some scholars have chosen to add a second *t*. See Catherine L. Holmes, "'The Darling Offspring of Her Brain': The Quilts of Harriett Powers," in *Georgia Quilts: Piecing Together a History*, ed. Anita Zaleski Weinraub (Athens: University of Georgia Press, 2006), 176–87.

3. He must have seen the quilt soon after it arrived at the Smithsonian in 1969, for he mentioned it in his landmark essay of that year. Robert Farris Thompson, "African Influence on the Art of the United States," in *Black Studies in the University*, ed. Armstead L. Robinson, Craig Foster, and Donald H. Ogilvie (New Haven: Yale University Press, 1969), 122–70. In an e-mail to me on February 21, 2008, Thompson affirmed that he was the first scholar to suggest Dahomean influence.

4. Doris M. Bowen to Larry Salmon, May 25, 1971, and Larry Salmon to Doris Bowman, June 29, 1971, Museum of Fine Arts, Boston, curatorial files, 64.619. A photograph and description of the quilt had already appeared in Museum of Fine Arts, Boston, *Bulletin* 62 (1964). Maxim Karolik, a Russian-born tenor and folk art collector acquired the Powers quilt sometime in the 1950s. It came to the Museum of Fine Arts, Boston, in December 1963, after his death. Carol Troyen, "Maxim Karolik Folk Art," *Magazine Antiques* 159 (April 2001): 588–99.

5. Fry, "Sermon in Patchwork," 92–93.

6. Gladys-Marie Fry, "Harriet Powers: Portrait of a Black Quilter," in *Missing Pieces: Georgia Folk Art, 1770–1976*, ed. Anna Wadsworth (Atlanta: Georgia Council for the Arts and Humanities, 1976), 16–23; reprinted in Gladys-Marie Fry, *Stitched from the Soul: Slave Quilts from the Ante-bellum South* (New York: Dutton, 1990; reprint, Chapel Hill: University of North Carolina Press, 2002), 84–91.

7. The bibliography in Kyra E. Hicks, *Black Threads: An African American Quilting Sourcebook* (Jefferson, N.C.: McFarland, 2003), which runs over 100 pages, gives some sense of the vitality and breadth of this field.

8. Cuesta Benberry, *Always There: The African-American Presence in American Quilts* (Louisville: Kentucky Quilt Project, 1992).

9. Roland L. Freeman, *A Communion of the Spirits: African-American Quilters, Preservers, and Their Stories* (Nashville, Tenn.: Rutledge Hill Press, 1996), 149–55, 103, 131–33; Alvia Wardlaw, "Introduction: The Quilts of Gee's Bend," in *Gee's Bend: The Women and Their Quilts* (Atlanta: Tinwood Books in association with the Museum of Fine Arts, Houston, 2002), 10.

10. Freeman, *Communion of the Spirits*, 101–3. On the broader controversy, see Judith Elsley, "The Smithsonian Quilt Controversy: Cultural Dislocation," *Uncoverings* 14 (1993): 119–36; *The Great American Quilt Revival*, a documentary film produced by Bonesteel Films (http://www.bonesteelfilms.com) in 2005; and an interview

with Bonnie Leman at "Quilt Treasures," Center for the Quilt Online, http://www
.centerforthequilt.org/treasures/index.php.

11. The exhibit is now closed. For an online overview, see "Treasures of American History: Online Exhibition," http://americanhistory.si.edu/exhibitions/small_exhibition.cfm?key=1267&exkey=143&pagekey=250.

12. See Museum of Fine Arts, Boston, Collections, Textile and Fashion Arts, http://www.mfa.org/collections/index.asp?key=31.

13. Jennie Smith, "A Biblical Quilt," National Museum of American History Files, Accession no. 183472, 4-23-1969, Textile Department. I thank Doris Bowman for providing me with a photocopy of this document. Almost all accounts of Harriet's life quote at least some of this material either directly or secondhand through Fry or others.

14. I first saw the picture in Hicks, *Black Threads*, 210. She found it in Judy Lorraine Larson, "Three Southern World's Fairs: Cotton States and International Exposition, Atlanta, 1895; Tennessee Centennial, Nashville, 1897; South Carolina Inter-state and West Indian Exposition, Charleston, 1901–1902; Creating Regional Self-Portraits" (Ph.D. diss., Emory University, 1999). For Hicks's description of how she found the picture, see "The Coffee Tree Quilt," *Quilters Newsletter* 34 (March 2003), http://qnm.com/issue/350.

15. Diver, inscription on photograph, Harriet Powers's Bible Quilt, Files, Textile Department, National Museum of American History. Doris Bowman kindly supplied a copy of this material. Kyra E. Hicks discovered the second copy in Keokuk, as well as an autobiography of Powers and a brief note from Jennie Smith. See Kyra E. Hicks, *This I Accomplish: Harriet Powers' Bible Quilt and Other Pieces* (Black Threads Press, 2009), 37–39.

16. Lucine Finch, "A Sermon in Patchwork," *Outlook Magazine*, October 19, 1914, 493–95. Fry republished Finch's article alongside her own essay in *Singular Women*. Hicks (*This I Accomplish*, 52) suggests that Finch borrowed her accounts from Diver. I do not find this argument credible. Although there are a few similar passages in the two accounts, there is enough unique material in both to suggest a third, common source (either Powers or Smith). Fry ("Sermon in Patchwork," 85) suggests that Finch may have known Jennie Smith's brother, Wales Wynton Smith, who was for a time a journalist in Birmingham, but he died in 1886, when Finch was still very young. Since Smith, Diver, and Finch all traveled extensively, I see no reason to doubt that they all saw the quilt (perhaps at the Atlanta Exposition) or that one or more of them may have known the other. Smith, of course, had the quilt in her possession until her death in 1946.

17. Smith, "A Biblical Quilt," 3.

18. Finch, "A Sermon in Patchwork," 495.

19. Diver, inscription on photograph.

20. Finch, "A Sermon in Patchwork," 494.

21. Smith, "A Biblical Quilt," 3; Finch, "A Sermon in Patchwork," 495.

22. Fry, "New Light on Harriet Powers," 91.

23. LCT, "Applique Quilt, American, Athens, Georgia, 1895–1898," *Bulletin* (Museum of Fine Arts, Boston) 62, no. 330 (1964); and Curatorial Files, Textile Department, Museum of Fine Arts, Boston.

24. Key to the Harriet Powers quilt, Museum of Fine Arts, Boston, also published as a chart in Marie Jeanne Adams, "The Harriet Powers Pictorial Quilts," *Black Art* 3 (1979): 15, and quoted verbatim in Regenia Perry, *Harriet Powers's Bible Quilts* (New York: Rizzoli, 1994), 6.

25. A recent essay that cites much earlier scholarship is Thomas J. Campanella, "'Mark Well the Gloom': Shedding Light on the Great Dark Day of 1780," *Environmental History* 12, no. 1 (2007): 35–58. For an example of contemporary interest in these phenomena, search "Dark Day," "Moon Turned into Blood," and "Stars Fall from Heaven" on BibleUniverse.com.

26. Jane Wilson Joyce, "Bible Quilt, circa 1900," in *Quilt Stories*, ed. Cecilia Macheski (Lexington: University Press of Kentucky, 1994), 183–85.

27. John Michael Vlach, *The Afro-American Tradition in Decorative Arts* (Cleveland: Cleveland Museum of Art, 1978), 44–54. The earliest of the African textiles in his exhibit dated from the late nineteenth century to the early twentieth. Others he acquired in Benin in the 1960s. Fry gave no source for her discussion of Dahomey. Conversations with Thompson may have been a factor. Both are listed as members of the "Black Folklore Committee" in "Proceedings of the Annual Business Meeting," *Journal of American Folklore: Annual Supplement* 86 (May 1973): 85. For Thompson's larger argument, see *Flash of the Spirit: African and Afro-American Art and Philosophy* (New York: Random House, 1983).

28. Marie Jeanne Adams, "The Harriet Powers Pictorial Quilts," *Black Arts* 3, no. 4 (1979): 12–28. This essay is reprinted in William R. Ferris, ed., *Afro-American Folk Art and Crafts* (Jackson: University Press of Mississippi, 1986), 66–76. Unfortunately, some scholars have ignored Adams's reservations about the Vlach argument, quoting in their work only the single paragraph noting similarities. See, e.g., Michelle Cliff, "'I Found God in Myself and I Loved Her / I Loved Her Fiercely': More Thoughts on the Work of Black Women Artists," *Journal of Feminist Studies in Religion* 2, no. 1 (1996), reprinted in *Feminism-Art-Theory: An Anthology, 1968–2000*, ed. Hilary Robinson (Oxford: Blackwell, 2001), 613–14. For a scathing critique of the use of visual analogies in cultural analysis, see Sally Price, "Seaming Connections: Artworlds of the African Diaspora," in *Afro-Atlantic Dialogues: Anthropology in the Diaspora*, ed. Kevin A. Yelvington (Santa Fe: School of American Research Press, 2006), 83–114. Thanks to Vincent Brown for letting me know about this essay. Price has high praise, however, for Gladys-Marie Fry's locally based fieldwork.

29. Mary E. Lyons, *Stitching Stars: The Story Quilts of Harriet Powers* (New York: Charles Scribner's Sons, 1993), 31–37.

30. Perry, *Harriet Powers's Bible Quilts*, 2, 4. For an assessment of the early twentieth-century anthropology popularized in Temple's book, see Walter E. A. van

Beek, "Haunting Griaule: Experiences from the Restudy of the Dogon," *History in Africa* 31 (2004): 43–68; and "Dogon Revisited," with comments by ERLINK"http://www.jstor.org.ezp2.harvard.edu/search/BasicResults?Search=Search&Query=aa:%22R.%20M.%20A.%20Bedaux%22&hp=25&si=1&wc=on"R. M. A. Bedaux, Suzanne Preston Blier, and others, *Current Anthropology* 32 (1991): 139–67. On the importance of context in understanding symbols, see Suzanne Preston Blier, "Words about Words about Icons: Iconology and the Study of African Art," *Art Journal* 47 (1988): 75–87.

31. Maude Southwell Wahlman, "The Art of Afro-American Quiltmaking: Origins, Development, and Significance" (Ph.D. diss., Yale University, 1980); and *Signs and Symbols: African Images in African-American Quilts* (New York: Studio Books in association with the Museum of American Folk Art, 1993).

32. Robert Ferris Thompson, "From the First to the Final Thunder: African-American Quilts, Monuments of Cultural Assertion," in *Who'd a Thought It: Improvisation in African-American Quiltmaking*, ed. Eli Leon (San Francisco Crafts and Folk Art Museum, 1987), 12.

33. Leon, *Who'd a Thought It*, 59.

34. Freeman, *Communion of the Spirits*, 118–19.

35. Sally Price has been the most vehement in challenging the work of Thompson and his associates, but see the extremely interesting comments by Suzanne Blier cited in Janet Catherine Berlo, "'Acts of Pride, Desperation, and Necessity': Aesthetics, Social History, and American Quilts," in *Wild by Design: Two Hundred Years of Innovation and Artistry in American Quilts*, ed. Janet Catherine Berlo and Patricia Cox Crews (Lincoln, Neb.: International Quilt Study Center, 2003), 20–21, 139n98. Most of these issues were raised, though very gently, in Monni Adams's early essays.

36. The oldest, according to a note attached to it, was said to have been made by a slave in 1810. Just over 3 percent of the quilts were attributed to African Americans. Of those, 5 percent appeared to be based on original designs (compared with 3 percent of those made by whites). See Anita Zaleski Weinraub, "Introduction," and Margie Rogers, "Appendix A: Statistical Summary of Documented Quilts," in *Georgia Quilts*, 4, 250–51.

37. Irene McLaren, "Early Quilts," in *Georgia Quilts*, 65, 66. For other examples of starlike shapes within circles, see 62, 68, 71, 85, 89, 93, 94.

38. Berlo, "Acts of Pride," 15–21; and many examples in Sandi Fox, *Wrapped in Glory: Figurative Quilts and Bed Covers, 1700–1900* (London: Thames and Hudson in conjunction with Los Angeles County Museum of Art, 1990).

39. Wahlman actually pointed this out but did not follow through on the implications of the point. She noted, for example, two literary sources that referred to Bible quilts by African Americans—but she was apparently unaware of biblical imagery in other nineteenth-century American quilts. See Wahlman, *Signs and Symbols*, 67; Eleanor C. Gibbs, "The Bible Quilt," *Atlantic Monthly*, July 1922, 65–66; Julia Peterkin, *Black April* (New York: Bobbs-Merrill, 1927), 159–79; and on the broader tradition among both African Americans and Euro-Americans, Benberry,

Always There, 43–47, 89; Fox, *Wrapped in Glory*, 84–87, 114–17, 126–27, 150–53; and for the very early work of Sarah Warner Williams, Linda Eaton, *Quilts in a Material World: Selections from the Winterthur Collection* (New York: Abrams, 2007), 50–53; and Amelia Peck, *American Quilts and Coverlets in the Metropolitan Museum of Art* (New York: Dutton, 1990), 16–19.

40. *Wild by Design*, 74–75; Patricia T. Herr, *Quilting Traditions: Pieces from the Past* (Atglen, Pa.: Schiffer, 2000), 71–81; Ellen Harding Baker, "Solar System Quilt," National Museum of American History, http://americanhistory.si.edu/collections/object.cfm?key=35&objke y=53.

41. Benberry, *Always There*, 44–45.

42. William Gilcher, "Anything for Wisement: The World of Harriet Powers," unpublished manuscript shared by the author, 23–26. Twenty-nine African American lodges were active in Athens at the end of the nineteenth century, enrolling roughly 75 percent of the adult black population. See T. J. Woofter Jr., *The Negroes of Athens, Georgia*, Phelps-Stokes Fellowship Studies, no. 1, *Bulletin of the University of Georgia* 14, no. 4 (December 1913): 35, 36.

43. This was not easy to do. See Joan Halimah Brooks to Malcolm Rogers, October 17, 1995; Nicola J. Shilliam to Joan Halimah Brooks, October 20, 1995; Janice Srkow to Joan Halimah Brooks, February 14, 1996, Museum of Fine Arts Curatorial Files; and Freeman, *Communion of the Spirits*, 103.

44. Lee Shearer, "Student spent 2 years looking for grave site of renowned quilter," *Florida Times-Union*, January 11, 2005. Catherine Holmes is now writing a doctoral dissertation on Harriett Powers.

45. Al Hester, "Slavery—and what happened when the Yankees came," On-line Athens, Friday, June 15, 2001, http://onlineathens.com/stories/061701/ath_0617019009.shtml; and "Reminiscences of a Negro Preacher," by Mrs. Ina B. Hawkes, Research Field Workers, Georgia Writers' Project, ed. Mrs. Maggie B. Freeman, WPA Area 6, November 7, 1939, in *American Life Histories: Manuscripts from the Federal Writers' Project, 1936–1940*, Manuscript Division, Library of Congress, http://lcweb2.loc.gov/wpaintro/wpahome.html.

46. Hicks, *This I Accomplish*, 38. On the census, see Holmes, "Darling Offspring of Her Brain," 271n10. On the efforts of freed slaves to achieve literacy, see Tera W. Hunter, *To 'Joy My Freedom: Southern Black Women's Lives and Labors after the Civil War* (Cambridge: Harvard University Press, 1997) 42–43, 69.

47. "Colored Fairs" were held in Athens from 1886 onward, usually in association with the Northeast Georgia Fair. See Hicks, *This I Accomplish*, 25–27, for a brief summary of stories from the *Athens Banner*. Other notices of the fair can be found in *Macon Telegraph* (Macon, Ga.), November 19, 1886, 5, 6; November 16, 1888, 3; and *Columbia Enquirer-Sun* (Columbus, Ga.), November 6, 1887, 2.

48. Smith, "A Biblical Quilt," 1.

49. Diver, inscription on photograph.

50. Key to the Harriet Powers quilt.

51. Anne Firor Scott, "On Seeing and Not Seeing: A Case of Historical Invisibility," *Journal of American History* 71 (1984): 15.

52. Anne Firor Scott, "Most Invisible of All: Black Women's Voluntary Associations," *Journal of Southern History* 56 (1990): 12.

53. Fry, "Sermon in Patchwork," 84–86; Hicks, *This I Accomplish*, 22, 32; membership list, Athens Women's Club Papers, 1899–1911, Digital Library of Georgia, http://dlg.galileo.usg.edu/athenswomansclub/index.php.

54. *Atlanta Constitution*, August 29, 1895, 3; September 19, 1895, 5; October 6, 1895, 14.

55. Winona Evans Reeves, *The Blue Book of Iowa Women: A History of Contemporary Women* (Mexico, Mo.: Missouri Printing and Publishing Company, 1914), 143–47, accessed through Internet Archive, http://www.archive.org.

56. Fry, "Sermon in Patchwork," 84–86; Hicks, *This I Accomplish*, 53; David Allan Robertson, *The Quarter-Centennial Celebration of the University of Chicago* (Chicago: University of Chicago Press, 1916), 149; "Chautauqua Assembly Program," *Chautauquan* 42 (March–August 1905): 436–37, 442, 452; "News and Notes," *English Journal* 4 (October 1915): 536; Harriet Monroe, "Review: Negro Sermons," *Poetry* 30 (August 1927): 293; Gertrude E. Johnson, *Modern Literature for Oral Interpretation* (New York: D. Appleton, 1920); *Poet Lore: A Magazine of Letters*, vol. 21, ed. Charlotte Porter and Helen A. Clarke (Boston: Poet Lore, 1910), 401; and many references in newspapers, including *Atlanta Constitution*, August 24, 1907, 2; *Chicago Daily Tribune*, February 27, 1910, G2; *New York Times*, October 7, 1923; June 23, 1929, 24; March 29, 1931; April 25, 1931, 26; April 6, 1933, 2; May 13, 1934, N6; December 12, 1936, D2. For the larger context of such performances, see Micki McElya, *Clinging to Mammy: The Faithful Slave in Twentieth-Century America* (Cambridge: Harvard University Press, 2007), 58–73. Although McElya does not discuss Finch, she shows how middle-class white women refined motifs familiar from nineteenth-century minstrel productions.

57. *Daughters of the American Revolution Magazine*, July 1914, 13, 14, 17. On the life and death of Keokuk, see Thomas Burnell Colbert, "'The Hinge on Which All Affairs of the Sauk and Fox Indians Turn': Keokuk and the United States Government," in *Enduring Nations: Native Americans in the Midwest*, ed. R. David Edmunds (Urbana: University of Illinois Press, 2008), 54–71; Patrick J. Jung, *The Black Hawk War of 1832* (Norman: University of Oklahoma Press, 2007), 202; and John W. Hall, *Uncommon Defense: Indian Allies in the Black Hawk War* (Cambridge: Harvard University Press, 2009), 135. In Hall's summary, "The cost of alliance with the Great Father was considerable and manifest; the dividends, however, were hard to discern."

58. Sarah Harper Case, "Renegotiating Race and Respectability in the Classroom: Women and Education in the New South" (Ph.D. diss., University of California, Santa Barbara, 2002), 13, 47, 48, 49, 51; McElya, *Clinging to Mammy*, 52–59.

59. Case, "Renegotiating Race," 46.

60. Anne Firor Scott, *Natural Allies: Women's Associations in American History* (Urbana: University of Illinois Press, 1991), 90, 168, 169. On one woman's effort to enlist the mammy stereotype in the interest of reform, see Glenda Elizabeth Gilmore, *Gender and Jim Crow: Women and the Politics of White Supremacy in North Carolina, 1896–1920* (Chapel Hill: University of North Carolina Press, 1996), 189, 190; and Kimberly Wallace-Sanders, *Mammy: A Century of Race, Gender, and Southern Memory* (Ann Arbor: University of Michigan Press, 2010), 113.

61. *Independent* 63 (December 26, 1907): 1582, 1583.

62. Minutes, Athens Women's Club Papers, 90. The leaders of the Athens Women's Club were white supremacists, but they seem to have preferred more subtle forms of social control than some of their neighbors. In *Behind the Mask of Chivalry: The Making of the Second Ku Klux Klan* (New York: Oxford University Press, 1994), 30, Nancy MacLean notes that in the 1920s only one member of the Athens Women's Club had a husband in the Klan.

63. June O. Patton, ed., "Moonlight and Magnolias in Southern Education: The Black Mammy Memorial Institute," *Journal of Negro History* 65 (1980): 149–55. See also McElya, *Clinging to Mammy*, 217–21; Wallace-Sanders, *Mammy*, 105–14. An article in the *Atlanta Constitution* ("Servant Problem Being Settled at Athens, Ga.," August 27, 1911, A6) made clear the impetus for the new school—household servants had been abandoning their posts. The *Constitution* published nine articles on the black mammy memorial between July 6, 1910, and June 8, 1912; then the institution and perhaps the idea disappeared. S. F. Harris continued to preside over Athens's segregated black school. He died in 1935. *Atlanta Constitution*, July 2, 1935, 2.

64. Holmes, "Darling Offspring of Her Brain," 185.

65. Theda Purdue, *Race and the Atlanta Cotton States Exposition of 1895* (Athens: University of Georgia Press, 2010), 1–2.

66. "The Colored Race at Atlanta," *Broad-Ax* (Salt Lake City) 1, no. 15 (December 7, 1895): 1. For a brief account of the Dahomean soldiers in relation to other reputed "Amazons," see Laurel Thatcher Ulrich, *Well-Behaved Women Seldom Make History* (New York: Alfred A. Knopf, 2007), 49, 50.

67. Clara R. Jemison, "Exhibit of the Negroes," *Chicago Daily Tribune*, November 24, 1895, 30. According to the byline, Jemison's account first appeared in the *Boston Transcript*. The editor of Salt Lake City's African American newspaper, the *Broad-Ax*, also published parts of it in a synthesis of various accounts of the Negro Building.

68. Miss S. S. Revels, "Negroes at the Atlanta Exposition," *Seattle Republican*, 1896. Also see Arana Bontemps and Jack Conroy, *Anyplace But Here* (1945; Columbia: University of Missouri Press, 1966), 260, 261.

69. Alice M. Bacon, *The Negro and the Atlanta Exposition* (Baltimore: Trustees of the John F. Slater Fund, 1896), 9, 12, 15, 22–23.

70. Hicks, *This I Accomplish*, 38. Hicks believes this document was a letter written to Lorine Diver. I see no evidence of that. In tone and form, it reads as a more general

statement, an autobiography of the sort an author or artist might compose for public purpose.

71. Purdue, *Race and the Atlanta Cotton States Exposition*, 45–48, quote 58. On earlier organizational activities by working-class Atlanta women, see Hunter, *To 'Joy My Freedom*, 71, 72, and, on the voluntary work of women associated with Atlanta University, 136ff.

72. Inscription on back of photo, Textile Files, National Museum of American History; Finch, "A Sermon in Patchwork," 493.

73. Fox, *Wrapped in Glory*, 62–65, 74, 76–79, 104–7, 118–21, 150–57, and many others.

74. "Aunt Liza's Porch, 1921," in *The Art of Lucy May Stanton* (Athens: Georgia Museum of Art and University of Georgia, 2002), 97.

Taking Care of Bodies, Babies, and Business

Black Women Health Professionals in South Carolina, 1895–1954

—DARLENE CLARK HINE

Anne Firor Scott enjoined my generation of students and scholars to make women and their activism for social reform visible, to relocate their experiences and contributions from the intellectual, cultural, and political margins to the core of American and southern history. She, in her own body of work, made centering and seeing critical processes essential to truth telling and the reconstruction of our nation's past.[1] Without her scholarship and friendship, and her enormous mentoring of countless women scholars, myself included, women's history would not today stand as a legitimate and respected field of inquiry. Her gifts and our debts are beyond measure.

I published my first essay in black women's history, "Female Slave Resistance and the Economics of Sex," in 1979.[2] I theorized about enslaved women's strategies to thwart their owners' economic profiting from the exploitation of their reproductive labor. I suggested that black women's biological resistance to slavery, that is, the assumption of control over reproduction, was manifested in the practices of sexual abstinence, abortion, and infanticide. In a follow-up theoretical piece, I historicized how rape and the threat of rape informed the development and practice of the art of dissemblance, that is, the cultivation of psychic space within which black women in slavery and freedom shielded or masked their innermost selves and were thus able to craft identities, at once positive and empowering, in opposition to widely accepted dehumanizing stereotypes of their morality.[3] The historian Deborah Gray White concedes that dissemblance "was a good strategy," one that was deployed to great effect by leaders of women's clubs in the early twentieth century. Accordingly, they allowed "their public identities to stand in for the private."⁴ These theoretical and conceptual ruminations inspired and informed my monographic study of black women's social activism, community building, and emergence as professional nurses in the first half of the twentieth century. In *Black Women in White: Racial Conflict and Cooperation in the Nursing Profession, 1890–1954*,⁵ I focused on the struggles of nurse leaders to break down the barriers of segregation, discrimination, and exclusion that characterized black professional life during the era of Jim Crow.⁶ The historian Stephanie Shaw astutely observed, "Professional women worked both to repair and to prevent the damage that frequently resulted from systematic discrimination, and thus their work reflected, if it was not defined by, the neglect of existing public institutions."⁷

Returning full circle, I now engage a different set of questions concerning black women professionals who devoted their private lives and public works not to the destruction of fetuses or the prevention of birth but to building programs and institutions that would facilitate black survival by keeping black babies and their mothers alive and healthy "on the black side of town," where, as the sociologist Aldon Morris observed, "life expectancy was lower because of poor sanitary conditions and too little income to pay for essential medical services."⁸ I focus on one central question: what were some of the political implications and incremental consequences of the work of black medical and nursing professionals who provided health care to impoverished black residents in segregated southern communities?⁹ Or framed another way, how did a small core group of black women health-care personnel transform health care from being a private affair or privilege into a civic right and a government responsibility? How did their early local struggles to heal black bodies and save black babies prepare and inspire the subsequent activist generation that would lead and serve as foot soldiers in the modern civil rights movement of the 1950s and 1960s?¹⁰

Before introducing the four representative black women health-care activists and reformers—nurse Anna De Costa Banks (1869–1930), physician Lucy Hughes Brown (1863–1911), physician Matilda A. Evans (1872–1935), and nurse-midwife Maude Callen (1898–1990)—who, throughout the first half of the twentieth century, took care of business, bodies, and babies, it is important to underscore the dehumanization and disfranchisement of African Americans that prevailed after the collapse of Reconstruction. The fear of black and white bodies sharing intimate relations became one of myriad forces that propelled white disfranchisement of black men. Miscegenation erupted as a divisive issue during South Carolina's 1895 constitutional convention. The convention essentially ended black male participation in state politics and simultaneously called attention to the low regard of black women. Whereas 88 black men (and 67 white delegates) had participated in the 1868 constitutional convention, by 1895 only five African Americans, all representing Beaufort County, served as delegates: Thomas E. Miller, James Wigg, Isaiah R. Reed, William J. Whipper, and Robert Smalls.

According to the historian George Brown Tindall, white delegates to the 1895 convention sought to write a measure into the new constitution that would prohibit interracial marriage.[11] Robert Smalls proposed a counteramendment providing that any white man guilty of cohabiting with a Negro woman should be barred from holding office; moreover, any child resulting from such a relationship should bear the father's name and inherit property as if the parents were married. Predictably, uproar followed. According to the *Columbia State* (October 4, 1895), James Wigg of Beaufort, noting the consternation that Smalls had provoked, commented that the "coons" had the dogs up the tree for a change and intended to keep them there until white delegates admitted that they must accept such a provision. Not to be trumped, Governor Benjamin Tillman (who after his reelection to the governorship in 1892 was determined to push through a constitutional referendum that would forever disfranchise black men) introduced a substitute amendment that would have punished perpetrators of miscegenation. Such measures were warranted, he averred, to "protect negro women against the debauchery of white men degrading themselves to the level of black women." The convention rejected both motions and enacted a law that made interracial marriage a crime.[12]

The historian Thomas Holt put it succinctly: "At the 1895 constitutional convention, the five black delegates were simply a forlorn reminder of the earlier Republican majority. At that convention Benjamin Tillman made certain that blacks would not regain their political majority in that century; henceforth even the blackest districts would have white masters."[13] By 1900 Tillman proudly claimed credit for the concentrated determination to end black voting. "We have done our level best. . . . We have scratched our heads to find out how we could eliminate the last one of them. We stuffed ballot boxes. We shot them. We are not ashamed of it."[14] It would take over fifty years for a black man to receive a political appointment to a state position. In 1949 Democratic governor Strom Thurmond appointed Dr. T. Carr McFall, head of the Charleston Hospital and Nurse Training School, to a seat on the hospital advisory council.[15]

Racial segregation became an established and unquestioned fact by the end of the nineteenth century. A new social arrangement emerged and was maintained by statute and customary practice. The hierarchy of white over black was reflected in the institutional segregation of schools, churches, hospitals, and private organizations. The caste system permitted white and black personal contact primarily as employer and worker, and as servants and caregivers in white households.[16] The period from 1895 to 1954, characterized by white domination and black powerlessness, required black women to develop diverse and multifaceted relations with white women to provide essential services, particularly in the health-care arena, to black women and children, and paradoxically also to white women and their families. In South Carolina and across the South, the majority of black women worked as domestics. Because "germs recognized no color line," the health of black workers became a concern of white women and their families who employed them.

The urgency of protecting the health of white families opened a space for black women health-care professionals to seize the initiative to make accessible health care available in their own communities. Black women were essential partners in the health-care business. In the late 1890s, Alonzo McClennan, a physician in Charleston, South Carolina, urged African American professionals to establish their own hospitals. In 1899 he wrote, "The time has come when it is necessary for colored physicians to establish hospitals and infirmaries in towns where there are three or four physicians." A year earlier, McClennan had joined with eight medical colleagues—one of whom was the first African American woman physician in South Carolina, Lucy Hughes Brown, and another the state's first trained black nurse, Anna De Costa Banks—to launch the Hospital and Nurse Training School.[17]

McClennan, Brown, and Banks were determined to create and sustain a health-care and nurse training institution servicing their community and the greater Charleston low-country region. The tragic murder of black postmaster Frazier Baker and the killing of one of his children in nearby Lake City underscored the need for a black hospital. The attack on Frazier Baker was part of a statewide effort to violently eliminate black men from all appointed and elective offices. While no one could have saved Frazier Baker on that ill-fated night, had the Charleston hospital not existed, there would have been even more casualties. The wounded members of the Baker family found refuge at the Charleston hospital, where they received treatment for their injuries and protection.

Banks, the head nurse at the Charleston Hospital, described the three-stage process that culminated in the establishment of the hospital and nurse training school. First, she wrote, "We started the work by giving lectures three times a week to those who wished to take up the training. The lectures were given in one of the rooms of the Presbyterian school house." The second stage began with the realization that "it was impossible to train the girls without practical work of some kind. This was followed by efforts to get our nurses into the city hospital to take charge of the colored wards, but this was refused." When white city officials refused to allow black student nurses to care for patients, Banks, McClennan, and Brown ignited the third stage of the process. They appealed "to all of the colored churches and societies, asking [them] to help raise money to buy or build a hospital of our own." Banks reported, "They all responded, some sending five, ten and fifteen dollars. In six months we raised $900."[18] McClennan and his colleagues used the money to purchase a building for the hospital, which opened in late 1897.

On February 24, 1898, a white mob attacked the Frazier Baker residence, which was also the post office, in nearby Lake City. The mob set the building on fire and killed Baker as he came out the front door. Anna De Costa Banks implicitly affirmed the importance of establishing black hospitals and nurse training schools in a straightforward account of the aftermath of the murder of Frazier Baker and his infant child and the attack on the family survivors who made their way to the Charleston hospital.

> Our work is not confined to the city of Charleston and its vicinity, but patients come from all parts of the State. On the 24th of February, 1898, a wagon drove up to our door with four patients, and two children besides. It was the Baker family from Lake City. You remember how the mob went out to the post office at midnight and set it on fire. They put shavings under the building and poured kerosene oil over it; then struck a match to it. The family had retired for the night and were sleeping soundly. The little fellow named Lincoln was the first to awaken. He was sent out to see about the fire, but as soon as he opened the door he was shot down. The father and mother then ran out, and each one was fired upon. The postmaster and babe, about six months old, were killed. The rest of the family made their escape by running through the woods and jumping into a ditch. Lincoln Baker was shot in the abdomen; the ball passed through the coating of the abdomen. For days his life hung on a thread. Mrs. Baker's right arm

was broken in two places and had to be put in plaster of paris. Cora Baker's left arm was broken above the elbow. Rosa Baker was shot in the hand. The ball was taken out the next day. Postmaster Baker and his child were consumed in the flames. His watch was all that could be found the next day. We took care of them until they were well, and then we had to beg clothing for them and get a place for them to stay. The Colored Preachers' Union gives them five dollars a month for rent and friends help to furnish food for them.[19]

Black professional women were the individuals most capable of effective yet subtle manipulations of the complex intersection of race, class, and gender power relations within white supremacy. Critical to the success of their negotiations and the development of strategic contingent alliances with white women was their construction of flexible identities allowing the projection of nonthreatening images of accomplishment, respect, and devoted service to their people. Similarly, southern white women modified definitions of themselves in ways that permitted collaboration with black women without detracting from or imperiling their own social stature. White southern women projected Christian altruism, advocated for social order, and represented moral authority. Health-care arenas became the sites where black professional women could project these same "white-woman" characteristics in their own communities, as well as to powerful white elites from whom they sought and received financial support. Within a space that was public yet private, both groups expanded and fashioned new dimensions of their respective racial identities and social responsibilities as women of the New South. As the historian Alisa Klaus notes, "The rudimentary nature of public health and welfare institutions outside of metropolitan areas allowed women's voluntary organizations to retain a greater degree of autonomy."[20]

Rural and urban African Americans in the South were caught in the grip of exploitative and dangerous labor occupations where injuries were frequent. They were captives of inadequate and inaccessible health-care systems that foreordained much suffering and early death. Black women health professionals were all too often the only barrier between injured and ill black rural southerners and their compromised lives. Women health workers—such as nurses Anna De Costa Banks and Maude Callen and physicians Lucy Hughes Brown and Matilda A. Evans—bore burdens that were, in the words of Deborah Gray White, entirely "too heavy." But they embraced their work as if it was a mission and as if they were responding to a Christian call to do good deeds. For them, the work became the all-consuming focus of their lives, making their private identities indistinguishable from the public service, social activism, and inspiration they provided their communities. They shared many other dreams of adequate, efficient, and accessible health care. Health was one of the most pressing concerns among a staggering array of needs.

Nurses Anna Banks and Maude Callen and physicians Lucy Brown and Matilda Evans were representative of black women of the New South in one important respect. They were the pioneer black professional women in nursing and medicine in South Carolina. Although they each acquired above-average education and professional training and enjoyed a rare degree of economic security, they never forgot the hardships they had overcome. They never refused to respond to pleas for assistance by less-advantaged members in their communities. They remained connected to their people.

Not unlike the majority of black women, these stalwarts of the black professional class constructed blended families that included blood relatives, adopted children, and close friends. Lucy Manetta Hughes, born in 1863 and orphaned as a young girl, helped to rear her brothers after the death of their parents. She and her husband, Reverend David Brown, had one daughter, Myrtle. Callen and Evans both adopted children. While their families gave them common cause with the people they took care of, Banks and Brown, Evans and Callen, each in her own way, built close relationships within their larger respective communities across a bridge of common concern for the health and welfare of the children. They all believed in the gospel of providing service to the people in ways that allowed them to help themselves.[21]

The struggles of southern black women professionals such as Banks, Callen, Brown, and Evans illuminate theories about the matrix of race, class, and gender inequalities, on the one hand, and conceptions of representation, voice, and resistance, on the other. It is important to examine fully the remarkable demonstrations of self-reliance, autonomy, and agency in South Carolina's black communities and simultaneously to excavate the areas in which black and white southern women collaborated against the backdrop of Jim Crow segregation.[22] Considerable urgency exists to research and analyze the impact of southern states' neglect of black health care, the failures of American medicine, and the seemingly intractable inadequacies of social welfare policies.

Anna De Costa Banks (September 2, 1869–November 29, 1930) was the daughter of Samuel and Elizabeth De Costa Banks of Charleston, South

Carolina. She received her early schooling at Avery Institute in Charleston and in 1891 earned an undergraduate degree at Hampton Institute. Banks entered the newly founded Dixie Hospital and nurse training program in Hampton, Virginia, and graduated in its first class in 1893. African American nurse administrators were in short supply. Dixie Hospital offered Banks the position of head nurse, and she served in that capacity from 1895 to 1897. During her stay in Hampton, Banks married Isaiah Harrison and gave birth to a daughter, Evangeline Banks Harrison. The status of the marriage was hard to discern, but within a matter of months, Banks returned to Charleston with her daughter and participated in the establishment of the Hospital and Nurse Training School. For the next thirty years, from 1898 to 1930, Banks served as first head nurse and later as superintendent of nursing. She was influential in training more than one hundred black woman nurses.

Banks was quick to nurture working relationships with prominent white women in Charleston. In 1906 Banks became a visiting nurse for the Ladies Benevolent Society of Charleston. It was while operating in the dual capacity as head nurse at the Charleston Hospital and Nurse Training School and visiting nurse for the Ladies Benevolent Society of Charleston that Banks honed her organizational and management skills and demonstrated an effective capacity for intragender and interracial mediation. Banks oversaw the care of an average of 250 patients annually under the aegis of the Ladies Benevolent Society. It was through the development of mutually beneficial collaborations with the white women of the Ladies Benevolent Society that Banks was able to enlarge the reach of the services provided to the members of the greater black community in Charleston.

Significantly, Banks assigned student nurses to serve in white homes as needed, but she also deployed the student nurses in black homes even when the clients were not able to pay. When the fees were paid, Banks collected and used those sums to sustain the hospital. These funds were essential to pay for building repairs and to purchase needed equipment and supplies. Banks gradually "accustomed the white community to using Black women who were trained as nurses." This was an important facet of her work, although it was rarely touted. Banks revealed the thoughts that guided her actions; she insisted that "the care of the sick of the South has always been the work of the colored women," and she argued that with the advent of the trained nurse, it was imperative "to keep this work from drifting into the hands of white nurses." Banks declared, "We have to train these girls," adding, moreover, that it was the community's responsibility to relieve the suffering of the poor "by placing hospitals and medical aid within their reach."[23] Banks, deferentially but with unrelenting determination, mediated relations between black and white citizens by providing frequent reminders and evidence of the lifesaving contributions that her student nurses made to the improvement of the health of all, without regard to race.

To be sure, the hiring out of student nurses provided the hospital with much-needed money. While this financial support was critical to survival, the student nurses also provided invaluable assistance to women and children and families who did not have access to health-care facilities owing to poverty, distance, or lack of transportation, as well as fear and superstition. The testimony of a hired-out student nurse in Alabama, Bessie Hawes of Tuskegee Institute, opens a window onto the variety of experiences and services offered by young women on assignment away from their hospitals. Hawes wrote:

> I shall tell you of an experience of which I am very proud. Eight miles from Talladega [Alabama] in the back woods, a colored family of ten were in bed and dying for the want of attention. No one would come near. I was glad of the opportunity. As I entered the little cabin, I found the mother in bed. Three children were buried the week before. The father and the remainder of the family were running a temperature of 102–104. Some had influenza, others had pneumonia. No relatives or friends would come near. I saw at a glance I had work to do. I rolled up my sleeves and killed chickens and began to cook. I forgot I was not a cook, but I only thought of saving lives. I milked the cow, gave medicine, and did everything I could to help conditions. I worked day and night trying to save them for seven days. I had no place to sleep. In the meantime, the oldest daughter had a miscarriage and I delivered her without the aid of any physicians. I didn't realize how tired I was till I got home. I sat up at night alone, and one night with a corpse in the house. The doctor lived about twenty miles away. He came every other day. He thought I was very brave. I didn't realize till it was over just how brave I was. I did feel happy when they were out of danger. I only wished that I could have reached them earlier and been able to have done something for the poor mother.

Hawes's experiences mirrored the range of conditions that student nurses encountered in isolated rural communities in the early twentieth century.[24]

In Charleston, South Carolina, the white assistant secretary of Associated Charities affirmed that the black student nurses provided essential, indeed lifesaving, service to the larger community. He wrote, "It is with sincere feeling that I speak of the work of Charleston's Colored Hospital, it is sending forth women who are not only capable, but tender and faithful. . . . I particularly mention Gussie Davis who during an epidemic of typhoid fever, at our Episcopal Church Home, fought hard often night as well as day for the lives of those children and through the Master's blessing many were saved."[25] The Hospital and Nurse Training School became a notable example of interracial cooperation. The historian Todd Savitt's detailed examination of the *Hospital Herald* underscored that "fundraising efforts on behalf of the hospital and nurse training school depended on the generosity and good will of whites."[26] The lines between black and white southerners permitted mutual exchanges of money, goods, and services that both strengthened black institution building and preserved racial segregation in the Jim Crow era.[27]

In addition to collaborating with the white members of the Ladies Benevolent Society and serving as an agent with the Metropolitan Life Insurance Company responsible for collecting payments from black policyholders, Banks was a single mother. In her role as mother she benefited from the assistance of her own mother, Elizabeth De Costa, who was a talented and well-connected dressmaker with an interracial clientele. Nurse Banks became the image, voice, and ambassador of the institution to the larger white world and throughout the greater black community. She worked tirelessly to ensure the survival of the institution. The extent and range of Banks's labors were recalled by her daughter, Evangeline Banks Harrison, who as an infant had returned to Charleston with her mother to live with her grandmother. Harrison remembered: "Under my mother's supervision and guidance many young women were trained as nurses. Working under less than adequate conditions, with very little equipment and supplies her and Dr. McClennan and the student nurses somehow managed to care for large numbers of Negro patients. Charges to each patient covered only the cost of board and medicine. Repairs to the old building, supplies and equipment were always needed."[28] Harrison continued, "I hardly ever saw my mother out of nurse's uniform. I would be sent to spend the day with her and the nurses at the hospital, and I came back to my grandmother's at night. Actually I grew up in the hospital."[29] In 1959 the hospital was relocated closer to the Medical University of South Carolina and renamed McClennan-Banks Hospital to honor Anna Banks's lifelong service to the facility and to recognize the importance of her efforts to extend health care throughout the greater Charleston community.[30]

Arguably, nurse Anna De Costa Banks was the heart and soul of the Hospital and Nurse Training School throughout the course of its decades-long existence. Still, the work of Dr. Lucy Manetta Hughes Brown (April 1863–June 26, 1911) was a major factor in the success of the nurse training program. It is imperative to convey both the significance of their collective accomplishments and to analyze what I refer to as the "Christian missionism" that motivated Brown and Banks in the execution of their work. Indeed, each of the pioneering black women health professionals under study was sustained by a deeply felt Christianity and a conviction that service centered on education and social progress strengthened individuals and their communities. From their perspective, health was a people's wealth.[31]

After completing Scotia Seminary and marrying a clergyman, Reverend Robert Brown, Lucy Manetta Hughes Brown entered medical school and in 1894 was graduated from the integrated Woman's Medical College in Philadelphia. Brown passed the medical examination and practiced in Wilmington, North Carolina, for two years before moving to Charleston to become the first black woman to join the medical fraternity in South Carolina.[32] Shortly after her relocation, she joined a group of black professionals, led by physician Alonzo McClennan, and established the Hospital and Nurse Training School in late 1897. Indeed, black male physicians in virtually every southern state established parallel hospitals and clinics to attend to black patients and to circumvent their exclusion from white health-care facilities and organizations. The inclusion of a black woman physician in the founding of the Charleston hospital attracted attention. Newspapers in the North as well as publications in England provided coverage of Lucy Hughes Brown's early career. In 1902 the *British Journal of Nursing* noted that "Charleston had for fifteen years enjoyed the distinction of having more colored physicians than any other city in the State. This woman physician [Lucy Hughes Brown] soon became one of the recognized leaders in the profession, and was foremost in the establishment of a hospital and training-school for nurses."[33]

Brown had oversight of the two-year nurse training program, graduating the first class in 1898. During the first year, students worked in the hospital and attended lectures. In the second year, they spent considerable time attending to patients outside the hospital in surrounding counties. They acquired expertise in implementing and translating physicians' instructions and performing tasks that helped patients manage their own illnesses.

Brown emphasized the healing effects of sanitation, fresh air, and healthy food. Under Brown's guidance, student nurses learned that "great adaptability, good judgment, the ability to hold one's tongue and a willingness to do work outside the usual line," along with a sense of humor and the grace to "take for their services what their patients can afford to pay," were necessary attributes of the good nurse. While textbook instruction remained important, the mastery of practical nursing skills was also essential.[34]

In addition to serving as the first superintendent of nurses at the Charleston Hospital and Nurse Training School, Brown assisted with the editing of the first black medical periodical in South Carolina, the *Hospital Herald*, which began in 1898. Anna De Costa Banks described the *Hospital Herald* as "a little journal which gives you an idea of what is going on in the hospital, the number of patients, the amount of money collected and how it is used, and also its needs." Banks reported that in the early years approximately half of the 135 hospitalized patients and 42 outside cases were unable to pay full medical expenses. She added that instead of cash, the hospital usually received "potatoes, rice, corn, eggs and chickens." Of course, all these things helped, she declared, while rightfully insisting, "I cannot buy medicine, bedding, wood and coal with such articles."[35] When Brown retired from the hospital in 1904 due to ill health, head nurse Anna De Costa Banks assumed the position of superintendent of nurses.

The *Hospital Herald* lasted for a couple of years, through sixteen issues. Every issue telescoped the twin objectives of transmitting health advice and soliciting material and financial donations from the larger Charleston public. The journal fostered black identification with the hospital and deepened the black community's psychological investment and commitment to the success of the fledgling enterprise. The publication duly noted each item and the amount of money contributed by both white and black residents. It also recorded the number of nursing services rendered. The hospital became a space in which community building occurred. In the *Hospital Herald*, Banks and Brown publicized the hospital's sponsorship of cultural events such as fund-raising fairs, performances, and dinners. Ultimately the hospital brought people together in common cause and in so doing joined the schools, churches, and women's clubs as vital civic spaces. After a long illness, Brown died on June 26, 1911.[36]

Black women in the professional class, out of necessity, nurtured a consciousness of race, gender, and class uplift. The examples of their lives may have helped to alleviate some of black citizens' apathy and alienation or mediated the hostility and anger they felt toward powerful white citizens who denied them access to better health and education facilities. In ways similar to those who would follow, the first substantial cohort of black women professionals scraped together available community resources and breached the race divide as they solicited assistance from white women of means, in the process underscoring that they were often what Anne Scott referred to as "natural allies." Anna De Costa Banks worked closely with white club women in Charleston to garner their support for the Charleston hospital. Matilda Evans in Columbia, South Carolina, sought support from white women to sustain her hospital and to help her student nurses secure funds for advanced training. The tacit agreements and unspoken bargains, always implicitly understood, helped to relieve some of the suffering among the poor in both black and white communities. As one white commentator observed in 1923, "It is an established Southern tradition that Negroes should have their own preachers, teachers, physicians. . . . Such a mode of living for the two races has come about because it represents the sanest sort of common sense with regards to the social contacts of whites and blacks."[37]

Matilda A. Evans (May 13, 1872–November 17, 1935) was born in Aiken, South Carolina, to Anderson and Harriet Evans. Martha Schofield, the white founder of a school for black children, was impressed by Matilda Evans's industriousness even as a child. Evans, with Schofield's assistance, attended Oberlin College in Ohio and the Woman's Medical College in Pennsylvania. After graduating in 1898, Matilda Evans returned to her native South Carolina to become the first licensed black woman physician to found her own hospital and nurse training school. In the closing years of a career that spanned over three decades, Evans spearheaded a movement to force the state to provide inoculations and dental examinations to poor black children.[38]

In 1901 Evans founded the first of her three hospitals, Taylor Lane Hospital and Nurse Training School in Columbia. After a fire destroyed Taylor Lane, Evans opened St. Luke's Hospital in 1916. In 1918 she relocated and renamed it St. Vincent Hospital. Finally, in the 1930s she opened a smaller facility, Evans Clinic. The Taylor Lane Hospital facility was both similar to, and different from, the Charleston venture. Whereas a group of black physicians collaborated in the establishment of the Charleston hospital, the Columbia group of black male professionals refused to assist Evans in her efforts, perhaps out of fear of competition or perhaps because of gender bias.[39] Evans turned her attention to securing material and financial support from white men and women. Her acute understanding of the etiquette of southern race and gender power relations proved critical. She acknowledged the importance of white patronage to the growth of her private practice and to the success of her efforts to institutionalize healthcare access for an impoverished, exploited, and racially segregated black population. By the 1930s, however, Evans earned the widespread support and reverence of the black professional community, religious leaders, and women's clubs, which enabled her to launch the Evans Clinic and the free clinic movement.

In their work in both the Charleston and the Columbia hospitals, these professional women demonstrated a strong commitment to mentoring nursing students and to promoting their interests. Reminiscent of the ways in which Martha Schofield had intervened in her life, Evans interceded to help others. In March 1907 she wrote to Alfred Jones, a wealthy white male supporter and friend of Martha Schofield who had helped her attend the Woman's Medical College of Pennsylvania, to enlist his support for one of her nursing students, Melissa Thompson, who wanted to attend medical school. "I have known this young woman for nine years and she has been in my nurse-training department and has helped in the dispensary at the hospital. She is a most worthy and reliable woman. Her means are quite limited; but she would be of great service, if she could get a few years in medicine and surgery. . . . I would be greatly pleased, if you can do something for her! I am sure that she will be of great service to the race and to suffering humanity. I need her greatly in my work. The poor people of her race need her."[40] Thompson was admitted to the Woman's Medical College and in 1910 received her medical degree.[41]

Even as Jim Crow laws, customary practices, intimidation, and economic disparities separated black and white citizens, for mutual benefit in specific circumstances they crossed the racial divide. Evans manipulated the fact that prominent whites could support black initiatives, as the historian Mark Schultz observes, "without creating any sense of ambiguity." Under the cloak of noblesse oblige, elite white South Carolina women could, if they were disposed to do so, assert a right "to maintain close relationships" with individual black men and women or, in other words, "condescend to assist those who were not their social equals" without threatening the tenets of white supremacy.[42] Adam David Miller, a black resident of Orangeburg, South Carolina, who as a teenager escaped a threatened lynching by leaving home in the 1930s, later elaborated on the racial power dynamics. He recalled that "any whites would patronize black businesses or employ black skilled craftsmen if it was convenient, if it was for an essential service, if what was offered by blacks was of high quality and not readily available elsewhere, and if as was often the case, they saved money—and if their patronage did not imply either friendship or social equality."[43] Within this context, professional black women across the South often made effective appeals, privately and publicly, to white patrons and allies to act on their behalf as long as the appearance of white supremacy was maintained.[44]

In 1916 Evans launched a new initiative for public health care and her own periodical, the *Negro Health Journal*, with objectives similar to those that had motivated McClennan, Brown, and Banks to found the *Hospital Herald*. Evans used the short-lived publication to solicit white financial contributions for the development of a public-health nursing project by appealing to white self-interest and simply manipulating racist stereotypes and white fears of black contamination. Evans argued that "private families would profit by . . . having cleaner healthier servants in their homes. . . . Cheap help contaminates your home even the food you eat because they can not be clean healthy and honest on the wages they get." She pointedly asked whites to help her to establish a visiting-nurse health program to eradicate tuberculosis in black communities. She continued, "With a few hundred dollars which is absolutely essential to the success of our work we could prevent the communication of this disease to many whose time and potential earnings to society would exceed the cost of our services by hundreds of thousands of dollars." Sounding the alarm, she entreated, "Will not somebody help us immediately before it is everlastingly too late?"[45]

The historian Susan L. Smith elaborates on the tuberculosis threat as being "a disease that carried a social stigma in the early twentieth century because of its association with poverty, immigrants, African Americans, and Native Americans. At the time, doctors urged institutionalization as part of the treatment."[46] As Evans and other black health-care professionals in South Carolina knew, many cases of tuberculosis went undetected and untreated in their communities. The state's tuberculosis sanitariums accommodated relatively few black men and women patients in the institutions' segregated wards.[47] Evans rightly deemed the deployment of public-health nurses with access to black communities to be an essential first step toward identifying patients in need of attention. Only after her death in 1935 would the state of South Carolina employ black public-health nurses.

In 1930 Evans launched the last major health project of her long and distinguished career, the free black clinic movement. A passionate subscriber to the belief that she shared with Banks that "the health of a people is that people's wealth," she preached that "the ounce of prevention is better than a pound of cure."[48] Through a carefully executed plan, she enlisted the support of diverse constituencies, including black male physicians, dentists, women's club leaders, and the black clergy. She welded them into a virtual movement to demand health-care services as a right that the state should recognize and support. She created a movement that generated enough publicity and pressure that the secretary of the state board of health deemed it wise to accommodate. Evans recalled the mobilization process: "We went from church to church and from school to school." She confided, "Before we were able to set up our work we had to educate people up to the idea of having such an institution."[49] According to her, the secretary of the state board of health promised vaccines, and the Richland County delegation made an appropriation of five hundred dollars to the Columbia Clinic Association to launch the experiment by establishing a temporary free clinic housed in the basement of the Zion Baptist Church.[50]

On the day in July 1930 that the clinic opened to provide free vaccinations, an overwhelming number of children and their parents and guardians stood in line. The *Palmetto Leader*, a black newspaper, heralded the effort: "The first day the clinic was opened 700 came in for service[,] which showed that the people were anxious for the service and also the need of bigger and permanent headquarters." For three months, the *Palmetto Leader* provided extensive coverage of the operation of the clinic and the efforts of black leaders to secure a permanent home and state allocations for it.[51] Evans lectured across Richland County and gave interviews to the media. She declared, "I am determined I have sworn it that in whatever else our group in Columbia be negligent or indifferent, our children shall not be deprived of the advantages which a first class, most modern clinic can give."[52] By September the *Palmetto Leader* reported that "already 3,187 have been examined as well as 1,108 vaccinated. And a steady stream of hundreds continues each day to come."

In October 1930 the *Palmetto Leader* offered an exuberant assessment of Evans's free clinic movement, declaring that "evidence keeps on piling on top of evidence to the effect that the Columbia Clinic is just proving to be, and will yet stand as the most important effort sponsored for our group in Columbia within the last half century."[53]

The deteriorating economic conditions of both the state and the people and the ravages of the Great Depression made it impossible to sustain the effort. But the ramifications of the Columbia Clinic movement continued well into the next decade. It taught the citizens a powerful lesson concerning the processes of black mobilization and thus raised, as Evans anticipated, black consciousness about the necessity of applying pressure on the state to achieve changes that permitted greater access to opportunity and to state-supported health care.[54]

Maude Callen (November 8, 1898–January 23, 1990) was the daughter of Harrison and Amanda Daniels of Quincy, Florida. When her mother died, the seven-year-old Maude went to live with her uncle, Dr. William John Gunn, in Tallahassee, Florida. She attended Saint Michael's and All Angels Parochial School and enrolled at Florida A&M University. In 1921 she entered the Georgia Infirmary to pursue nurse training. She married William "Dick" Callen, and the couple relocated to Pineville, South Carolina, after Maude accepted an appointment as a missionary nurse sponsored by the Protestant Episcopal Church. For the thousands of black citizens of Berkeley County, Maude Callen was the only accessible black health professional. Not only did she attend them in their homes, but she and her husband constructed a two-room addition to their own dwelling to serve as a community clinic. In 1927 Callen passed the examination to become a registered nurse. As one newspaper story summed up these early years, "Pineville was [twenty-two] miles from the nearest hospital or [ten miles to the local] doctor and people sent for Miss Maude when they became ill. She was available day and night."[55]

During the early years of her nursing practice, Callen addressed black women's urgent birthing issues. She launched training workshops for local midwives in an effort to bring them into compliance with state registration laws and worked to improve the quality of care for mothers and infants. White public-health nursing reformers routinely maligned black "granny" midwives, as did many obstetricians, who accused midwives of being responsible for the South's high rates of infant and maternal mortality. As the historian Laura E. Ettinger argues, "Maternal mortality rates actually increased from 61 deaths per 10,000 live births in 1915 to 70 in 1929, during exactly the same period when many women first chose to give birth in the hospital."[56] Black women were a distinct minority among American women, most of whom embraced hospital birthing. Rigid adherence to segregation laws combined with poverty and long distances to discourage pregnant black women from entering white hospitals and clinics.

In 1934 Maude Callen conducted the first prenatal class in Berkeley County. A few years later, in 1936, impressed by her successful interventions that improved the lives of black citizens, the county's top public-health officer, William Fishburne, hired Callen. In her capacity as a paid public-health nurse with the Berkeley County Health Department, Callen continued to organize health clinics and opened the county's first venereal disease clinic. She visited the public schools, inoculating hundreds of students, and delivered hundreds of babies. Callen found an ally in Dr. Hilla Sheriff, director of the state division of maternal and child health, who shared her passionate commitment to decreasing black infant and maternal morbidity by strengthening the practices of the state's large number of midwives.

The disparities between black and white health-care and death rates haunted both Dr. Sheriff and Nurse Callen. When Sheriff made funds available to Callen to acquire additional training in midwifery, Callen did not hesitate. She enrolled in the three-year-old Tuskegee School of Nurse-Midwifery in Tuskegee, Alabama, and completed the six-month course, graduating in 1943. She returned as the first black trained nurse-midwife in South Carolina.[57] Together, Callen and Sheriff coordinated annual summer two-week-long midwife training institutes at St. Helena Island.[58]

The significance of the midwife training institutes was reflected in lower rates of infant and maternal mortality. This noticeable decline in mortality statistics and the recognition of South Carolina's midwife training program as one of the best in the nation attracted the attention of the photojournalist W. Eugene Smith, who in a ten-page spread in the December 3, 1951, issue of *Life* published powerful images of Maude Callen at work in Pineville. The anthropologist Gertrude Jacinta Fraser maintains that "the *Life* photo-essay also influenced the state legislature to increase funds to public health, which previously had been steadily cut." She interpreted the photographs of Maude Callen as "reassuring in some ways . . . because they allowed whites into the homes and communities of the racial and economic outsider."[59] *Life* readers responded by sending Callen over $18,000, which she used to build a health clinic in Pineville.

The response of the readers of *Life* caught many by surprise, including Callen. The unexpected, but greatly appreciated, donations enabled her to transform a long-held dream into a reality. A follow-up story appeared in the April 6, 1953, issue of *Life*, replete with more of Smith's photographs. The title summed it up best: "Maude Gets Her Clinic: *Life* Readers Donate $18,500 to Nurse Midwife of Pineville, S.C." The Berkeley County Maude Callen Health Center bore her name; the symbolic significance was enormous. Few, if any, public buildings in South Carolina bore the names of black women and men to signal that the state and general public should acknowledge and value their contributions. Ironically, the clinic's existence also stood as a reminder of the historical and contemporary disparities between black and white health-care facilities and educational opportunities in South Carolina and across the Jim Crow South.[60]

Although Callen retired from her nursing career in 1971, she continued to perform voluntary work for senior citizens. In the last decade of her life, she received many honors from white leaders and honorary doctorates from leading institutions in the Palmetto State. The accolades poured forth. In 1981 Governor Richard W. Riley awarded her the Order of the Palmetto. In 1986 Berkeley County Supervisor Johnnie T. Flynn presented Callen with the annual County Chamber of Commerce's Honorary Citizen's Award, remarking that "Mrs. Callen did vaccinations for nine schools in her district and performed eye and dental examinations. She kept records on the many deliveries made by her and in her estimation she has delivered more than 800 babies in the past 62 years."[61]

Callen, by all accounts, was more interested in serving her people than in receiving plaques. While official state recognition was important, she would perhaps have been more pleased with the fact that years after her death in 1991, those whom she had served, inspired, and helped to survive dismal conditions remained eager to share their recollections. Her adopted son Sinclair Callen, retired from the army at age sixty-three, remembered her as a parent and missionary nurse. "She insisted that I go to school and never expected anything but the best." He added, "I always thank the Good Master for Maude Callen. . . . She was sent here as a missionary. I have seen many nights that Maude would get up and go out at ten or eleven and tend to people having trouble delivering. . . . Berkeley County was truly blessed to have her. She was a true pioneer in her field."[62]

In an interview with the *State* newspaper in 1998, seventy-two-year-old Martha Butler spoke of her meetings with Maude Callen and the instructions she received when she attended Callen's annual summer institutes for midwives. Callen made an indelible impression on the then twenty-seven-year-old Butler, who recalled, "She would teach you all she could and have good patience with you." She declared, "I don't know what would have happened [to the people] if Miss Maude had not been there." Butler specified the many ways that Callen helped mothers and families in her community. "She did the blood work, she visited the home and visited with the mother and baby. . . . She told families what to eat and how to get rest."[63] Taking good care of babies and mothers often entailed attending to other problems within the many impoverished black households. Where there was no running water, Maude would get it from the well, and she often prepared meals and sterilized the home, all while on call.

According to one of the schoolboys whom she vaccinated, Maude was "dedicated to her profession and had a great concern for the health of the children." Seventy-year-old Thomas L. Myers elaborated, "She came in to give us shots and we were afraid; there was a lot of running and hollering in the classroom. But she held us and did her job. She would dress so neat. She wore a gray uniform with a white collar and white shoes. She was a beautiful lady. She went all over the county."[64] Callen's personal motto, according to those who knew and loved her, was "Let me live in the house by the side of the road and be a friend to man."[65] That was how she lived her life. Her adopted children, students, and licensed midwives unanimously credit her for being a pioneer professional who took care of babies, bodies, and business in one of the poorest counties in South Carolina. She saved lives.

By the dawn of the twentieth century, a gender division of civic work became more apparent in the institutional infrastructure that connected disparate elements of South Carolina's black population. Black women activist professionals assumed responsibility for health care and primary education, while black male professionals and businessmen occupied visible positions of leadership in the public arenas of state and local politics and in private and state-funded higher education. Professional black men were often more visible in the larger-scale agricultural operations, as well as in key economic enterprises such as the major black insurance companies in Atlanta, Georgia, and Durham, North Carolina. To be sure, gender boundaries were frequently more porous within the black community than within white communities. Still, the significance of the medical, health care, and social welfare institutions—especially the hospitals, clinics, and nurse training schools founded or nourished by black women—was tremendous. They saved lives. Thus the many women who managed and supported hospitals, clinics, and nurse training schools proved essential to black survival in the Jim Crow era. Few of the women who inspired and initiated the founding of health-care facilities could have anticipated that those institutions, both figuratively and symbolically, would become launching pads for civic mobilization campaigns and help to raise a collective consciousness that challenged inequitable resource distribution and demanded health care as a human right, not a privilege.

Future investigations will continue to layer our understanding of the lives and work of black and white women who, through their respective professional service and leadership of voluntary associations, made important contributions to ensuring the survival of black bodies, babies, and communities.[66] Ultimately, through a process of incremental changes and an occasional bridging of the racial divide, intrepid black and white southern women propelled a movement toward the modern civil rights struggles and the eventual birth of a more progressive South.

Notes

It gives me great pleasure to thank William C. Hine at South Carolina State University for sharing his expertise in South Carolina history. I am grateful to Georgette Mayo and Marvin Dulaney at the Avery Research Center, College of Charleston. I appreciate the assistance of the staffs at the Waring Historical Library at the Medical University of South Carolina and the South Caroliniana Library at the University of South Carolina. A special word of gratitude is owed to my research associate, Marshanda Smith at Northwestern University.

1. Anne Firor Scott, *Natural Allies: Women's Associations in American History* (Urbana: University of Illinois Press, 1991); Scott, "On Seeing and Not Seeing: A Case of Historical Invisibility," *Journal of American History* 71 (June 1984): 9–18; Scott, "Women's Voluntary Associations: From Charity to Reform," in *Lady Bountiful Revisited: Women, Philanthropy, and Power*, ed. Kathleen D. McCarthy (New Brunswick, N.J.: Rutgers University Press, 1990), 35–47.

2. Darlene Clark Hine, "Female Slave Resistance: The Economics of Sex," *Western Journal of Black Studies* 3 (Summer 1979): 123–27.

3. Hine, "Rape and the Inner Lives of Black Women in the Middle West: Thoughts on the Culture of Dissemblance," *Signs* 14 (Summer 1989): 95.

4. Deborah Gray White, *Too Heavy a Load: Black Women in Defense of Themselves, 1894–1994* (New York: W. W. Norton, 1999), 88.

5. Hine, *Black Women in White: Racial Conflict and Cooperation in the Nursing Profession, 1890–1950* (Bloomington: Indiana University Press, 1989).

6. Stephanie J. Shaw, *What a Woman Ought to Be and to Do: Black Professional Women Workers during the Jim Crow Era* (Chicago: University of Chicago Press, 1996), 185–88.

7. Ibid., 188.

8. Aldon D. Morris, *The Origins of the Civil Rights Movement: Black Communities Organizing for Change* (New York: Free Press, 1984), 3. For views of black people's alleged inadequacies, see Michele Mitchell, *Righteous Propagation: African Americans and the Politics of Racial Destiny after Reconstruction* (Chapel Hill: University of North Carolina Press, 2004), 10.

9. C. Calvin Smith, "Serving the Poorest of the Poor: Black Medical Practitioners in the Arkansas Delta, 1880–1960," *Arkansas Historical Quarterly* 62 (Autumn 1998): 287–307. For an alternative analysis, see Thomas J. Ward Jr., *Black Physicians in the Jim Crow South* (Fayetteville: University of Arkansas Press, 2003). Ward posits

that while a number of black physicians during the segregation era objected to the subordination of African Americans, "many others refused to take a stand against the segregated system that permeated southern society and that provided them with valuable economic opportunities" (299).

10. Hine, "African American Women and Their Communities in the Twentieth Century," *Black Women, Gender, and Families* 1 (Spring 2007): 1–23; Susan L. Smith, *Sick and Tired of Being Sick and Tired: Black Women's Health Activism in America, 1890–1950* (Philadelphia: University of Pennsylvania Press, 1995).

11. George Brown Tindall, *South Carolina Negroes, 1877–1900* (Columbia: University of South Carolina Press, 1952), 296–98.

12. Ibid., 298–99; Thomas C. Holt, *Black over White: Negro Political Leadership in South Carolina during Reconstruction* (Urbana: University of Illinois Press, 1977), 220.

13. Holt, *Black over White*, 224.

14. Omar H. Ali, "Standing Guard at the Door of Liberty, 1886–1895," *South Carolina Historical Magazine*, July 2006, 190–203. Dr. Alonzo McClennan, *Hospital Herald*, November 12, 1899, 4, quoted in Todd L. Savitt, "Walking the Color Line: Alonzo McClennan, *Hospital Herald*, and Segregated Medicine in Turn-of-the-Twentieth Century South Carolina," *South Carolina Historical Magazine*, October 2003, 256.

15. Cassandra Maxwell Birnie, "Race and Politics in Georgia and South Carolina," *Phylon* 13 (3rd Quarter, 1952): 236–44, 238.

16. Tindall, *South Carolina Negroes*, 302; Joan Marie Johnson, *Southern Ladies, New Women: Race, Region, and Clubwomen in South Carolina, 1890–1930* (Gainesville: University Press of Florida, 2004), 68.

17. McClennan, in *Hospital Herald*, November 12, 1899, 4.

18. Anna De Costa Banks, "The Work of a Small Hospital and Training School in the South," in *Eighth Annual Report of the Hampton Training School for Nurses and Dixie Hospital* (Hampton, Va., 1898–99), 23–28; reprinted in *Black Women in the Nursing Profession*, ed. Darlene Clark Hine (New York: Garland, 1985), 3–6.

19. Banks, "Work of a Small Hospital in the South," 23–28; Karen Buhler-Wilkerson and Sarah A. Johnson, "Anna De Costa Banks, R.N.," in *Black Women in America*, 2nd ed., ed. Darlene Clark Hine (New York: Oxford University Press, 2005), 68–70.

20. Alisa Klaus, "Women's Organizations and the Infant Health Movement in France and the United States, 1890–1920," in *Lady Bountiful Revisited: Women, Philanthropy, and Power*, ed. Kathleen D. McCarthy (New Brunswick, N.J.: Rutgers University Press, 1990), 157–73, 159.

21. Matilda A. Evans, *Martha Schofield, A Pioneer Negro Educator: Historical and Philosophical Review of Reconstruction Period of South Carolina* (Columbia, S.C.: DuPre, 1916), 86.

22. Sonya Ramsey, *Reading, Writing, and Segregation: A Century of Black Women Teachers in Nashville* (Urbana: University of Illinois Press, 2008); R. Scott Baker, "Schooling and White Supremacy: The African American Struggle for Educational

Equity and Access in South Carolina, 1945–1970," in *Toward the Meeting of the Waters: Currents in the Civil Rights Movement of South Carolina during the Twentieth Century*, ed. Winfred B. Moore Jr. and Orville Vernon Burton (Columbia: University of South Carolina Press, 2008), 300–318; Amilcar Shabazz, *Advancing Democracy: African Americans and the Struggle for Access and Equity in Higher Education in Texas* (Chapel Hill: University of North Carolina Press, 2004).

23. Banks, "Work of a Small Hospital," 28.

24. Quoted in Hine, *Black Women in White*, 24–25.

25. Ibid., 60.

26. Savitt, "Walking the Color Line," 252–53.

27. Glenda Elizabeth Gilmore, *Gender and Jim Crow: Women and the Politics of White Supremacy in North Carolina, 1896–1920* (Chapel Hill: University of North Carolina Press, 1996), 151–54. Gilmore examines the work of black women's home missionary societies as "a para-political tool" (151).

28. Thomas R. Waring, "Hospital and Training School Depended on Dedicated Staff," *Charleston News and Courier* (South Carolina), Hospital and Nurse Training School Clipping File, Waring Historical Library, Medical College of South Carolina, Charleston, December 30, 1979, 2B.

29. Ibid.

30. Elizabeth D. Schafer, "Banks, Anna De Costa," in *South Carolina Encyclopedia*, ed. Walter Edgar (Columbia: University of South Carolina Press, 2006), 45.

31. Steven J. Peitzman, *A New and Untried Course: Woman's Medical College and Medical College of Pennsylvania, 1850–1998* (New Brunswick, N.J.: Rutgers University Press, 2000), 116.

32. Gilmore, *Gender and Jim Crow*, 21, 240.

33. "The American Nursing World: A Training School for Coloured Nurses," *British Journal of Nursing*, September 13, 1902, 215, http://rcnarchive.rcn.org.uk/data/VOLUME029-1902/page215-volume29-13thseptember-1902.pdf.

34. Hine, *Black Women in White*, 54, 58.

35. Ward, *Black Physicians in the Jim Crow South*, 166.

36. Maxine Smith Martin, "Dr. Lucy Hughes Brown (1863–1911): A Pioneer African-American Physician," *Journal of the South Carolina Medical Association* 89 (January 1993): 15–19; Ward, *Black Physicians in the Jim Crow South*, 166. Hine, *Black Women in White*, 58. In 1949 the twenty-six-bed hospital and nurse training school closed, no longer able to meet state regulations concerning minimum patient load for an accredited nursing program.

37. Lester A. Walton, "Southern Opinion on the Tuskegee Hospital," *Outlook* (New York) 135 (September 5, 1923): 14, quoted in Vanessa Northington Gamble, *Making a Place for Ourselves: The Black Hospital Movement, 1920–1945* (New York: Oxford University Press, 1993), 42. Gamble notes that in 1923 approximately 202 black hospitals existed.

38. Gamble, *Making a Place for Ourselves*, 117.

39. Ward, *Black Physicians in the Jim Crow South*, 160.

40. Matilda A. Evans to Alfred Jones, March 13, 1907, Matilda A. Evans File, Waring Historical Library, Medical College of South Carolina, Charleston.

41. Peitzman, *New and Untried Course*, 116: Lucy Hughes-Brown (1863–1911; graduated 1894), Matilda Evans (1872–1935; graduated 1897).

42. Ward, *Black Physicians in the Jim Crow South*, 64.

43. Adam David Miller, *Ticket to Exile: A Memoir* (Berkeley: Heyday Books, 2007), 64.

44. Mark Schultz, *The Rural Face of White Supremacy: Beyond Jim Crow* (Urbana: University of Illinois Press, 2005), 95, 199.

45. Matilda A. Evans, "Cheap Living, Poverty, Disease, and Death Lay Heavy Annual Tax on People Everywhere!" *Negro Health Journal* 1 (September 1916): 1; Hine, "The Corporeal and Ocular Veil: Dr. Matilda A. Evans (1872–1935) and the Complexity of Southern History," *Journal of Southern History* 70 (February 2004): 3–34; Leslie Brown, *Upbuilding Black Durham: Gender, Class, and Black Community Development in the Jim Crow South* (Chapel Hill: University of North Carolina Press, 2008), 156–59.

46. Susan L. Smith, *Japanese American Midwives: Culture, Community, and Health Politics, 1880–1950* (Urbana: University of Illinois Press, 2005), 92; Sheila M. Rothman, *Living in the Shadow of Death: Tuberculosis and the Social Experience of Illness in American History* (Baltimore: Johns Hopkins University Press, 1994). In South Carolina, the Poppenheim sisters (Louisa and Mary), as leaders of the state's Federation of Women's Clubs, embraced the necessity of participating in tuberculosis eradication work, asserting that "TB germs are easily transmitted from gentle black mammies to white babies . . . and so the protection of the black nurse may save its white charge." Quoted in Johnson, *Southern Ladies*, 67.

47. Peter McCandless, *Moonlight, Magnolias, and Madness: Insanity in South Carolina from the Colonial Period to the Progressive Era* (Chapel Hill: University of North Carolina Press, 1996).

48. "Dr. Matilda A. Evans: Noted Physician and Surgeon, Humanitarian, Outstanding Citizen of Columbia," *Columbia (S.C.) Palmetto Leader*, March 22, 1930, 1.

49. Evans, quoted in "The Columbia Clinic Association: This Institution Offers Medical Inspection and Free Vaccination to All Negro Children of This City," *Columbia Palmetto Leader*, September 20, 1930, 1.

50. John R. Wilson, "The Columbia Clinic an Effective Reality: Has Temporary Quarters in the Basement of Zion Baptist Church; A Number of Children Treated," *Columbia Palmetto Leader*, August 16, 1930, 1; [Evans], "Brief History of the Evans Clinic," Evans Folder, South Caroliniana Library, University of South Carolina, Columbia.

51. Wilson, "Columbia Clinic an Effective Reality," 1; "Columbia Clinic Association," 1.

52. "Dr. Matilda A. Evans Interviewed," *Columbia Palmetto Leader*, September 20, 1930, 1. In another story, the *Palmetto Leader* noted in passing that Evans "gives poor heed to both her physical and financial limitation when a question of service arises" (October 18, 1930, 3).

53. *Columbia Palmetto Leader*, September 13, 1930, 1, and October 18, 1930, 1.

54. Evans, *Martha Schofield*, 86.

55. Claire Pooser, "MUSC Honors Nurse-Midwife-Teacher Callen," *Charleston News and Courier/Charleston Evening Post*, May 20, 1989, 9A, Maude Callen Biographical File, Waring Historical Library, Medical College of South Carolina, Charleston.

56. Laura E. Ettinger, *Nurse-Midwifery: The Birth of a New American Profession* (Columbus: Ohio State University Press, 2006), 9; Kathy Dawley, "Origins of Nurse-Midwifery in the United States and Its Expansion in the 1940s," *Journal of Midwifery and Women's Health* 48 (March–April 2003): 86–95. For oral histories of southern midwives who were contemporaries of Maude Callen, see Onnie Lee Logan, *Motherwit: An Alabama Midwife's Story as Told to Katherine Clark* (New York: E. P. Dutton, 1989); Margaret Charles Smith and Linda Janet Holmes, *Listen to Me Good: The Life Story of an Alabama Midwife* (Columbus: Ohio State University Press, 1996). In the language of religious missionism that many black midwives used to explain their devotion and competence, Margaret Charles Smith declared, "Oh, I have been through it, been through the wringer but I did what the Lord wanted me to do 'cause the Lord loves His people, especially children" (156).

57. Ettinger, *Nurse-Midwifery*, 150.

58. Ibid., 151; Patricia Everidge Hill, "Maude E. Callen," in *Doctors, Nurses, and Medical Practitioners: A Bio-bibliographical Sourcebook*, ed. Lois N. Magner (Westport, Conn.: Greenwood Press, 1997), 49–54; Hilary Mac Austin, "Callen, Maude," in *Black Women in America*, 2nd ed., ed. Darlene Clark Hine (New York: Oxford University Press, 2005), 1:184–86.

59. Gertrude Jacinta Fraser, *African American Midwifery in the South: Dialogues of Birth, Race, and Memory* (Cambridge: Harvard University Press, 1998), 4–5.

60. Hine, "African American Women and Their Communities," 15.

61. "'Miss Maude' Honored in Berkeley," *Charleston News and Courier*, November 7, 1986, 16A, Maude Callen Biographical File, Waring Historical Library, Medical College of South Carolina.

62. Mike Livingston, "An Angel of Mercy: Dedicated Midwife Helped Assist Poor in Berkeley County," *Columbia (S.C.) State*, February 22, 1998, E1.

63. Ibid.

64. Ibid.

65. "Nurse and Midwife Maude Callen Dies," *Charleston News and Courier*, January 24, 1990, Maude Callen Biographical File, Warning Historical Library, Medical College of South Carolina.

66. Belinda Robnett, *How Long? How Long? African-American Women in the Struggle for Civil Rights* (New York: Oxford University Press, 1997). Robnett's conceptualization of "bridge leaders" is especially helpful in understanding the processes of building strong mobilizing bases from which to launch effective challenges to problems of racial inequities such as the disparity in health care.

From Jim Crow to Jane Crow, or How Anne Scott and Pauli Murray Found Each Other

—GLENDA ELIZABETH GILMORE

Guion Johnson was home alone on an early spring afternoon in 1939 when the ringing telephone pierced the silence. It was a school day, and she was president of the PTA at Chapel Hill High School. Her husband, Guy Johnson, was up in New York talking to a visitor from Sweden, Gunnar Myrdal, whom the Ford Foundation had hired to study race relations in the United States. Guy might have learned more about race relations if he had stayed at home that day.

A male graduate student from the University of North Carolina was on the line, and his words tumbled out in a rush. A white mob had headed out to lynch a "Negro farmer who lived on the edge of town." The farmer was accused of raping a white Chapel Hill High student during the school lunch period a couple of hours earlier. Graduate students from the sociology department were heading out to confront the lynch mob. Would Guion Johnson gather some townspeople to come and back them up?

Johnson asked who had been raped, and when she heard the student's name, she stopped the torrent of words. "That can't possibly be true," she exclaimed, "I saw and talked with this girl during the noon recess." Johnson had seen the girl at the Rose's 5-10-25 Cent Store, "whispering and giggling with one of the salesgirls." Johnson reprimanded her: "What are you two giggling about? And why are you off the schoolgrounds? It's against the rules, you know." "I'm going right on back to school now," the girl promised.

Johnson described the girl as belonging to "one of the few poor-white families" in Chapel Hill. The girl was fatherless and lived near the black farmer whom she had accused of raping her. In Johnson's capacity as PTA president, she managed a small emergency medical fund for poor students. Months earlier, the girl had needed a tonsillectomy; Johnson had taken her to the hospital to have the procedure, and paid for it.

Fearful that a mob of graduate students might prove unequal to a lynch mob, Johnson hung up and called the chair of the sociology department, the famed race-relations expert Howard Odum. She told him that his students needed him and that she had proof that the girl was lying. He responded, "I can't join these boys. I would not like to face my white farmer friends and confront them when they think they are doing what is right." He advised her to "leave the matter alone because he was sure the police would handle" it.

Muttering to herself that she "knew the police better than he did," Johnson then called the mayor, who took the farmer from the tiny jail in Carrboro to safety in the Durham jail. Despite Johnson's eyewitness testimony that the young white woman was elsewhere at the time of the alleged rape, the black farmer stayed in jail for months.

There are thousands of southern stories like this one, but in this case, we know *why* the white woman cried rape. Johnson was already aware of the girl's "general reputation." Here is how she conveyed it to the mayor that day: "She has been slipping out of classes and going next door to the basement of the Baptist Church to meet her boy friend. . . . She is pregnant and . . . she has concocted this tale to get a legal abortion."[1]

Such an embarrassment of riches, the plethora of connections between race, class, and gender that radiate from this story, ready to ensnare the historian. Let's start at the end: "She is pregnant and . . . she has concocted this tale to get a legal abortion." That explanation is astonishing to us, yet it seemed perfectly logical to Guion Johnson. In the pre-*Roe* South, at least in the ninety square miles that Johnson and I shared in the 1950s and 1960s, pregnant girls went to the drugstore for quinine tablets, threw themselves down the stairs, or wondered if they knew anyone who knew anyone in New York City. Wealthy girls might find their private doctors helpful. I remember choosing a gynecologist in Charlotte in 1969 because, it was rumored, he would help "if you got in trouble."

But what's a poor white southern high school girl to do when she finds herself pregnant and desperately wanting an abortion in 1939? If she said that she had been raped, the abortion was legal, and the state paid for it. However, if this girl said she had been raped by a Chapel Hill High boy— indeed, by any random white man in Chapel Hill—her social class would have worked against her. Few would believe that she had been raped; hence there would be no abortion. She was a poor white girl with a bad reputation. Her sister had "an illegitimate child" already. To guarantee the abortion, she had to finger a black man. This chilling fact joins race and sex in a devil's bargain. How could the state create a conundrum in which desperate white girls had to weigh that bargain: the death of a black man for the chance to escape her mother's wrath, the community's scorn, and a lifetime of drudgery as a single mother without a high school diploma? Perhaps her boyfriend told her to frame the black man or else . . .

The black farmer must have wondered what in the world he had done to deserve this. Had he been too neighborly or not neighborly enough? Actually, he had done absolutely nothing. Yet he "stayed in the Durham jail all through the planting season and was finally released without trial in the fall." We do not know what his family ate while he sat in jail or what passed between him and his white neighbors when he walked up the red clay road past their house on his way home after six months. It would be dangerous to stay on his land now. Hundreds of thousands of black families in similar situations abandoned their southern homes and went north and west.

It is as if the black farmer and the white schoolgirl were bound together by barbed wire in a tight embrace. If one of them moved, the other one bled. That is another way of saying that race and gender are socially constructed and mutually constitutive. In this story, class is the barbed wire. Both characters are dependent on—and at the mercy of—the middle-class white people around them. The white schoolgirl is known, marked, and under surveillance. She cannot go to the dime store without notice. The black farmer is figuratively and literally marginalized on the edge of town; then his notoriety immobilizes him. He is innocent, but stuck in jail. His release back into the community would disturb the peace.

The view from the white southern middle-class panopticon was expansive. Guion Johnson did not hesitate a second before she upbraided the schoolgirl in Rose's. "What are you two giggling about?" is an amazing opener, followed by "Why are you off the school grounds?" Imagine accosting one of your teenage acquaintances at the mall in this way. It takes a village, indeed. Why did the girl simply answer meekly that she was on her way back to school? If you ever had tonsillitis, you know the answer. You would do anything to get rid of those tonsils. Dependent on the kindness of middle-class strangers, she was in thrall to them as well. Yet the story reveals conflict within the white middle class as well. Guion Johnson and Howard Odum chose different courses of action in the face of race trouble.

As students of women's history now turn to the latter half of the twentieth century to research, for example, conservative women or the connections between the movements of the sixties and seventies, much remains to be done on the long women's movement itself and its connections to what Jacquelyn Dowd Hall so famously called the "long civil rights movement." Little-known white southern women like Guion Johnson, or Hall's protagonist Katherine Dupree Lumpkin, exemplified activism from the 1920s to the 1960s as their pro-feminist work included an antiracist critique on which the next generation drew. At the same time, little-known black southern women such as Pauli Murray exemplified activism as their antiracist work included a pro-feminist critique on which the next generation drew.

World War II was a key moment for all women as they stepped into opportunities vacated by men and welcomed younger women such as Anne Scott into public life. Moreover, black civil rights activists such as Pauli Murray began during the war to develop a theory of human rights that included women's rights. In 1944, Pauli Murray began to articulate "like race" analogies for women's issues when she compared racism, or Jim Crow, to sexism, which she called Jane Crow.[2]

The corpus of Jacquelyn Hall's work, from *Revolt against Chivalry* to her writings on the Lumpkin sisters and their worlds, demonstrates close connections between the two long movements.[3] Sarah Wilkerson Freeman's articles and dissertation document southern women's activism from the Progressive Era to the Equal Rights Amendment, and Lorraine Schuyler probes southern women as new voters in the 1920s. Sara Evans's *Personal Politics*, Casey Hayden's prominence in the movements, and Doug Rossinow's *Politics of Authenticity* all indicate that southern white women became feminists through civil rights activism.[4]

But to our students, if not to us, a generational chasm yawns between Jessie Daniel Ames and Sara Evans. How do we write this *other* greatest generation—women, especially southern women, who came of age in World War II—into the historical canon so indelibly that our students reflexively look to the South for the roots of the second women's movement and to women for the roots of the civil rights movement? One way is to consider Anne Scott's generation. To do so, we must untangle the historical barbed wire that bound Jim and Jane Crow and draw a map of how Anne Scott and Pauli Murray found each other. That map has to include an intergenerational model of feminist activism, a more prominent place for southern women in second-wave feminism, a fuller cost accounting of the Cold War, and a prehistory of the "like race" analogies that influenced feminist strategy in the 1960s.

We might start by trying to figure out how and why Guion Johnson stopped a lynching while Howard Odum sat on his hands. They both operated from a position of middle-class privilege when they interacted with the poor and often rural white people around them. Odum did not want "to face my white farmer friends and confront them when they think they are doing what is right." Johnson worked behind the scenes; her power was indirect. Odum *was* the scene; his power came from imagining himself as spokesperson for his "white farmer friends," not just in Chapel Hill but across the South.

Regarded as the foremost authority on the "Negro Problem" in the South, the sociologist Howard Odum was born in 1884 on a small farm in Georgia and earned a master's degree in classics at the University of Mississippi in 1906. In 1908 at Clark University in Massachusetts, he studied under the psychologist G. Stanley Hall and attended a seminar on psychoanalysis taught by Sigmund Freud himself, which seems not to have made even the slightest impression on Odum. His Ph.D. dissertation at Clark, arguing for biological racial differences, took only twelve months, and he dashed off another dissertation at Columbia University the next year with the sociologist J. Franklin Giddings.[5] In 1920 Odum founded the School of Public Welfare (later Social Work) and the Sociology Department at the University of North Carolina. He recruited Guion's husband, Guy Johnson, to teach there. Odum remained chair of the Sociology Department when the Supreme Court handed down its *Brown v. Board of Education* decision thirty-four years later. He saw himself as a liberal; indeed, after 1937, he was president of the Commission on Interracial Cooperation, headquartered in Atlanta. He held that position on the afternoon that Johnson called him about the imminent lynching.[6] It is particularly galling to think of Jessie Daniel Ames's enormous success in organizing white women all over the South to stop lynchings in light of the fact that her boss, Odum, refused to drive two miles to stop one.

Odum had every academic and professional advantage and sat at the head of what C. Vann Woodward called "the most thriving academic empire in the South." Odum's close links with private foundations and his cautious diplomacy tided his enterprise over the shoals of the Great Depression.[7] He supervised students and researchers who were more liberal than he on race and labor issues, even as he drew fire from many white southerners more conservative than he. Yet he cared the most for those conservative white southerners. According to Odum, change came achingly slowly, only over generations, since people behaved according to folkways forged in a regional context. As a common farmer from Georgia, he understood "why certain people joined the Ku Klux Klan, lynched Negroes, and did other unjust things." "But for the Grace of God you or I might be doing these same things. Let us condemn their evil deeds, but still love the people," he told his colleagues.[8] Without the support of the folk, law could not force social change, Odum cautioned. In an article titled "Lynchings, Fears, and Folkways," Odum took the viewpoint of a lyncher. After musing that "we" worried that "the Negro" was rising, he wrote: "We struggle with fear and misgivings and rage that we should get into such a fix. And the Negro must pay. And then we are afraid of what we have done. Our conscience is the conscience of a religious people. . . . We have done right and will stand by it and . . . the sacred whiteness of our race." "The Negro must pay," "what we have done," and "it" are all euphemisms for lynching.[9] When Odum explained lynching, he made it seem normal, and his critique remained muted or missing.

Guion Johnson, on the other hand, carved out a professional career on the margins of the academy as the "foremost organizer of women in North Carolina," as Anne Scott put it.[10] Johnson was born in 1900 in Texas and attended Baylor College for Women, where, as Scott noted, she was a "wunderkind." She married Guy Johnson upon graduation—yes, they were Guy and Guion—with the understanding that she would "continue with an independent career."[11] Noticeably absent from her papers is any sort of complaint about the difficulties of marrying and bringing up two children; in fact, noticeably missing are any complaints at all. She comes across not so much as selfless but as someone who made herself through her causes.

Guy got a job at the University of North Carolina, and Howard Odum offered Guion a spot as a research assistant. But Guion Johnson clashed with Odum, and she migrated over to the history department to earn her doctorate degree. Her dissertation was published as *The Social History of Ante-bellum North Carolina* in 1937, and she coauthored sociological studies with Odum's researchers, including her husband. Although she pioneered social-history methodology, Johnson could not make the history department come through with the job that they had promised her when she was finishing her doctorate. When she brought up that promise again years later, after World War II, she was pointedly told not only that she could not have a job, but also that Guy was likely to lose his because of their support of desegregation. The chancellor advised her to "join as many women's organizations as she could find in order to make friends with the wives of influential men who might soften their husbands' views so that when the Board of Trustees had to vote on the reappointment of her husband there would be no problem."[12]

As marginalized as Guion Johnson might have been in the academy, she saw her professional life as being much wider than that. She chose every activity she pursued for its potential to push women toward social change and civil rights—the more innocuous the activity, the better. For example, for the better part of thirty years, she served as faculty adviser to the Chi Omega sorority at UNC because "there were the daughters of the leaders in the state who make the decisions for North Carolina and I considered it very important for me to work with them, to develop some kind of liberal, rational approach to the problems of the state."[13] During World War II, she moved to Atlanta with her husband, who went to direct the Southern Regional Council. Guion Johnson got a job as director of the Georgia Conference on Social Welfare. She taught a 250-member adult Sunday school class because it was filled with "the wives of the men who make the decisions for Georgia." She thought that she must get to know them to influence them. Johnson saw stopping a lynch mob as part of her job; Odum saw it as antithetical to his position.

In 1938, several weeks before Guion Johnson single-handedly stopped a lynching by telling the truth, Pauli Murray applied to enter the University of North Carolina to get a master's degree in Howard Odum's Department of Social Work. Pauli Murray was a black woman who had grown up in nearby Durham. Her grandmother, Cornelia Smith Fitzgerald, was the daughter of Sidney Smith, son of one of the foremost white families of North Carolina, who had raped his father's slave Harriet. Sidney's father, James Strudwick Smith, was one of North Carolina's most prominent men, a member of the General Assembly and a trustee of the University of North Carolina. He "protected" Harriet and Cornelia by selling them to his daughter Mary around 1846.[14]

The drama seething at James Strudwick Smith's house in the 1840s— one of rape and interracial sex—was not so unusual for the times. After all, the governor of North Carolina, Charles Manly, recognized two families, one white, one black. What was unusual about the Smiths was the aftermath. The white Smiths—Mary, Sidney, and Frank—never married, and they lived out their lives with Harriet and the children. Throughout the Civil War, emancipation, and the return of white supremacy in the 1890s, the Smiths were the Smiths, white and "black."[15]

After James Smith died, Mary assumed authority over Harriet and her children, and she ruled her brothers with an iron hand. Although it was illegal to teach slaves to read and write, Mary's own governess stayed on to tutor the "black" Smiths. On Sunday mornings, Mary gathered the children in the family buggy and drove them to services. They sat up in the slave balcony overlooking their white relatives, and here they were baptized in 1854.[16] In her will, Mary Smith provided a small settlement for Harriet's daughters and left the rest of her considerable estate to the Episcopal Church and to the university.

Fifty years later, in 1938, Cornelia's granddaughter, Pauli Murray, attempted to claim her heritage when she applied to the University of North Carolina to enroll at the Graduate School of Social Work.[17] Murray's campaign for admission to the university opens a window on civil rights strategies before the period that historians now designate as *the* civil rights movement. Fifteen years before *Brown v. Board of Education*, Murray's application warned the white South that integration was coming. Murray saw herself as a perfect plaintiff for the NAACP's graduate school desegregation initiative in the states of the upper South. She had left North Carolina at seventeen "determined not to attend a segregated college."[18] Part of her goal had been to gain academic credentials that white people could not deny, and she earned a degree in English from Hunter College.[19] She applied to UNC in sociology, a discipline in which the state would be hard-pressed to open an "instant" department at the nearby North Carolina College for Negroes.[20]

Howard Odum, still chair of the Department of Sociology, must have felt like Job when he heard about her application. No one, he thought, had done more for the Negro than he had. Despite that, he was being challenged on his home ground only a year after becoming the secretary of the regional Commission on Interracial Cooperation.[21] No doubt he thought it would have been better if Murray had wanted a graduate degree in history. Then she would have to contend with a real southern conservative like J. G. de Roulhac Hamilton, who might have told her that her mind had frozen at age twelve. Hamilton was Guion Johnson's chair in the Department of History at UNC. Howard Odum was her husband Guy's chair in sociology. If Murray had applied in history, Odum could have rushed in, explained the conflict, lamented southern white folkways, and advised Murray that the time was not right. But Murray thought it was the right time. The late 1930s offered a propitious moment to challenge educational segregation, particularly at the graduate level, where the absence of black graduate programs and professional schools in many states defied *Plessy v. Ferguson*'s mandate for equal institutions.

For her part, Pauli Murray always claimed that she "knew nothing of the Lloyd Gaines case" when she applied to UNC to do graduate work in sociology; indeed, she sent in her application a month before the court ruling.²² But her claim was disingenuous. She had known for years of the NAACP's broad call for graduate school applicants, which included women graduate students. Three years earlier, the NAACP had helped a black Virginia woman apply to do graduate work in English at the University of Virginia. She was refused and given money to attend graduate school out of state. Second, in the previous spring, Murray had spoken with someone at NAACP headquarters, probably Walter White, about the desegregation campaign. Moreover, Charles Houston and William Hastie were Murray's "heroes"; surely she knew what they had been up to.²³ And perhaps most telling, it was on November 10, 1938, the day after the Supreme Court heard *Gaines v. Canada*, that Pauli Murray first wrote to the University of North Carolina, requesting the graduate school catalog and an application. Murray would not have wanted her own case to seem too "fomented," and she was aware that folks back home would welcome an insider more quickly than an outsider inspired by a national campaign. A month later, Murray wrote to Gaines himself, identifying herself as a "fellow pilgrim." She noted ruefully, "Our own Southern Negro leaders may not be willing to support us in this battle for equality of human rights." "Accept your admission," Murray urged Gaines, no matter how "uncomfortable" whites might make it.²⁴

Murray quickly realized that she had an uncomfortable fight on her own hands. The UNC dean who answered her letter replied to "Mr." Murray, signing "cordially yours."²⁵ But when the application arrived a few days later, someone had typed "Race____" and "Religion____" on the printed form.²⁶ Murray proposed to earn a master's in Public Welfare Social Work, the applied sociology program.²⁷ Murray's application arrived just as the Swedish economist Gunnar Myrdal visited UNC to seek advice on how to begin his monumental study on southern white supremacy and recruit Guy and Guion Johnson to work on the project. Both of the Johnsons would advise Myrdal for years to come and write papers that he incorporated into his book *An American Dilemma*.²⁸

When Murray's application became public in Chapel Hill after the Christmas break, the all-male, all-white undergraduate students moved in and out of the houses on fraternity row, talking big about what they would do if the news proved to be true. Several vowed to "tar and feather any ——— 'nigger' that tried to come in class." One declared, "I think the state would close the University before they'd let a Negro in. I've never committed murder yet but if a black boy tried to come into my home saying he was a 'University student . . .'"[29]

The rarefied Supreme Court decision in *Gaines* could not change much on the ground. One undergrad warned, "Prejudices in Southern minds can never be removed if they are suppressed and denied by external forces from without. For, the roots of prejudice grow healthier when the branches are clipped." The student's statement reflected an understanding of human behavior consistent with Howard Odum's regional sociology: people could not be forced by law to do something that betrayed their folkways. After all, the student cautioned, white southerners had proved this fact after Reconstruction, which brought on, he said, "seven decades of lynchings and close-mindedness." Others reported an "ante-bellum spirit" on campus.[30]

Local white newspapers struggled to give shape to the threat that Pauli Murray posed to the Carolina boys. Four headlines sorted it out: "New York Woman Seeks to Enter Grad School," "Administration Confronted with 'Liberalism' Issue," "Negress Applies to Enter Carolina," and "Colored, Tries to Enter Carolina U."[31] To translate: A brazen black Yankee woman (not *from* here) had decided to trap UNC president Frank Graham in a snare of his own foolish liberal making. Murray had an army of contacts sending her press clippings from back home, the student newspaper office at Columbia University held the latest exchange copy of the *Daily Tar Heel* for her, and recent UNC graduate George Stoney advised her in New York.[32] She learned, for example, that the white *Durham Morning Herald* responded with a call to found graduate schools at North Carolina College for Negroes; after all, "No one in his right mind favors trying to abandon" segregation.[33] When the *Daily Tar Heel* cabled the NAACP to ask for its stand on the case, staffer Roy Wilkins answered, "We have opposed separate schools for the races . . . [for] 30 years . . . because all surveys and statistics show conclusively that there does not exist in America a so-called equal school system."[34]

As students at UNC began to debate Murray's application, it became clear that a substantial minority of them actually supported her matriculation. In a law school vote, 18 voted to "admit Negroes to the University"; 65 voted against.[35] In a similar straw poll, the graduate students voted 82 to 38 to admit Murray, and 10 wrote to the *Daily Tar Heel* to condemn as a "disgrace" the university's noncompliance with recent Supreme Court decisions. From New York, the communist *Daily Worker* called the election a "resounding rebuke" to "Jim Crow campus regulations."[36]

The Baptist Student Union took up the matter at a discussion led by Guion Johnson, who was not ready to support Murray's admission. Rather, she used the occasion to point out the inequality in black education from first grade through college, and she also read papers written by black college freshmen elsewhere who opposed integration because they feared unjust treatment, certainly a possibility, and preferred to "build up their own schools."[37] Guion Johnson was at the white-liberal edge of race relations, but that edge did not include desegregation as an immediate goal.

Finally, Howard Odum spoke out against Murray's admittance in *Carolina Magazine*. "It is not possible that the South can forever go on being different in many fundamental aspects of life," he said, but for now "it is asking too much of a region to change over night the powerful folkways of long generations." Odum supported the *principle* of "the gradual admission of well-equipped Negro students, tested by the same standards of preparation and equipment as are the whites, into selected professional and graduate schools, followed by critical and progressive experimentation to the end that ultimate adjustments might be made." He just didn't support application of that principle right now. Alas, Odum sighed, it would be illegal under state laws—he did not reconcile that with the recent Supreme Court decision—and "the facts of race relations and culture of the South" would not permit any such thing immediately. Instead Odum advocated setting up regional centers for black graduate education across the South.[38] The idea of regional centers was so perfectly Odum: it would buy time while upgrading black education; it would take a good deal of regional planning, happily supplied, no doubt, by Odum; and it would bring the society back into Odum's imagined equilibrium. When Howard Odum condemned graduate school integration at a time when others endorsed it, including the editor of the state's largest newspaper and the state's most beloved playwright, he compromised his usefulness to the interracial movement.

Murray had never expected Howard Odum to support her application. Her own reading of his work led her to believe that he had "grown more progressive," but he was still "too close to the Old South" to offer his support.[39] Murray pointed out the irony: "Sociologists who . . . realize the necessity for giving the Negro equal opportunity" could not accept Negroes in their own universities. Moreover, "Negro educators, whose prestige and influence depend upon the improvement of their own segregated institutions," found themselves in the position of defending "segregation with fervor." Even so, Europe's clouds threatened to rain on America's South: "White southerners with a social conscience are beginning to squirm," Murray observed, "because they cannot howl against Hitler with self-righteous integrity" and hold African Americans in "social bondage" without endangering freedom.[40] How could the global onslaught of fascism be turned back by temporizing?

A few weeks later, the NAACP turned Murray down as a plaintiff. The diverse forces that combined to thwart Murray's homecoming had succeeded, if only for the time being. North Carolina lost a social worker, and the nation gained a social activist.

For the next two years, Pauli Murray worked in New York, primarily for a socialist organization that tried to ameliorate the conditions of sharecropping. She bargained some speaking engagements on sharecropping for a cabin at a socialist camp in the Catskills, where she wrote several short stories about "Bennie," a young black girl growing up in the South. She had applied to Howard Law School the preceding fall and even convinced Thurgood Marshall to write her a letter of recommendation. Marshall wrote Leon Ransom, acting dean of the law school, that Murray had "the courage and initiative, as well as the ability, to take an active part in the legal battles to secure full citizenship rights for Negroes." Finally, a letter arrived at her cabin from Ransom: "You have been admitted to law school and awarded a scholarship." It was perfect. If she could not be a plaintiff, she would be a lawyer.[41] After a decade of trying to find a place in the world, the perfect place found her. Or so she thought.[42]

Murray was one of two women in the class. She had not been there three days when one of her professors prefaced his assignment to her with the words "We don't know why women come to law school anyway, but since you're here . . ." Then all the "male members of the first year class" were invited—through a poster on the bulletin board—to a "smoker" at a dean's house. There in the bosom of Howard University, "the racial factor was not the problem," but "immediately the sex factor was isolated," Murray recalled. If you have been fighting injustice alone and finally find yourself invited to a place where you are among like-minded friends, do you protest the way that they do things? Sure. Murray marched up to her professors and asked, "Well, if it is a legal fraternity, why am I not eligible?" They suggested she form a "legal sorority." This kind of "crude," "unvarnished" sexism, she came to believe, thrived in "minority groups." "It is not a smooth, kind thing," Murray learned. "It is a kind of straight out machismo."[43] She began to wonder if it might be a long three years.

In wartime Washington, Murray joined the March on Washington Movement and became its expert on Gandhian methods of protest while she studied law. Murray conducted a class on nonviolent direct-action techniques using Fellowship of Reconciliation lesson plans that argued, "One reason why racial prejudice has flourished in the South has been the docile acceptance by Negroes of segregation in principle." Her lesson, of course, ignored the hundreds of black southerners who challenged segregation individually every day during the war. The lesson instructed those who sat in to respond to an order to move by asking "Why?" Then when the manager or bus driver explained that there were segregation laws or that the accommodation served whites only, the protester should ask again, "Why?"⁴⁴ All the students she trained had to sign an "oath of nonviolence." Murray reminded them that "a tactful man can pull the stingers from a bee without getting stung."⁴⁵ The students approached on another front as well. The Howard chapter of the NAACP set up a civil rights committee to encourage passage of bills pending in the House and Senate to "assure to all persons within the District of Columbia full and equal privileges" in public accommodations.⁴⁶

They chose the Little Palace Cafeteria as their target. Owned by two Greek men, the restaurant was in a black neighborhood close to the Howard campus, but it did not serve African Americans. Murray scrupulously planned the sit-in for a Saturday afternoon in late April 1943. The students were organized into teams of four: three students would go in, one would stay outside to picket. After servers refused four groups of students, they sat down with their empty trays at tables, pulled out books, and "assumed an attitude of concentrated study. Strict silence was maintained." Outside, the pickets began marching, carrying signs such as "We Die Together— Why Can't We Eat Together?" and "There's No Segregation Law in Washington, D.C. What's your story, Little Palace?"⁴⁷

Murray had lined up the Washington bureau reporters for the nation's black newspapers, and they stood on the sidewalk interviewing confused whites who tried to enter the restaurant. When told what was happening inside, a white man from Charlotte, North Carolina, exclaimed, "Well, now isn't that something! I eat here regularly and I don't care who else eats here." He did not know that there was a black Charlottean seated inside. Neither of them would eat that evening. The owner called the police, who arrived led by the city's only black police lieutenant, who "ordered his men to keep distance and simply to be alert for any disorder." Then the owner closed early, explaining, "I'd rather close up than practice democracy this way."⁴⁸ But the students returned the next day, and the next, and the next. Finally, the owner declared that he was "licked and ready to serve anyone." Murray felt sympathy for the owner. "He's a little man. He's a Greek. He has no country, and sometimes I think I don't have a country, too," she wrote in the poem "Prayer of a Solitary Picket." When it was all over, Ransom confirmed that he had helped the students organize and told the press that he was proud of them.[49]

One can only imagine how the sit-in would have rocked the rest of the segregated South—if they had heard about it. They did not. While the black press broadcast the story nationwide, the white press, even locally, ignored it. This would be the policy for most of the next decade, until television began to cover civil rights protests. The only surviving white response is from a man who wrote, "Who wants to sit down to a table to eat with a dirty, greasy, stinking nigger; no matter how many times he bathes, he still 'stinks'? Instead of wasting your time by picketing, start at the beginning and educate the NEGRO—not to steal, lie, rape and assault women." The students reprinted the letter in their newspaper, telling their peers, "THIS IS TO YOU!! What are you doing about it?"

Murray had come to know Eleanor Roosevelt through her work on sharecroppers. Now she wrote Roosevelt a long letter describing the sit-ins and included a copy of the nasty letter. Roosevelt put down her copy of the letter with disgust and invited Pauli Murray over for tea. If she could not eat in most places in town, Roosevelt would make sure that she could eat at the White House. Murray wrote home, "Dear Mother, the tea with Mrs. Roosevelt was exquisite." Scheduled for thirty minutes, they talked for an hour and a half, and "you would have thought I was talking to either you or Aunt Sallie, the way she talked to me."[50]

Summer vacation put a stop to the Washington sit-ins, but not before Murray and three friends on the civil rights committee resolved to go "downtown" next time. That summer Pauli Murray attended a March on Washington Movement conference that debated launching a similar sit-in movement across the country. A white minister who attended as a resource person in nonviolent direct action came away converted and told a meeting of white religious leaders, "Brethren, it looks very much like the Revolution is upon us."[51] Murray probably didn't tell Eleanor Roosevelt that the conference inspired her to "join the Socialist Party." She confided that to her friend Caroline Ware, a white woman who had begun teaching Howard undergraduates the year before. She also told Ware something that she surely didn't tell Eleanor Roosevelt, "FDR is unhappily wedded to white supremacy, I'm afraid."[52]

The violence that broke out that summer came not from a civil rights revolution but from a white supremacist rebellion. In 1943 forty-seven cities experienced 240 racial incidents, with full-blown race riots in Detroit, Los Angeles, and Mobile. In Beaumont, Texas, several hundred whites burned and looted the black section and killed two men in a "week end of terror, worse than anything visited upon the Jews by Nazi fanatics at the height of their pogroms." Whites beat African Americans bloody in Detroit, and police "used the ultimate in force" against African Americans but "persuaded" whites, reported Thurgood Marshall, counsel for the NAACP. He characterized police action as "the Gestapo in Detroit." Reporters captured the carnage in photographs that ran nationwide, yet little was done to punish the white bullies.[53]

Pauli Murray wrote a poem about the Detroit violence that appeared in *Crisis* along with Marshall's report. She had hoped that FDR would speak out more forcefully and say something more than the statement he issued, which read: "I share your feeling that the recent outbreaks of violence in widely spread parts of the country endanger our national unity and comfort our enemies. I am sure that every true American regrets this." That sounded so "mealy-mouthed" that it made Murray furious, so she penned "Mr. Roosevelt Regrets."

> What'd you get, black boy,
> When they knocked you down in the gutter,
> And they kicked your teeth out,
> And they broke your skull with clubs,
> And they bashed your stomach in?
> What'd you get when the police shot you in the back,
> And they chained you to the beds
> While they wiped the blood off?
> What'd you get when you cried out to the Top Man?
> When you called on the man next to God, so you thought,
> And you asked him to speak out to save you?
> What'd the Top Man say, black boy?
> "Mr. Roosevelt regrets..."

Murray sent a copy to Eleanor Roosevelt, who returned it with a note scribbled on top, "I'm sorry, but I understand."[54]

Because of the Detroit riot, the March on Washington Movement decided to "defer, for the time being," the planned sit-ins. The *New York*

Times reported the postponement with palpable relief.⁵⁵ Three weeks after A. Philip Randolph called off the planned sit-ins in Washington, thus freeing up Pauli Murray's summer, Anne Firor was learning the ropes as a congressional aide for Horace Jeremiah Voorhis, a representative from California. If there was ever a case for the argument that the Progressive Era did not end in World War I, Jerry Voorhis's life made it. Born in 1901 in Kansas, Voorhis graduated from Yale and set out to find authentic experience. He worked as a cowboy, a roustabout on the rails, a YMCA representative in prostrate Germany in 1923, and an assembly line worker in an automobile factory in Charlotte, North Carolina. Then he started a folk-farm school before his election to Congress in 1937, where he stayed until he lost his seat in 1947. Anne Firor loved working for him. Her job as a congressional aide would normally have gone to a young man, but the war had taken all of them away. Four days after Eleanor Roosevelt wrote to Pauli Murray, "I'm sorry, but I understand," the First Lady met Anne Firor at the interns' annual tea at the White House. Anne described Roosevelt and the occasion: "She is a charming person, make no mistake. We all sat around her in one of the living rooms of the White House and asked questions which she used as springboards for discussions." Anne was quite aware of black protest and white backlash. She noted, "The first question, *quite naturally I suppose*, was about race relations" (italics mine). Eleanor Roosevelt told the interns that the problem was not a problem of blacks and whites but one of intolerance to those who are different, including Mexicans and "Orientals." The problem lay with "both the majority group and the minority group. Many of the causes of our difficulties lie in inertia of citizen groups." Roosevelt said that in Detroit "the mayor of the city and the governor of the state had both been more concerned with keeping the city intact than with solving the housing problem." The interns' questions moved quickly from minority rights to women's rights. Her answer to the young woman who asked for suggestions for breaking down prejudice against women in the federal service was to "keep quiet and do a good job." Scott remembered seeing Eleanor Roosevelt in a small group once again, when the interns invited her to supper at their "hang out at the Brookings Institution, then on Jackson Place." She came, Scott remembered, and "sat on the floor and again led a discussion."⁵⁶

While Anne Firor remained in Washington into the next year, Murray and her Howard classmates decided to press on with sit-ins there. In April 1944 they were ready to start what they called a "civil rights campaign" near the Capitol. Students signed a pledge of commitment against discrimination, promised to execute their "patriotic duty," and went through nonviolent direct-action training. They anticipated confrontation and were taught to ignore it, even as they were to try to engage sympathetic people around them. For this "campaign of 'sitting' in restaurants," Murray secured the names and addresses of the parent companies of chain establishments and came up with ideas for picket signs. She disabused herself of some slogans ("We are the paratroopers—March on Washington"), but others ("Is this Hitler's Way or the American Way?") stuck. Most of the campaigners were women. Murray gave them some final advice: "No matter what happens to you temporarily, whether you are served in a restaurant, or go to prison, or get slapped down, the resources of human history are behind you and the future of human society is on your side, if there is to be any human society in the future. You have nothing to lose and everything to gain."[57]

The protesters targeted Thompson's Restaurant, headquartered in Chicago, with three locations in Washington, when it refused to serve two "scouts" sent earlier.[58] Forty-three Howard students and three sympathetic white adults entered Thompson's in small groups, each leaving a picket on the sidewalk. Again they sat reading at tables with empty trays. They were shocked when nine black soldiers in uniform joined them, sitting separately from the white soldiers and sailors in the restaurant. By now the police had arrived, and they called the Military Police. Things got tense when the black soldiers refused the MPs' order to leave, and Murray brokered a deal through which the MPs escorted all the soldiers, white and black, out of Thompson's. Four and a half hours later, the Thompson's Chicago office ordered the restaurant to serve the protesters. "It is difficult to describe the exhilaration of that brief moment of victory," Murray recalled. On the next day, the students put up posters on campus that listed the protesters' names and asked, "Were you there when we all took a chair at dear old Thompsons?" They sent out press releases and gloried in headlines such as "New Technique" and "Howard Students Break Color Bar in D.C. Café." Again the white press, except for I. F. Stone at *PM* magazine, ignored them. Nonetheless the students believed that this would be the first of many victories.[59]

It was the first of many victories for the country, but it was the last victory for the Howard students. When Thompson's again refused service to two scouts in the following week, students planned another sit-in. Howard's president, Mordecai Johnson, had been widely criticized during the war for "militant" statements, so the students were stunned when he called them in and told them to stop. His prohibition covered all "officially recognized organizations" that were "now engaged in a program of direct action in the City of Washington, designed to accomplish social reform affecting institutions other than Howard University itself." They could not demonstrate as school-sponsored groups, only as individuals through other groups. The problem was that Howard's annual appropriation was then before the Senate's District of Columbia Committee, chaired by Mississippi senator Theodore Bilbo. The protest's faculty sponsor, law school dean Leon Ransom, had no choice but to back up Johnson.[60]

The radicalized students immediately formed a Howard free speech movement. They asked Johnson to define "direct action" and "social reform" and protested free speech infringement.[61] With the help of Howard Thurman, dean of the chapel and a supporter of nonviolent action, Murray articulated the students' position in a meeting with the administration. President Johnson reiterated that they should work with outside groups, not student groups, to protest. After a week, they met with the entire faculty and administration and agreed to refrain from demonstrations, in exchange for the chance to appeal to the trustees in the next month. Thus the students stood up for their rights, and Mordecai Johnson quietly encouraged them to demonstrate outside school-sponsored organizations.[62]

At the meeting with the faculty, Murray realized that a new militancy had taken hold of the younger students. Scary as it was to protest against white supremacy, it was just as scary to stand up to President Johnson, who held their futures in his hands. Henceforth Murray would have company as she went through the continuous protest that was her life. She had seen the future, and it was on her side. She thought that the contretemps ended "magnificently." As she had so many times in the past, Murray belatedly contacted the NAACP to notify them of the sit-ins, the "confrontation" with the administration, and the appeal to the trustees, adding weakly, "I hope we have done the wisest thing all along the line." Then she sat down to explain herself to someone else. "Dear Mother," she wrote, "We have had quite a controversy on the Howard campus, but part of it ended magnificently with a conference with President Johnson today. But oh, we've taken a terrific pounding today. We really had to stand up and meet our responsibilities as students." She closed with "My Love, A Very Tired Fighter—it's that old Smith Fitzgerald Murray spirit."[63]

Pauli Murray invited Eleanor and Franklin Roosevelt to her law school graduation in June 1944, but Eleanor wrote back quickly to say that they could not come. Instead the First Lady invited Murray and her mother, Pauline Dame, to tea at the White House. On the day before commencement, they went, the brash valedictorian and the seventy-three-year-old Dame, still an elementary schoolteacher. The next day, as Dean William Hastie prepared to confer degrees, a huge bouquet of flowers arrived at President Johnson's office, a gift from Eleanor to Pauli. The flowers ended up on the platform for all to see as they listened to President Johnson urge graduates to move to the South to organize labor and work for the NAACP. The *Baltimore Afro-American* scoffed, "Go South, Commit Suicide."[64] But Murray wrote an open letter to the entire class, urging them to take Johnson seriously. She proposed that all seven law graduates head to Mississippi and invited the class of '44 to come as well.[65]

As ecstatic as Pauli Murray was that day, one remaining battle nagged at her. Dean Hastie had suggested to Murray that she apply for a Rosenwald Fellowship to do graduate study in law. Howard Law School's valedictorian had traditionally attended Harvard Law School for graduate work.[66] She won the fellowship, but Harvard Law responded to Murray's application this way: "Your picture and the salutation on your college transcript indicate that you are not of the sex entitled to be admitted to Harvard Law School." She felt the blow as sharply as she had when the University of North Carolina told her, "Members of your race are not admitted to the University." Murray appealed the decision to the Harvard Law faculty, and her appeal was still pending on graduation day. As she shook Dean Hastie's hand and reached for her diploma, she was already looking forward to her next campaign, against an evil she called "Jane Crow."[67] Murray's rejection from Harvard melded women's rights and African American rights in her thinking, and nevermore were the two to part for her.

When the war ended with the bombings of Hiroshima and Nagasaki, Pauli Murray and Anne Firor faced a postwar world in which they recognized the terror of ultimate destruction. Anne recalled the moment: On "a hot August night in 1945 . . . [we] constituted ourselves a Ten Years to Live Club. . . . The postwar world for which we had thought we were preparing, would clearly be somewhat different from our hopes. . . . The league [of Women Voters] put me to work writing pamphlets about the control of atomic energy. That task made me again uneasily aware of how little I knew and how much there was to know, but if the world was doomed to self-destruction, did it matter?"[68]

For her part, Pauli Murray was in San Francisco when she heard about Hiroshima, living with forty-four women from all over the world in San

Francisco's International House. By the time that the international conference on the United Nations began there in late April 1945, Murray had already started her own "embryonic United Nations" with her housemates: a Japanese American woman who had been interned, a Jew who had fled Germany as a child, a Chinese woman, a Mexican American, and a white American whose parents had been Chinese missionaries. The six women's last names—Murray, Takita, Schiff, Li, Garcia, and Tutell—reflected their diversity. They formed a panel to speak to Bay Area groups about "the interrelatedness of minority problems" and "breaking down barriers."[69] Murray may have gotten the idea from her friend Caroline Ware, who had written a few months before: "We had a race relations forum which blew the lid off & has caused revelations a-plenty [from] Jewish, Negro, Chinese & white gentile Americans. The group was shocked to hear what the Negro women tend to think of whites. Ever since they have been trying to get me to tell them it wasn't true."[70]

Anne Scott's dreams of Harvard fared better than Murray's; she earned her Ph.D. from Radcliffe in 1958. While writing her dissertation, Scott had rediscovered a group of women whose daughters she had grown up with: white Methodist female activists. "At first, I was puzzled since none of the people who had written on . . . [Progressivism in the South] (luminaries such as C. Vann Woodward and Arthur Link) had prepared me to find women there at all."[71]

Those same sorts of Methodist women, albeit slightly younger than Scott's subjects, rescued Pauli Murray when she returned to the East Coast after earning her master's in law in California. The Women's Division of Christian Service of the Methodist Church's Board of Missions and Church Extension, which included white Georgia ladies whom Anne Scott might have known, organized the Committee to Study Racial Policies and Practices. Black and white southern women vowed to review their own Methodist practices first and then "all of the segregation ordinances of all communities in which the Women's Division has institutions." The Methodist women ran settlement houses, social service agencies, and health centers in cities across the nation. They hoped to sort out "law or custom" and to equip Methodist women to stand up for desegregation in their own communities. It was the same sort of political model that the Methodist women had used in the Southern Association of Women for the Prevention of Lynching: getting the facts out to prominent Methodist women to empower them to challenge local racial practices. The guiding lights behind the project were the manager of the Women's Division, Thelma

Stevens from Georgia, and a North Carolina black woman, Susie Jones, the wife of the president of Bennett College. At the division headquarters in New York City, the staff worked with the United Nations and ran training programs for thirty-six thousand local Methodist Women's units.[72]

Gathering the legal data to sort out local segregation laws would be an enormous job, but the Women's Division found the perfect person to do it: Pauli Murray. After working for the State of California for a few months on antidiscrimination issues, Murray returned to New York and took a job with the American Jewish Congress. When the congress retrenched after nine months, Murray took the small retainer from the Methodist Women's project and opened a law practice. She passed the New York bar exam but refused to take the North Carolina bar exam because she would have had to swear that she would uphold the laws of the state—including those supporting segregation. Rather than affirm them, she compiled them. Two years and 746 pages later, Murray and the Women's Division published *States' Laws on Race and Color*. They presented one of the first copies to representatives of the United Nations.[73] Murray's publication would serve as a critical source for Thurgood Marshall and his team as they prepared arguments for *Brown*.

Meanwhile Guion Johnson was faced on a local level with the practical aspects of the laws that Murray had cataloged. Governor Kerr Scott decided in 1952 that Johnson would be the perfect candidate to run for lieutenant governor on the Democratic ticket. A newcomer, Luther Hodges, a businessman who was head of a Charlotte bank, had declared his interest in the spot, and Scott wanted to stop him by putting up the most famous woman volunteer in the state. Johnson was aghast and responded, "No woman can be elected lieutenant governor in this state for a long time to come, and I don't want to be the first woman defeated." But the real reason, she added, was, "I'm vulnerable." She continued, "I think that any person who has any strong commitment toward desegregation or towards the improvement of the lot of the Negro is vulnerable."[74] She declined the overture. Luther Hodges won the race for lieutenant governor and, upon the death of the incumbent, became governor in 1954.

Hodges responded to *Brown v. Board of Education* with the Pearsall Plan, a freedom-of-choice plan. Through the American Association of University Women, Johnson fought the proposal. She called it an attempt "to delay or nullify the Supreme Court decision." She told her fellow AAUW members that "North Carolina should go along and work slowly and cooperatively, because [integration is] coming." To Johnson's chagrin, the AAUW was the only organization to which she belonged that would speak out against the plan.[75]

In 1958 Anne Scott moved to Chapel Hill, and in 1961 she joined the faculty at Duke University in Durham, Pauli Murray's hometown. During the 1950s, Murray had honed her critique of sexism, and her denunciation of Jane Crow became sharper. She came to understand the linkages between oppression because of race and because of sex. A year later, the governor of North Carolina, Terry Sanford, asked Anne Scott to head North Carolina's Commission on the Status of Women. Scott hesitated because she thought that the honor should perhaps go to Guion Johnson, whom Scott modestly thought was the best qualified to lead the commission.[76] For her part, Guion Johnson thought that "Anne Scott did an excellent job for North Carolina" on the commission. Scott assigned Johnson to write about women's voluntary organizations, which she did, Scott recalled, "with her customary intelligence and efficiency." Ever resourceful, Johnson held three meetings across the state with white women's organizational leaders, took a stenographer, and typed up the results as her report. In 1967 the North Carolina Council of Women's Organizations published the study as a "handbook for would-be leaders of voluntary associations."[77]

One happy result of Scott's leadership of the North Carolina Commission on Women was that in 1964 Lyndon Johnson appointed her to the Advisory Council on the Status of Women, where she met Caroline Ware, the Howard professor who had by then been Pauli Murray's friend for two decades. Three years earlier, President John Fitzgerald Kennedy had appointed Lina Ware to serve on the President's Commission on the Status of Women, which Eleanor Roosevelt chaired. Only one black woman served on the commission itself, but Murray was appointed to a subsidiary committee, the Committee on Civil and Political Rights. The commission credited Murray's work as follows: "The opinion of the members of the Committee and the Commission were strongly influenced by a document prepared at the request of the Committee by . . . Miss Pauli Murray." Murray had argued for a "re-examination of the Fourteenth Amendment with respect to state discriminatory laws and practices with regard to sex."[78]

Murray also seems to have read Scott's 1962 article "The 'New Woman' in the New South." When Murray heard that Anne Scott, whom she had never met, was heading the North Carolina Women's Commission, she marveled at the changes in her old home state. She excitedly wrote to a friend, telling her that she had heard that Anne Scott from North Carolina had come up with the insight that women were the only oppressed group who slept with their oppressors. Murray had attributed that insight to the wrong woman—it is one of the few insights Anne Scott did not have—but by the early 1960s, the paths of Guion Johnson, Murray, and Scott were intertwined ideologically.

For many years at Duke, Scott taught Pauli Murray's family autobiography, *Proud Shoes*, which was on the reading list for her course in women's history. One of her students recalled, "My friends and I debated signing up for her 8 a.m. survey class. We'd heard about her high standards, her piercing questions. We knew she expected that our research papers, preferably about overlooked women in American history, use only primary sources." She continued, "The braver among us enrolled, well aware that we dared not be absent and dared not fail to answer.... We grew accustomed to her famous question: 'What do you think?'" Another recalled of Scott, "She seemed to have accomplished everything and conveyed the unstated message, 'This is what a woman can be and do.'"[79] It was in that class in 1966 that Scott overlooked Sara Evans's absence when she "skipped class to participate in antiwar demonstrations and union support work."[80]

Caroline Ware had given Scott her first copy of *Proud Shoes*, but she never managed to introduce her to Pauli Murray. Scott writes regretfully, "Pauli Murray I never met, but our paths had crisscrossed in intriguing ways.... Crisscross though we did, the fundamental division of race meant that her life was inevitably different from mine." Of Ware's friendship with Murray, Scott wrote, "In their different but overlapping struggles for justice, Ware and Murray became lifelong allies and personal friends."[81]

If in life they merely crisscrossed or overlapped, in the practice of social justice Scott's and Murray's paths converged. Scott had come to realize through the civil rights movement of the 1960s that "much of what I had thought I knew about Southern black women needed rethinking; that *their* history had not yet begun to be written."[82] When Guion Johnson, Anne Scott, Caroline Ware, and Pauli Murray joined African American rights and women's rights, they ultimately folded their analyses into the concept of human rights. Murray recalled that after World War II, she had learned "to see the civil rights struggle within the wider context of all human rights."[83] Anne Scott remembered that in the civil rights movement, she "began at last to gain a faint glimmer of what it must have been like to have been part of the progressive excitement in the first two decades of the century or how it might have felt to be an ardent suffragist."[84]

Scott wrote of Murray and Ware, "Had they been able to work for another decade they might have been recognized by members of the movements that followed as forebears and pacesetters who made the point that the status quo wouldn't do." She observed, "Reading what these two wrote about the burning issues of their time reminds me how much we are all creatures of the context in which we live and work, and how differently some events are viewed by historians from the way they were perceived at the time."[85]

Eleanor Roosevelt, Guion Johnson, Caroline Ware, Pauli Murray, and Anne Firor Scott were part of the same context, separated by age, color, and prominence, but they all were enmeshed in the burning issues of their times. The two issues that mattered most to them were civil rights and women's rights. For most of the twentieth century, those issues played out in separate arenas, and those who worked for them did not assume that the same issues were at stake.

Women such as Johnson, Ware, Murray, and Scott came to understand that women's rights and civil rights were inseparable. Certainly, the issues have different histories, with complicated trajectories that overlap and diverge. But World War II provided the crucible that demonstrated to the women who lived through it that women's rights and black civil rights are subsumed under universal human rights: rights that know no regional or national boundaries, reside in the individual, and are not bestowed by a government or a social system. If Enlightenment thinkers such as Thomas Jefferson believed in equality and inalienable rights, they extended them only to white men. We would not be exaggerating to term the recognition that these rights existed in no lesser measure in women and African Americans a New Enlightenment.

We must make certain that when the history is written of the mid-twentieth-century intellectual paradigm shift that forged a new language of human rights, local women take their places beside, or perhaps in front of, international statesmen. They believed, shaped, and practiced the ideas of the New Enlightenment. We must make certain that historians who write about the civil rights movement or the women's movement recognize the one to be the wellspring of the other.

Notes

Works frequently cited are identified by the following abbreviations:

ER	Eleanor Roosevelt Papers on Microfilm
PM	Pauli Murray Papers, Arthur and Elizabeth Schlesinger Library, Radcliffe Institute for Advanced Study, Harvard University
SHC	Southern Historical Collection, Wilson Library, University of North Carolina, Chapel Hill
SOHPC	Southern Oral History Program Collection

1. Guion Johnson, interview by Jacquelyn Hall and Mary Frederickson (pt. 1), and pts. 2, 3, and 4 by Mary Frederickson, April 1974, G-29, SOHPC no. 4007, 52, SHC. Johnson did not date the incident; however, Myrdal came to the United States for the first time in 1938 and was in Chapel Hill in the spring of 1939. See http://nobelprize.org/nobel_prizes/economics/laureates/1974/myrdal-bio.html; and Glenda Elizabeth Gilmore, *Defying Dixie: The Radical Roots of Civil Rights, 1919–1950* (New York: W. W. Norton, 2008), 265.

2. Pauli Murray to Mrs. Roosevelt, June 24, 1944, r14, ER; Pauli Murray, *Song in a Weary Throat: An American Pilgrimage* (New York: Harper and Row, 1978), 239–44.

3. Jacquelyn Dowd Hall, "The Long Civil Rights Movement and the Political Uses of the Past," *Journal of American History* 91 (March 2005): 1233–64; Hall, *Revolt against Chivalry: Jessie Daniel Ames and the Women's Campaign against Lynching*, rev. ed. (New York: Columbia University Press, 1993); Hall, "Women Writers, the 'Southern Front,' and the Dialectical Imagination," *Journal of Southern History* 69 (January 2003): 3–38; Hall, "'You Must Remember This': Autobiography as Social Critique," *Journal of American History* 85 (September 1998): 439–65.

4. Sarah Wilkerson-Freeman, "The Creation of a Subversive Feminist Dominion: Interracialist Social Workers and the Georgia New Deal," *Journal of Women's History* 13 (Winter 2002): 132–54; Wilkerson-Freeman, "The Second Battle for Woman Suffrage: Alabama White Women, the Poll Tax, and V. O. Key's Master Narrative of Southern Politics," *Journal of Southern History* 68 (Spring 2002): 333–74; Wilkerson-Freeman, "Women and the Transformation of American Politics" (Ph.D. diss., University of North Carolina, 1996); Lorraine Gates Schuyler, *The Weight of Their Votes: Southern Women and Political Leverage in the 1920s* (Chapel Hill: University of North Carolina Press, 2006); Douglas C. Rossinow, *The Politics of Authenticity: Liberalism, Christianity, and the New Left* (New York: Columbia University Press, 1998); Sara Evans, *Personal Politics: The Roots of Women's Liberation in the Civil Rights Movement and the New Left* (New York: Alfred A. Knopf, 1979).

5. George Brown Tindall, "The Significance of Howard W. Odum to Southern History: A Preliminary Estimate," *Journal of Southern History* 24 (August 1958):

285–307; John T. Kneebone, *Southern Liberal Journalists and the Issue of Race, 1920–1944* (Chapel Hill: University of North Carolina Press, 1985), 86–88; Michael O'Brien, *The Idea of the American South, 1920–1941* (Baltimore: Johns Hopkins University Press, 1979), 32–36; Wayne D. Brazil, *Howard W. Odum: The Building Years* (New York: Garland, 1988), 72–123; Morton Sosna, *In Search of the Silent South: Southern Liberals and the Race Issue* (New York: Columbia University Press, 1977), 43.

    6. Brazil, *Odum*, 183; Guy B. Johnson and Guion G. Johnson, *Research in Service to Society: The First Fifty Years of the Institute for Research in Social Science at the University of North Carolina* (Chapel Hill: University of North Carolina Press, 1980), 3–5; George Brown Tindall, *Emergence of the New South, 1913–1945* (Baton Rouge: Louisiana State University Press, 1967), 283; David Joseph Singal, *The War Within: From Victorian to Modernist Thought in the South, 1919–1945* (Chapel Hill: University of North Carolina Press, 1982), 135, 151; Wilma Dykeman and James Stokely, *Seeds of Southern Change: The Life of Will Alexander* (Chicago: University of Chicago Press, 1962), 282; Sosna, *In Search*, 29, 51; Howard W. Odum, *Southern Regions of the United States* (Chapel Hill: University of North Carolina Press, 1936), 479; Paul Challen, *A Sociological Analysis of Southern Regionalism: The Contributions of Howard W. Odum* (Lewiston, N.Y.: Edwin Mellen, 1993), 4.

    7. C. Vann Woodward, *Thinking Back: The Perils of Writing History* (Baton Rouge: Louisiana State University Press, 1986), 20; Rupert Vance, interview by Daniel Singal, September 3, 1970 (B-030-1), SOHPC, 91.

    8. G. B. Johnson and G. G. Johnson, *Research in Service*, 5.

    9. Odum, "Presidential Address," f642, ser. 2.2, Howard Washington Odum Papers, SHC; Howard W. Odum, "Lynchings, Fears, and Folkways," *Nation* 133 (December 30, 1931): 719.

    10. Anne Firor Scott, telephone interview by author, January 10, 2008.

    11. Anne Firor Scott, *Unheard Voices: The First Historians of Southern Women* (Charlottesville: University of Virginia Press, 1993), 38.

    12. Scott, *Unheard Voices*, 42–43.

    13. Guion Johnson, interview by Jacquelyn Hall and Mary Fredrickson, pt. 1, 53.

    14. See biographical information in Gilmore, *Defying Dixie: The Radical Roots of Civil Rights, 1919–1950* (New York: W. W. Norton, 2008).

    15. Pauli Murray, *Proud Shoes: The Story of an American Family* (1956; reprint, New York: Harper and Row, 1978), 35; Trustee from Lou Kessler, "Legacy in Black and White," *New Carolinian*, March 1976, 19.

    16. Murray, *Song*, 433, baptismal record in 1854.

    17. Pauli Murray's legal name, which she never used, was Anna Pauline Dame Wynn. Her adoption papers changed her name to Anna Pauline Dame in 1919. She married William Roy Wynn in the early 1930s, and although they spent only a few days together, the marriage was not dissolved for two decades.

    18. Murray, *Song*, 65.

19. Ibid., 110.

20. Handwritten notes on Lin Holloway, "Around the Town," *Carolina Times*, n.d., f90, b4, PM; Murray, *Song*, 22, 23, 63; worksheet for application to bar, March 1948, f552, b28, PM. She worked for Spaulding's North Carolina Mutual and for Austin's *Carolina Times* in the summer of 1927.

21. Will Alexander to Friends, October 22, 1937, f59, b8, Frank Porter Graham Papers, SHC.

22. "To Times Letter Written to President Frank Graham," *Carolina Times*, [January 1939]; Murray, *Song*, 114.

23. "School Honors Legacy of Black Woman"; Pauli Murray to [unknown], January 19, 1939, pt. 3, ser. A, r18, National Association for the Advancement of Colored People Papers on microfilm; Pauli Murray, interview by Robert Martin, August 1968, PM.

24. Pauli Murray to Lloyd Gaines, December 18, 1938, f380, b15, PM.

25. For the November 10 date, see Pauli Murray to George T. Guernsey, February 6, 1939, f381, b15, and W. W. Pierson to Mr. Murray, November 16, 1938, f381, b15, both in PM.

26. Murray, *Song*, 110; "To the Editor," *Durham Morning Herald*, January 14, 1939, f380, b15, PM.

27. Will Alexander to Friends, October 22, 1937, f59, b8, Frank Porter Graham Papers; William Stevens Powell, *First State University: A Pictorial History of the University of North Carolina* (Chapel Hill: University of North Carolina Press, 1972), 210; Walter B. Weare, *Black Business in the New South: A History of the North Carolina Mutual Life Insurance Company* (Urbana: University of Illinois Press, 1973), 253–55; copy of page of *Catalogue, Issue 1937–1938*, Graduate School Division of Public Welfare Social Work, f381, b15, PM.

28. Walter A. Jackson, *Gunnar Myrdal and America's Conscience: Social Engineering and Racial Liberalism, 1938–1987* (Chapel Hill: University of North Carolina Press, 1990), 90.

29. *Daily Tar Heel*, January 5, 1939, f382, b15, PM.

30. "Mills of the Gods," *Daily Tar Heel*, January 7, 1939, f381, b15, and "Officials Faced Negro Entrance Application," *Daily Tar Heel*, January 5, 1939, f382, b15, both in PM.

31. "Officials Faced by Negro Entrance Application," *Daily Tar Heel*, January 5, 1939, "Negress Applies to Enter Carolina," *Durham Morning Herald*, January 6, 1939, and "Colored, Tries to Enter Carolina U.," *New York Daily News*, January 6, 1939, all in f382, b15, PM.

32. Thomas A. Krueger, *And Promises to Keep: The Southern Conference for Human Welfare, 1938–1948* (Nashville: Vanderbilt University Press, 1967), 27. George Stoney, a recent UNC graduate, then in New York, helped Murray. See Murray to Dear George, December 6, 1939, f381, b15, and Murray to Carl De Vane, March 6, 1939, f381, b15, both in PM.

33. "Negro Education," *Durham Morning Herald*, January 6, 1939, f382, b15, PM.

34. "Students Favor Negroes," *Carolina Times*, January 21, 1939, f383, b15, PM.

35. "UNC Law Students against Admitting Negroes to School," f381, b15, PM.

36. "Carolina Poll Favors Admission," *Norfolk Journal and Guide*, January 21, 1939, f382, b15, "Only One Negro Pressing," *Daily Tar Heel*, January 10, 1939, f381, b15, "To the Editor," *Daily Tar Heel*, January 12, 1939, 2, f382, b15, and "N.C. University Graduate Students Vote," *Daily Worker*, January 12, 1939, f382, b15, all in PM.

37. "Negro Entrance to UNC," *Daily Tar Heel*, January 26, 1939, f382, b15, PM.

38. Odum, "What Is the Answer?" 5–8, quoted in Glenn Hutchinson, "Jim Crow Challenged in Southern Universities," *Crisis* 46 (April 1939): 103.

39. Quoted in Murray, *Song*, 8; Olive Matthews Stone, interview by Sherna Gluck, March–November 1975 (G-059-1 to G-059-8), SOHPC; Pauli Murray to John Allen Creedy, March 6, 1939, f381, b15, PM.

40. Pauli Murray, letter to the editor [unpublished?], f381, b15, PM.

41. Pauli Murray to Leon Ransom, November 30, 1940, Murray to Thurgood Marshall, February 13, 1941, and Marshall to Ransom, February 26, 1941, all in f384, b15, PM; Murray, *Song*, 180–81.

42. Pauli Murray, interview by Robert Martin, PM; Pauli Murray, interview by Genna Rae McNeil, February 13, 1976 (G-044), SOHPC, 61, 63; Murray, *Song*, 182.

43. Pauli Murray, interview by Genna Rae McNeil, PM, 65; Murray, *Song*, 182–84.

44. "Lesson Plan on Non-violent Direct Action," f397, b18, PM.

45. Pauli Murray, interview by Robert Martin, PM; "Sit-ins," f397, b18, PM.

46. Juanita Morrow to James T. Wright, March 16, 1943, 78th Congress, H.R. 1995, and "Campus Campaign on 'Equal Rights Bill for the District of Columbia,'" [March 1943], all in f395, b18, PM.

47. Pauli Murray, interview by Thomas F. Soapes, PM; Murray, *Song*, 207.

48. Harry McAlpin, "Howard Students Picket," *Chicago Defender*, April 24, 1943 [handwritten], f399, b18, "Students Force Jim Crow Case," f90, b4, "HU Student Pickets Force Restaurant to Drop Color Bar," *Baltimore Afro-American*, April 24, 1943, f399, b18, all in PM. The black Charlottean was Thomas Wyche (Murray, *Song*, 207–8).

49. "HU Student Pickets Force Restaurant to Drop Color Bar," April 24, 1943, f399, b18, PM; Pauli Murray, "Prayer of a Solitary Picket," fM, b21, Benet Family Correspondence, Yale Collection of American Literature, Beinecke Rare Book and Manuscript Library, Yale University.

50. Murray to Mrs. Roosevelt, May 4, 1943, and *The Forty-Six*, May 4, 1943, both in r14, ER; Murray, *Song*, 195–97; Murray to Dear Mother, June 4, 1943, f253, b9, PM.

51. "Minutes Civil Rights Committee," May 3, 1943, f395, b18, and A. Philip Randolph to Murray, April 15, 1943, f265, b72, both in PM; [J. Holmes Smith], "March on Washington Movement," r30, and press release, August 19, 1943, r22, both in A. Philip Randolph Papers on microfilm; Herbert Garfinkel, *When Negroes March: The March on Washington Movement in the Organizational Politics for FEPC* (1959; reprint, with a new preface by Lewis Killian, New York: Atheneum, 1969), 133–38, 144–45; Paula F. Pfeffer, *A. Philip Randolph: Pioneer of the Civil Rights Movement* (Baton Rouge: Louisiana State University Press, 1990), 82.

52. Murray to Ware, July 31, 1943, reprinted in Anne Firor Scott, *Pauli Murray and Caroline Ware: Forty Years of Letters in Black and White* (Chapel Hill: University of North Carolina Press, 2006), 11, 25–26.

53. "Detroit Riot Toll 25" and "Nazi Pogroms Tame to Texas Rioters," both in *Baltimore Afro-American*, June 26, 1943, 1; Neil A. Wynn, "The 'Good War': The Second World War and Postwar American Society," *Journal of Contemporary History* 31 (July 1996): 472; Thurgood Marshall, "The Gestapo in Detroit," *Crisis* 50 (August 1943): 232.

54. "Mr. Roosevelt Regrets," July 22, 1943, r14, ER; Murray, *Song*, 212.

55. "Decides against March on Capital," *New York Times*, July 4, 1943, 12; Murray to Eleanor Roosevelt, June 4, 1944, r14, ER. (She joined a year earlier.)

56. Anne Scott, journal entry, July 26, 1943, read to the author.

57. "Pledge, Civil Rights Campaign," April 13, 1944, f395, b18, "Civil Rights Campaign," f397, b18, notebook, f395, b18, and "Suggested Instructions," f396, b18, all in PM.

58. Notebook, and "What Took Place on 11th and Pennsylvania," April 23, 1944, both in f395, b18, PM; Murray, *Song*, 223–25.

59. Press release, "Howard University Students Demonstrate New Technique in Securing Equal Rights," "Were You There?" and "What Took Place on 11th and Pennsylvania," April 23, 1944, all in f395, b18, PM; I. F. Stone, "One Elementary Step," *PM* magazine, April 29, 1944, f400, b18, and Horace Cayton, "New Technique," *Pittsburgh Courier*, April 30, 1944, both in f400, b18, PM; "Howard Students Break Color Bar in D.C. Café," *Pittsburgh Courier*, April 30, 1944, f399, b18, PM.

60. Ruth B. Powell and Marianne E. Musgrave to Dr. Johnson, April 30, 1944, f395, b18, Howard University Chapter, NAACP, to Professor Ransom, May 2, 1944, f396, b18, "We Just Ain't Ready Dept.," *Pittsburgh Courier*, April 30, 1944, f400, b18, Mordecai W. Johnson to Professor Ransom, May 2, 1944, f396, b18, all in PM.

61. "Among Howard University Students When President Bans Café Action," *Black Dispatch*, May 13, 1944, f400, b18, PM.

62. "Await Conference with President Johnson," *Pittsburgh Courier*, May 20, 1944, f400, b18, Report of Emergency Meeting, May 1, 1944, f396, b18, and *Non-violent Action Newsbulletin*, n.d., nos. 2 and 3, f400, b18, all in PM. Dean of the Chapel Howard Thurman counseled Murray and later advised Martin Luther King Jr.; see "Thurman-Murray Conference, May 5, 1944, Formulation of Principles on NAACP Student Controversy," f396, b18, PM. Pauli Murray, interview by Thomas F. Soapes, 65–67; Murray, *Song*, 225–28; Pauli Murray, "A Blueprint for First Class Citizenship," *Crisis* 51 (November 1944): 358–59.

63. Press release, Civil Rights Committee, May 10, 1944, Conference with President Johnson, May 10, 1944, Murray, Confidential Report on Howard Chapter NAACP, and Civil Rights Committee, all in f396, b18, PM. Murray to Dear Mother, May 20, 1944, f253, b18, PM.

64. Commencement at Howard, f81, b4, PM; Murray to Dear Mrs. Roosevelt, June 4, 1944, r14, ER; Murray, *Song*, 244–45; "Go South, Commit Suicide," *Baltimore Afro-American*, June 24, 1944, f18, b400, PM.

65. Pauli Murray, Open Letter to the Graduating Class of 1944, Howard University, Washington, D.C., May 29, 1944, f18, b396, PM.

66. Gilbert Ware, *William Hastie: Grace under Pressure* (New York: Oxford University Press, 1984), 149–50.

67. Murray to Mrs. Roosevelt, June 24, 1944, r14, ER; Murray, *Song*, 239–44.

68. Anne Firor Scott, "A Historian's Odyssey," in *Making the Invisible Woman Visible* (Urbana: University of Illinois Press, 1984), xiv.

69. L. S. Horne, "Aims of Security Conference," *New York Times*, April 1, 1945, B6; Anne O'Hare McCormick, "Road to Berlin Crosses the Road to San Francisco," *New York Times*, April 2, 1945, 18; Murray, *Song*, 258–61; Pauli Murray, interview by Thomas F. Soapes, February 3, 1978, 36–37, PM; Murray to Eleanor Roosevelt, March 30, 1945, r14, ER.

70. Lina Ware to Murray, August 8, 1944, reprinted in Scott, *Pauli Murray and Caroline Ware*, 27.

71. Scott, "A Historian's Odyssey," xix.

72. Murray, *Song*, 270–71, 283–89; Women's Division to Dear Friends, December 29, 1947, Murray to Mrs. M. E. Tilly, December 27, 1948, Tilly to Murray, January 5, 1949, all in f1322, b75, PM; Murray to Governor Hastie, f556, b28, PM.

73. "Fifty Years Marked by Jewish Group," *New York Times*, April 7, 1947, 12; Murray, *Song*, 270–71, 283–89; Pauli Murray, interview by Robert Martin, PM, 71; Thelma Stevens to Murray, February 1, 1950, and Murray to Stevens, February 2, 1950, both in f1324, b75, PM; Thelma Stevens, interview by Jacquelyn Hall, February 13, 1972 (G-58), SOHPC, 74, 82–84; Pauli Murray, "The Historical Development of Race Laws in the United States," *Journal of Negro Education* 22 (Winter 1953): 4–15.

74. Guion Johnson, interview by Mary Frederickson, 50.

75. Ibid., 45.

76. Anne Firor Scott, telephone interview by author, January 10, 2008.

77. Scott, *Unheard Voices*, 44–45.

78. Reprinted in Scott, *Pauli Murray and Caroline Ware*, 137.

79. Bonnie Vick Stone, "Great Scott," *Duke Magazine*, March–April 2007, http://www.dukemagazine.duke.edu/dukemag.

80. Stone, "Great Scott."

81. Scott, *Pauli Murray and Caroline Ware*, x.

82. Scott, "A Historian's Odyssey," xxiii.

83. L. S. Horne, "Aims of Security Conference," *New York Times*, April 1, 1945, B6; Anne O'Hare McCormick, "Road to Berlin Crosses the Road to San Francisco," *New York Times*, April 2, 1945, 18; Murray, *Song*, 258–61; Pauli Murray, interview by Thomas F. Soapes, 36–37; Murray to Eleanor Roosevelt, March 30, 1945, r14, ER.

84. Scott, "A Historian's Odyssey," xxii.

85. Scott, *Pauli Murray and Caroline Ware*, 187.

The Million Mom March

The Perils of Color-Blind Maternalism

—DEBORAH GRAY WHITE

On the first Mother's Day of the new millennium, a Connecticut mother told hundreds of thousands gathered for the Million Mom March the story of her son. He had survived a head shot by a gunman who took a .380 semiautomatic Beretta handgun to the top of the Empire State Building and opened fire. "I received a phone call that changed my life forever," she recalled. Another mother, a Californian, told a similar story with a familiar refrain: "I received the phone call that every parent dreads," she began. Her daughter, a camp counselor at a California community center, had survived a shooting that sent five-year-olds running for their lives. Other women spoke of loss, not survivors. A mother from Washington, D.C., described her son and daughter, who had been murdered as children, before they could go to their proms or high school graduations. "I will live with a broken heart for the rest of my life," pined a New Orleans woman whose child also fell victim to gun violence. A mother from Michigan said that she daily mourned her six-year-old: "There is not a day that goes by that I do not cry as I go on with my life without my daughter. A part of my heart went with her. It is so hard for me to think that I will never see her smile, laugh or play again. I can never hold her and kiss her again. Or see her grow up, get married, and have a happy life."[1]

The mass of mothers gathered on the National Mall in Washington that May 14 looked for peace and healing, but also for action. Those who knew the gut-wrenching pain of losing a child to gun violence came to share their pain with strangers. "There's strength . . . when you realize that there are lots of other people suffering," said a California grandmother who attended a similar gathering to commemorate the murder of her twenty-one-year-old granddaughter. At the Washington march, some, like a Brooklyn shooting victim's mother, found strength through song and prayer: "Father God, we're asking for joy where there is sadness. . . . We are asking for your healing power for those who have lost loved ones to this disease, gun violence. . . . We are also asking for your protection over those who have not lost a loved one to this disease . . . that you cover them and their loved ones from the heartache and pain." Others came to give support and to make a stand against senseless loss. A teacher at Columbine (Colorado) High School came with her husband, son, and two daughters. "Enough is enough!" she cried. "The safety of our students, our children must come first." In addition to hearing and participating in prayer, witness, testimony, song, and poetry, everyone who attended expressed a desire for action. "The mothers of the world are angry," said the mother of a Columbine victim, "and you never never tick off a Mother! Politicians take heed, we are watching you. The hand that rocks the cradle rules the world. We are united and we are here to protect our children."[2]

Motherhood and activism have been wedded ever since mid-nineteenth-century women organized against slavery, alcohol, and prostitution on the grounds that such social evils made America an unhealthy place for their children. Throughout the twentieth century, mothers mobilized for peace to safeguard their children's futures. While some women transformed motherhood into a weapon against environmental pollution so that their children could have clean air and water, others have fought for racial purity and heterosexual norms. The Million Mom March, hardly the first effort by cradle-rocking hands to change the world, was a first in other ways.[3]

For the first time, American mothers took aim at gun violence and gun control. In 2000, the United States had the highest rate of gun violence in the developed world, and in 1998 the Centers for Disease Control and Prevention reported that ten children and adolescents every day were killed by firearms. Though down from a high of sixteen deaths per day in 1994, it was, for those concerned, ten too many.[4] In calling for gun licensing and registration, child safety locks, and waiting periods, the million moms hoped to begin decreasing the number of deaths.

The Million Mom March represented the first coalition between suburban, mostly white mothers and urban mothers mostly of color. Politicians, commentators, seasoned activists, and even historians saw the potential of such an alliance: "Different women, different backgrounds, different neighborhoods, same cause," as one reporter put it. "It's a new group that's coming out," said an organizer of the march, excited about the diversity of the grassroots movement she had helped to build. When asked by a reporter for the *New York Times* about the alliance's significance, Annelise Orleck, a historian of working-class women's politics, spoke of the potential power of the movement: "It's a good way to bridge differences of ideology. . . . It makes possible at least a temporary coalition of a wider range of people than might have been drawn out by a march that was billed strictly as a gun control march." Emory history professor Mary Odem agreed. "When you use the word 'mother' it cuts across ideology, class, racial divisions. It goes beyond all that."[5]

Historically, black, brown, and white women have had a hard time coming together on anything. In the 1960s and 1970s, African American women and Chicanas organized feminist movements separate from those of white women. Even when they worked in small groups, white women had not always been receptive to tackling race issues and women's issues at the same time—something black and Hispanic women have had to do. Seldom did white women understand the inclination of black women to put race first, even in the face of rampant black sexism. For example, when radical white feminists met at Sandy Springs, Maryland, in 1968 to hammer out a radical feminist agenda, they admitted that they had "problems dealing with black people." They believed that black women "want to discuss different things, have different concerns." While describing a meeting of black and white welfare workers, a white feminist expressed her fear of black women: "Black militant women ruled the day. . . . They set the tone and they managed to completely cow the white women. . . . I don't want to go to a conference to hear a black militant woman tell me she is more oppressed and what am I going to do about it."[6] On the other hand, black women pointed to white women's history as enslavers, racial purists, and segregationists.[7] As the Nobel laureate Tony Morrison put it in 1971, black women see white women "and think of the enemy." They have "no abiding admiration of white women as competent, complete people" but rather see them as "willful children, pretty children, mean children, ugly children, but never as real adults."[8]

Since most women of color were more likely to be the housekeepers of those they were now paired with politically, the million-mom alliance that brought all these women together to pray, mourn, protest, and organize was as exceptional as it was promising. Could it be that their children had not died in vain? Could black, brown, and white mothers unite over their dead children and build a coalition strong enough to effectively challenge one of the most powerful lobbies this country has ever seen—the National Rifle Association? From a distance, on May 14, it appeared to be so, but only from a distance.

Maternalist politics seemed to be alive and well, in harmony with feminism and congealed around a unitary idea of what a mother was and the kind of citizenship she represented. But this too was only from a distance. Historically, maternalism has sparked controversy from left to right, and the Million Mom March held true to this tradition. Not surprisingly, it sparked heated debate over the meaning of, and relationship among, feminism, motherhood, and citizenship, a debate that impacted the cross-race alliance that the march tried to build. True to form, the Million Mom March, while building on a rich history of maternalist activism, also triggered age-old conflicts about the definition of good and bad domesticity, proving that at the beginning of the new millennium, maternalism was as perilous as ever.

Emotions matter, say sociologists, and this was never truer than in the case of the Million Mom March.[9] Though they came from different backgrounds, the marchers shared common feelings and a common frame of reference. When Donna Dees-Thomases, the founder of the Million Mom March, first heard, in August 1999, that a gunman had stormed the North Valley Jewish Community Center in Granada Hills, California, she described herself as "immobilized with shock." As she listened to television reports of the incident and the history of gun violence in America, she was "stunned," and then she was "mad." When she went online and typed in the words "gun control," fear overwhelmed her. When Dees-Thomases asked herself why the issue had not troubled her before the incident in Granada Hills, she speculated that unlike other reports of gun horror, even of Columbine, this one had "happened to children similar to my own." It was this realization that brought out her shame. This series of emotions transformed her from someone who, by her own admission, read the newspapers only for the gossip pages into a leading activist for gun control. Something else, however, drove her to lead hundreds of thousands of people to the National Mall on Mother's Day, 2000. As she describes it, she was driven by a "latent, fierce, maternal instinct." It was this "unleashed" instinct that drove her to organize the Million Mom March, which in 2002 became the Million Mom March United with the Brady Campaign to Prevent Gun Violence.[10]

Dees-Thomases's calling to antigun activism was not unlike that of countless others. Columbine was the impetus for Janet Mills, Karen Segal, and Renae Popkin, all of Marietta, Georgia, to march for gun control in Atlanta, Georgia, on Mother's Day, 2000. Mills said that when Columbine happened, "I was on the phone with Karen for hours just crying. Neither of us could hang up." April Rayborn went to the same march. As she held up a sign that read "Republican Mom for Gun Control," she explained that it was the killing of her daughter's classmate and mother that motivated her. Another mother, Shikha Hamilton, was sitting in a hospital at her sick daughter's bedside when she heard of the murder of a six-year-old girl by her six-year-old classmate right in the schoolroom. Infuriated by the killing, Hamilton resolved then and there to do something and subsequently became the president of the Michigan Million Mom March.[11]

Joining mothers like these were those who had been moved to action by immeasurable grief. Mary Leigh Blek, a staunch conservative from Orange County, California, got involved in gun control shortly after her son Mathew was shot down in New York by three fifteen-year-old boys who attempted to rob him. She became president of the Bell Campaign, a grassroots gun-control organization that preceded the Million Mom March and subsequently provided the financial oversight for Dees-Thomases's organization.[12] Carole Price took over the Maryland chapter of the Million Mom March after her thirteen-year-old son, John, was shot and killed by his friend's nine-year-old brother, who was showing off a gun. After her son's death, Price dedicated her life to encouraging parents to ask about the presence of guns when children visited their friends. She became honorary chairperson of Asking Saves Kids (ASK). After her son was murdered, Brenda Muhammad of Atlanta organized the group Mothers against Murdered Sons and Daughters. Loss also pushed Frances Davis into the fight for gun control. In separate incidents, all three of her sons—Rahlake, Andrew, and Frankie—were shot and killed.[13]

More than grief and anger, however, brought these women together. Whether their activism was forged before gun violence wreaked havoc in their lives or after, these women shared a common critique of America, especially the idea that something had gone terribly wrong with the country. According to marchers, the Million Mom March would send a message regarding the "bigger picture about guns and society." "Things cannot go on as they are," wrote an editorialist from Buffalo, New York. "It's not just about changing gun laws. It's about changing a society," said Maggie Escobedo-Steele at a Denver Million Mom March conference. "It's the violence, stupid," was the way a Chicago editorialist put it. As in the prayer quoted earlier, the metaphor of disease was widely adopted. "America is really sick," said Anne Van Prooyen of the Atlanta area. Guns were a major symptom of the problem, but violence was the disease.[14]

As with any disease, an antidote was needed, and Million Mom Marchers believed that mothers were that antidote. Theirs was an essentialist understanding of motherhood. Mothers were protective, mothers kept children safe; mothers were peaceful; mothers were nurturers; mothers put health, education, and welfare issues first; mothers knew best. It was a mother's duty to protect her children. "The gun lobby may be powerful, but a mother's love is more powerful," said Carol Kingsley, whose husband was shot to death in San Francisco in 1993. "Nobody feels the issue more strongly than mothers. We're the experts when it comes to protecting our children," declared Barbara Lee, a philanthropist from Brookline, Massachusetts. And no one was more powerful than an angry mom. "I think angry moms are the strongest force on the face of this planet," said Lisa Amspaugh, a thirty-eight-year-old mother of two. "A mother is someone whose anger is good," said Millie Webb, the president of Mothers against Drunk Driving (MADD). "Mothers are there to nurture and care for the world."[15]

Mothers, they argued, were multitaskers who combined good citizenship with motherhood. Like their forebears who since the American Revolution had rendered themselves, as the historian Mary Beth Norton tells us, "keepers of the nation's conscience, the only citizens specifically charged with maintaining the traditional republican commitment to the good of the entire community,"[16] Million Mom Marchers pledged themselves to crusade in the name of morality, to march to redeem a country stained by violence, to organize locally to enact antigun laws and unseat gun advocates, and to "make our tears a raging river of votes." "WE VOTE!" said Rosie O'Donnell to the hundreds of thousands gathered on the National Mall on May 14, 2000. "Are you listening, Congress, Senators? We vote and we will be watching you!"[17]

All of this does not surprise historians, who know that history does repeat itself. This mothers' movement for gun control followed a pattern that began in America in the late eighteenth century and continued during the nineteenth and twentieth. As explained by the historian Linda Kerber, in the early years of the Republic, politics and intellectual activity were thought to be the province of men. Women who addressed political issues were thought to threaten the sanctity of marriage and were ridiculed as masculine and insulted with impunity. Only the republican mother was spared criticism because her life and her intellect were dedicated to the service of civic virtue. As Kerber put it, the mother's "domestic behavior had a direct political function in the republic." Since republics were thought to be fragile, the republican mother was theorized (mostly by women) as the family member who was the bulwark against autocracy. As mothers socialized their sons and daughters to be moral and virtuous citizens, they strengthened the nation and simultaneously "justified women's absorption and participation in the civic culture." Republican motherhood redefined women as more than helpmates to their husbands, and the formulation became the foundation of the argument for women's education. Throughout the nineteenth century and into the twentieth, women, in the name of moral motherhood, fought not only for their educational advancement but against slavery, alcohol, and prostitution. They justified their fight for the vote on the grounds that as mothers and wives they were guardians of the family and nation. Facing fewer restrictions in the home than elsewhere, women, says the historian Carl Degler, expanded their influence and power by transforming the world into one large home.[18]

Just as mothers' movements have a long tradition, so too does opposition to them, and the opposition has always been as passionate as the mothers' movements themselves. This time around was no different. Coming as it did during a period of extreme anxiety about the meaning of American manhood, the issue of guns and mothers intersected with negative ideas about feminism and affirmative action in an explosive way. Put differently, the Million Mom March deepened anxiety about masculinity while it simultaneously helped fuel a backlash against blacks and women that was already well under way.

The catch-22 of mothers' movements has always been that when mothers take responsibility for the moral fiber of the nation, they leave themselves open to the charge that their failings as mothers have exposed the family, community, and nation to the ills that their movements address. If they had been better mothers, there would be no need for their movement. American history is full of this kind of rebuttal. For example, at the turn of the twentieth century, when America entered the imperial scramble and mothers staked their claim for temperance and the vote, they were chided for abandoning the home, for fostering an effeminate manhood, for being too masculine, indeed, for emasculating men by usurping their authority at home and in public.[19] Mother blaming reached new heights during the World War II crisis, when American manhood and patriotism were again put under a microscope. No one did more to institutionalize mother blaming than Philip Wylie, whose book *Generation of Vipers* (1942) virtually institutionalized what he called "momism." "Mom is a jerk," said Wylie before he went on to disparage "Mom's" consumption habits as trifling, her child-raising methods as doting and smothering, and her physical person as overweight and sexually unattractive. Mom, said Wylie in the 1955 edition, "is ridiculous, vain, vicious, a little mad. She is her own fault first of all and she is dangerous."[20] While Wylie let loose on white middle-class mothers, E. Franklin Frazier confirmed centuries of white commentary on black motherhood by proving that black mothers were the quintessential bad mothers. In *The Negro Family in the United States* (1939), Frazier described rural black mothers as "dominant," without morals, and possessive of only "elemental maternal sympathy." Frazier documented out-of-control illegitimacy, unwed urban mothers who, he claimed, were known to throw their babies in the garbage can, and working-class mothers who either neglected their children or focused overly on them. More than twenty-five years later, in 1965, Daniel Patrick Moynihan used Frazier's study as the basis for his description of black matriarchy, which was cited as the root cause of emasculated men, family and community disorganization, and even the urban riots of the early 1960s.[21] With this kind of history, the opposition to the Million Mom March promised to be fervent, if not fanatical.

Feminists were among the first to object. Many hoped that the Million Moms might succeed where other lobbying efforts had failed, and agreed that the "image of the bereaved and angry mother is the only one weighty enough to counterbalance that of the male hunter and patriot deployed so successfully by the NRA." Nevertheless some feminists were dismayed that the Million Moms did not address the issue of guns more expansively. "When will our culture have moved far enough beyond the view that women exist only to birth and care for [male] babies, that we witness the spectacle of huge numbers of women organizing to protect *themselves*?" wrote a male editorialist from Kalamazoo, Michigan. Another feminist critic complained about the equation of womanhood and motherhood. She winced when she thought of the number of times she heard "well-meaning people say that the most important job a woman can do is be a mother." Non-moms, she said, "have found tons of ways to nurture the globe and create productive lives. We baby-sit, teach, counsel other people's children; we heal, work in public policy, lead community groups, create art and have lives that are caring, conscientious, inventive and meaningful." This editorialist from Oakland, California, found the Million Moms' "pregnancy metaphors" "tiresome," their agenda too limiting ("Where's the Million Mom March to support public schools?"), and their constituency too exclusionary ("the issue of gun control is too big, too deadly serious to be addressed by mothers alone").[22]

These feminist critiques of maternalism were by no means new.[23] Maternalism and feminism have always had an uncomfortable relationship. Much like the seeming contradiction between affirmative action and equal opportunity for all, it has proved difficult and controversial for women to argue for equal rights and equal pay for equal or comparable work in the same breath as they justify maternity leave and tax-supported child care. The suffrage coalition divided on this point after the Twenty-first Amendment was passed. The National Women's Party supported the Equal Rights Amendment, which recognized no differences between men and women, while organizations like the Women's Trade Union League, the League of Women Voters, the General Federation of Women's Clubs, and the Young Women's Christian Association fought for legislation that gave women rights that recognized the differences between men and women.[24] Recent critics of maternalism not only lament the linking of women's politics and fate to biology—a potentially dangerous association in a period dominated by political conservatives whose political agenda includes limiting women's reproductive choices in the name of family values—but many feminists argue for their reproductive right not to have children or to have alternative families composed of same-sex couples. The 1990s were also marked by feminist critiques that bemoaned the child-centeredness of American society. In the context of the Million Mom March, they not only took issue with the lack of attention to the number of *women* who were victims of gun violence but also wondered why mothers had to take responsibility for a problem that was perpetrated mainly by men. As Katha Pollitt wrote in the *Nation*: "The gun culture is a highly masculine preserve, and so is most gun violence—drive-by shootings, mass murders by school kids, racist killing sprees, domestic murder-suicides. Who leaves those loaded guns around for kids to play with, anyway? Shouldn't it have been a Million Dad March?"[25]

As powerful as the feminist critique was, it was drowned out by pro-gun advocates. They made all the standard arguments: guns don't kill people, people kill people; gun control will not stop criminals; new laws are not needed if current laws are enforced. Moreover, it did not help that Donna Dees-Thomases's sister-in-law was a friend of Hillary Clinton. Although many Republican women numbered among the leaders and marchers, conservatives alleged that gun control was a liberal preserve, and support from Bill Clinton, who had by May 2000 been disgraced for sexual indiscretions, did not bolster the argument being made in the name of moral motherhood.

But against the Million Moms, pro-gun advocates went beyond the standard anti-gun-control arguments. They adopted the time-honored tactic of attacking the moms themselves, confirming feminists' fears that mothers who took responsibility for gun control would be blamed for all society's ills. Education, not regulation, was their answer. If moms stayed home and took time to teach their children right from wrong, respect for human life, and the difference between a real gun and a toy gun, the crime rate would be lower.[26] "Where were the moms when the six-year-old stole the gun from his home? Where were the moms when the Columbine kids were plotting their expedition? Where was the mom in Oregon when Kip Kinkel put together his arsenal?" asked Charles Sanborn, a resident of Washington State. Steve Kruse, from North Platte, Nebraska, blamed moms for everything from errant children to the lack of prayer in schools: "Where were they when their children got home from school, latchkey in hand, to find only an empty house? Where were the million moms when it was time for a daily family dinner? When it was time for a mother-to-child chat? . . . Where were the million moms when it came to keeping a family together rather than divorce? And most important . . . Where were the million moms when they banned my Lord and blessed Savior from school?"[27] An editorialist in the *Atlanta Journal* had an answer: "They should tear themselves away from the TV, shopping and marching up and down the street waving banners and spend more quality time with their children." While some pro-gun advocates pointed a finger at parents in general, most took direct aim at moms, moms who "wished the government to raise their children," moms who "turned their 'oven mittens' in too early for a career," and "lazy moms, who are trying to shirk their own responsibilities."[28]

With Wylie-like precision, pro-gun advocates hit their mark. The term "mom" was unfortunate, since, as we have seen, momism in America has negative connotations. The media's use of the term "soccer mom" was even more unfortunate, since it implied a particular kind of consumption and style of mothering, and not a caring, thoughtful person. In contemporary America, soccer moms are known for overscheduling, suffocating, and doting on their children, cowing their husbands, and for the SUVs they drive from kids' event to kids' event.[29]

When pro-gun advocates were not ridiculing Mom for the way she mothered, they caricatured her as overemotional, a familiar put-down of women who have from time immemorial been thought to be governed by their wombs. Rather than evoking compassion and concern about the death of so many children, the sight of mourning mothers evoked disgust, even rage, in pro-gun advocates. Suzanne Fields of the Cleveland area called the Million Moms "naive and emotional, short on facts and long on sentiment." Sonja Monsen of Tampa, Florida, complained that the Million Moms were "misguided" women who believed that "simply because they are moms their irrational, emotionally-driven beliefs should trump logical, fact-based reasoning." Not surprisingly, the conservative Camille Paglia weighed in. With her usual blistering, sharpshooter aim, she zeroed in on the Million Moms' emotionalism: "It doesn't take a weatherman to figure out that the average citizen doesn't want national policy determined by packs of weeping women."[30]

Emotionalism, then, was a double-edged sword. While effective in bringing mothers together, it nevertheless left them vulnerable. Although sociologists warn against the false dualism of emotionalism versus rationality, and instrumental versus expressive social movements, activists work hard to be perceived as rational and pragmatic, because social movements can be rendered ineffective if they can be dismissed as softhearted.[31] Too much emotionalism can be detrimental. Image is important, says Maurice Halbwach. Loaded with emotional content, images inform ideas about which people discern truth. The historian Temma Kaplan demonstrated how mothers acting in their capacity as caretakers challenged the authoritarian governments of Chile, Argentina, and Spain by using photos, paintings, and slogans, participating in mass spectacles to shame government officials. In Kaplan's cases, emotionalism met with some successes. In the United States, however, opponents of the Million Moms were able to counter the powerful image of mourning mothers and dead children by caricaturing mothers as spineless.[32]

The pro-gun opposition also offered up some effective images of their own. There was the patriot. Because it was untenable to claim that guns and children were a good mix, they subtly linked guns to freedom, masculinity, patriotism, and God, and then, while dressed in Revolutionary War attire, contrasted themselves to crying females.[33] Moms, they argued, threatened traditional liberties, especially the right of self-defense, which, they argued, was the principle that led to the severing of the colonies' ties to Britain. Repeating a dictum of Thomas Jefferson, they proclaimed, "What country can preserve its liberties if its rulers are not warned from time to time that its people preserve the right of resistance? Let them take arms."[34] Mike Ingle, from the Charlotte area of North Carolina, linked his Second Amendment rights to the First Amendment when he argued that "if that [right to bear arms] is taken away, then I don't understand how you'll defend your right to worship the way you want to." Charlton Heston, the National Rifle Association's spokesman and multiple-term president, struck the perfect patriotic pose. The actor, who in his role as Moses had liberated the Israelites, often talked about the Ten Commandments and the Bill of Rights in the same breath. "As an American and as a man who believes in God's almighty power, I treasure both," he said. He usually ended NRA meetings by holding a minuteman-like musket high over his head and vowing that his enemies would have to pry the musket from "my cold dead hands."[35]

It was not just that moms were espousing tyranny by government regulation and thereby leaving the nation exposed, but that gun control would leave families defenseless and men without means to protect them. Jeff Recycle, an Indiana resident, asked a familiar question when he challenged a reporter: "Do you think I should remain passive when there are criminals out there with guns?" Maria Hail, a pro-gun proponent, seconded Recycle's emotion. She was against gun control, in part because "criminals will not target men who appear to be strong." The *National Review*'s Andrew Stuttaford likewise made a pitch for strong men when he wondered where dads stood in the whole equation, and if American society was to be run first and foremost in the interest of its children by particular kinds of moms. He, for one, did not like being treated like a child. "The American people are not all children," he warned. Scott Mize agreed. His editorial ridiculed "plucky moms scolding the big boys." He thought that since American women were not encouraged to be strong, the Million Moms had unwisely "bought into the nanny state's prescription for safety."[36]

Ironically, at the same time that gun advocates painted the Million Moms as consuming, sobbing, and unpatriotic, they offered a different image of womanhood to Americans: a "pistol-packin' mama" who was strong, self-assured, and, they claimed, feminist.[37] Although the figure of the pistol-packin' mama seemed to contradict NRA fears of demasculinizing women, they claimed that these women would stand strong for liberty and defend the family against criminals. Good mothers embraced guns, argued Maria Hail; "If you care about your children, you should make sure you have the ability to defend them." Hail also made the case for feminism. Criminals, she said, target the weak, and since women "overall are seen as the weaker sex," criminals target women. Owning and knowing how to use a gun was "empowering," she said. "I don't like to use the word feminist but when a woman can carry a gun for self-defense the woman has equality, and if the so-called feminist movement is about equality then I guess I would be a feminist."³⁸

The Second Amendment Sisters felt justified in making the claim for maternalism *and* feminism because, unlike the Million Moms, they argued not just for children but for women. Suzanne Fields argued that while the pistol-packin' mama was not the most feminine image for a woman, "packing heat is beginning to make sense in a world where a woman is often defenseless without a man at her side." "When a gun is the only thing that stands between a woman and an attacker, that gun gives the woman a fighting chance to come out alive." A few argued against gun control because they wanted women to be able to protect themselves against husbands and other male relatives. Said one woman, "If Nicole [Brown] had [had] a gun, her kids [would] still have a mom. . . . I will not be a Nicole."³⁹

Finally, playing perhaps their most powerful card, pro-gun advocates zeroed in on the issue of rape.⁴⁰ They often carried signs reading "A Gunlock Is Safe Sex for a Rapist," or "Rapists Love Gun Laws." A picture of a blonde carrying a gun read: "As seen by would-be rapist, for about 0.2 seconds." "Rapists," said Dave Kopel, conservative research director of the Independence Institute, "are afraid of armed victims." Conservative *Boston Globe* columnist Jeff Jacoby told readers: "Make no mistake: Those who prevent law abiding women from arming themselves with guns make it easier for rapists to attack them with impunity." Another conservative, the blogger J. H. Huebert, likened gun control to putting a "Rape Me" sign on all unarmed women.⁴¹

Women are subject to many kinds of violence, so the preoccupation with rape should raise antennae. Why was there so little concern about domestic violence, a traditional feminist concern? Pro-gun advocates who focus on rape, an act that has a dramatically raced and gendered history, not only cast doubt on their feminist credentials but unveil their coded message.

Historically, when white women proclaimed their need for protection from rape, they usually meant, both explicitly and implicitly, that they needed protection from black men. It was a measure of white men's manhood and masculinity to provide that protection.⁴² This had been the case during the years of African American enslavement. It reached new heights after the Civil War, and near-hysterical proportions from 1882 to 1901, when more than a hundred people, most of them black men, were lynched every year. The pretext for the murder of black men was the same as that used to keep white women in their proper domestic place: black men, it was argued, were primordially driven to rape white women, who in turn needed to stay out of the public sphere, safely ensconced in the home, where white men could protect them. From the slaughter of Robert Moss, a Tennessee entrepreneur, to the 1923 pogrom in Rosewood, Florida, to the Alabama Scottsboro case of the 1930s, to the killing of fifteen-year-old Emmett Till in 1955, the murder of black men in the name of white womanhood served to maintain the traditional racial and sexual hierarchy that kept whites over blacks, and men over women.[43]

Ironically, it was the Million Moms who breathed new life into this time-old American dynamic of race and sex. When they made the case that Americans were not safe, that violence was spreading like a disease, they unwittingly helped to resurrect the template on which so many of America's racist and sexist practices were built. Said Cathy Kopecky, Western Pennsylvania coordinator for the Million Mom March, "I think people are really getting that it's not only happening to other people." "No one—and I mean no one—is immune from gun violence," warned Orange County Republican Mary Leigh Blek, one of the leaders of the Million Mom March.[44] When gun advocates like former NRA president Marion Hammer said, "I'll tell you what women want more than gun control. They want to be safe in their homes," they were only reiterating what the Million Moms had been preaching.[45]

But gun advocates and Million Moms did differ significantly in their approach to safety. The Million Moms took a fairly benign, color-blind approach to gun violence, a subject we will examine shortly. Gun advocates, however, put a race on the face of violence and thereby delivered an unsubtle, racially coded message. For them, violence was not just spreading; criminals disrupted the peace and made the public unsafe. When the Million Moms bolstered their argument for gun control with the claim that twelve children were killed by guns every day, gun advocates disputed their assertion on the basis that *children* weren't dying, *criminals* were. "You have to delve into how they define children," said Maria Hail. "Yes, there are twelve a day, but that's for twenty and under. That includes the highest crime group there is—the fifteen to twenty year olds. So most of that twelve children a day is including criminals, gang members who kill other gang members, police who kill criminals, citizens, ordinary citizens who defend themselves and kill a criminal." While Suzanne Fields argued that careless people and schizophrenics were part of the problem, she too identified the "bad people who shoot people" as "adolescent gangsters who kill each other over drug turfs."[46] Without the rabid racism that no longer accompanies right-wing rhetoric, this argument effectively racialized Field's fear of crime by redirecting attention onto black men, who since the 1830s had been constructed by the mainstream media as demons and in the 1990s had emerged in news reporting and prime-time police dramas as America's quintessential villains and predators.[47] Though hardly the perpetrators of most of America's crimes, in the year 2000, young black males between fifteen and nineteen years old did have the highest imprisonment rate for criminal activity and did (and still do) have the highest rate of death caused by firearms of any group in the country. In 2005 even the former secretary of education William Bennett linked African Americans to criminal behavior when he said: "I do know that it's true that if you wanted to reduce crime, you could—if that were your sole purpose—you could abort every black baby in this country, and your crime rate would go down."[48]

Gun advocates' argument about negligent moms (discussed earlier) also subtly evoked another familiar racialized trope: the bad black mother. This image took hold during the slavery era. Though perceived to be capable of mothering white children as mammies, black women were accused of carelessly smothering, starving, and neglecting their own children while they pursued sexual activity with abandon. After slavery the image of the black woman as promiscuous merged with one that maintained her sloth. Together they came to represent the black mother whom sociologists, public policy makers, and racists alike viewed with disgust. She was a single parent, a welfare queen, devoid of moral worth. With her libido out of control, she made babies so that she could live off the public dole. She was, as the critic Wahneema Lubiano writes, thought to be "a moral aberration, and an economic drain" who was blamed for the destruction of the "American way of life."[49]

In short, at the beginning of the new millennium, gun advocates reached back into history and drew on familiar tropes—the black male rapist, the helpless white woman, the white male protector, and the promiscuous black mother—to advance their argument against gun control. In coded language, they challenged the maternalism of the Million Moms by urging them to retreat to the domestic realm and raise their children more responsibly. They argued that moms could do more from the home to affect the contagion of violence that beset the nation. If mothers learned to use a gun, they could protect not only themselves but also their children from the criminal-rapist who plagued the land. Without ever identifying that criminal by race, they fingered him as the black male rapist who had for centuries threatened the country. Vividly they put a face on the images of the children who the Million Moms said were dying at a rate of twelve a day. It was not a picture that drew a sympathetic response.

This came as no surprise to African American women. Those who joined the Million Mom March had no illusions about the uphill struggle the maternalist gun-control movement faced. Along with their allies in the movement, they tried to educate the Million Moms. Ultimately the Million Mom March took a color-blind, race-neutral approach to the problem of gun violence and gun control.

Knowing that, historically, dead black children and especially dead black boys pulled no compassionate emotional strings, the few African American women who joined the movement knew that their first order of business was to educate.[50] Accordingly, Adrienne Young, the mother of Javon Thompson, a Carnegie Mellon art student killed in 1994, told a group of Pittsburgh Million Mom March organizers that they needed to acknowledge the gun violence ravaging black America: "I said whenever they hear about our children dying, it's always gang violence. When their children die, it's gun violence. If that angry boy did not have a gun, my son would not be dead. When I stood up and said this to these ladies at the meeting, they looked at me in astonishment, as if it had never dawned on them that it's the same thing."[51] The same black female reporter who reported Young's story told one of her own, about her own nephew Antonio Rykard Jr., who was shot in the back of the head and dragged to a wooded area. "His death didn't rate more than a newspaper brief," she wrote. As a reporter, a black female one at that, Monica Haynes probably knew better than most that "no one seems to care whether there is one little black man-child killed or a thousand."[52]

By all reports—from marchers, reporters, and commentators—black and Hispanic women made up an extremely small minority of the participants of the May 14 march and the movement as a whole, but those who did participate had a distinctive point of view.[53] On the one hand, they were bitter that white women came to the issue of gun violence only after white children became victims and gun violence seemed to be spreading to white American communities; on the other hand, they were grateful for help against a problem they knew they could not defeat alone. "We have lost the most children proportionately than any ethnic group. . . . Our voices need to be heard, our faces need to be seen and our pain needs to be known," said Adrienne Young.[54]

Young called for inclusion. Like Haynes, she understood that minority children were perceived as the other and devalued as children. On some level, the black mothers probably also understood that the nation saw them as bad mothers. Still, they fought along with other minority mothers for their children's rights. They spoke of "our children." Said Frances Davis of Philadelphia, "We have to start thinking not just my child but our children." Carol Ann Taylor agreed, "We must begin to look at each child like he or she belongs to us—no matter what color, what geographic area or economic background.... We must respond, because, if we don't save our children, who will?" Carolyn Macias, a participant from Los Angeles, said, "We are marching for all the children, whether we know them or not." Lillian Ileto, the mother of the Filipino American postal worker who was killed by the same white supremacist who shot up the Granada Hills Jewish Community Center, echoed Taylor's remarks. "I am asking you to reach out and to let your children know that we are all equal. Help our children to be tolerant of each other. . . . and let them know that gun violence has no place."[55]

Like other Million Moms, minority mothers argued that gun violence was a cancer spreading across America, but they also gently chastised the Million Moms for thinking that its spread was limited to minority neighborhoods. "You just don't know," said Frances Davis, who had three sons gunned down. "So you can't say not my child, it's not in my community. . . . It can happen to anybody at anytime, as long as there are so many guns available on the street and there's so much anger out there." Davis spoke these words not from a scholar's lectern, or from a pulpit, or from a campaign stump, but from her heart. Her message was clear: "Unfortunately the tragedies that happen in the schools, especially in suburban schools—it's like a wake-up call."[56]

Many white women in the movement agreed. Since they believed that violence was spreading throughout the nation, they could endorse the opinions of minority Million Moms. For example, Melinda Lee of Longmeadow, Massachusetts, saw the shooting of a Michigan six-year-old by another six-year-old as a "wake-up call that said, 'You can't sit around in your safe, little suburban town anymore.'" When the local headlines screamed about the murder of a college student who was shot to death by her boyfriend, Diana Bock, a resident of Clark, a suburb of New York City, took heed. "People say to me, 'It wouldn't happen here. Not in Clark.'" Bock, who decided to go to the Mother's Day march, thought, "But that's what Columbine people thought." It took the shooting of her child at the Granada Hills Jewish Community Center to transform Loren Lieb into an activist. According to Lieb, "Before the shooting, my approach to gun control was, 'Yes, it's a problem, but what can I do about it? I live in a safe community.' Then I found out that was very false thinking."[57]

Along with their newfound perspective, white women included mea culpas. "For too long we have ignored the gun violence epidemic because it was always in somebody else's back yard," said Donna Dees-Thomases, the founder of the movement, who credited New York Lt. Eric Adams of 100 Blacks in Law Enforcement with "bringing a sense of realism to our cause, because kids in his community were dying every day."[58] On the other side of the country, in the Los Angeles area, Kathy Friedman wrote an e-mail that was read and circulated at black church services in Los Angeles. "We will no longer stand silently on the sidelines as you walk through the shadows of darkness in your neighborhoods. We will instead walk side by side."[59]

And they tried. In some areas of the country, interracial maternalism seemed to succeed. Cathie Kopecky must have heard Adrienne Young speak of the different way that black and white death was perceived. As the western Pennsylvania coordinator for the Million Mom March, she filled five buses with participants and thought she would have to add two more. "So much of the black violence stuff was always talked about as gangs and we could reason it was gang stuff," she said. "I think people are realizing that that's not true, and shame on us for not acting sooner." Not only Kopecky but another Pittsburgh-area woman, who was in the room when Young made her appeal, got the message and anonymously sent Young $1,000 to help her rent buses to bring African American women to the march. An editorial in the *San Francisco Chronicle* likewise suggested interracial cooperation. While most commentators noted the mostly white marchers at the Washington and local area marches, this editorialist was buoyed by the diversity of the Oakland, California, march, reflecting the "rich racial and cultural makeup of the Bay Area."[60]

If Oakland was the exception, and by all accounts it seems that it was, we need to know why. The Pittsburgh incident is revealing. Many minority women lacked the resources to travel to Washington. Claudette Perry, a D.C. organizer, reasoned that black women did not get involved because much of the recruiting was done on the Internet, and "there are a lot of inner-city folks who don't have computers." When Brenda Muhammad, a black woman from Atlanta, Georgia, wondered why there was not more involvement of African American women, who were "the most affected by it all," as she put it, she reasoned that black mothers often had another child at home to care for. "Some aren't able to volunteer the time," she said. "Some don't have time to mourn." Mary Dejevsky, a reporter, gave yet another reason. She was told by some of the black women who did attend that their friends and neighbors resented the fact that gun violence had become a national issue only after white children were killed at Columbine.[61]

The Los Angeles march provides a laboratory for exploring other reasons why minority women's participation was low. Although the Million Mom March was held in Washington, smaller marches were held throughout the country for those who could not travel to the capital. Los Angeles was the only city to hold two marches, one in the predominantly white, affluent suburb of Westwood, and the other in downtown Los Angeles, on Olvera Street, close to minority neighborhoods. The march was originally planned as one big event, but participants could not agree on where to hold it. Minority women wanted to hold the event in their neighborhood, where gun violence wreaked the most havoc. But many, though not all, of the white women opted for Westwood. The sparks flew as the mothers tried to decide. Victoria Ballesteros, one of the organizers of the downtown march, fumed as she told a reporter, "I don't know how any organization that wants to make a difference on this issue can at the same time say: We don't want to work with communities of color.... And that's essentially what they are saying when they say they don't want to go east." Ballesteros became active in the gun-control movement after attending Million Mom meetings where Latinas were not well represented. She immediately started faxing Spanish-language radio and television stations and visiting churches and grandmothers' groups. Ballesteros's activities seem to have upset the march organizers, or so Joy Turner, an African American woman, surmised. Dawn Sinko, a mother from the predominantly white Westside area and cochair of the Southern California Regional Million Mom March, said she thought that the vote to hold the march downtown should stand. "We are really aware that this issue has been going on in communities of color for a really long time.... We chose Olvera Street because it serves people from five different counties of Southern California and it's the birthplace of L.A., and that's very much in keeping with our theme of birth and motherhood."[62]

But Ann Reiss Lane, the head of Women against Gun Violence, planned a separate march because participants from San Fernando Valley and Westside were unfamiliar with the downtown area and were afraid to venture there. Lane admitted that "there are some women who think that everything east of La Cienega is as crime-ridden as the Rampart Division." She added that for other women it was too much trouble to make the long trip downtown, and moreover the Federal Building in Westwood, at the busiest intersection in the city, was a traditional site of protests and therefore the perfect venue. When Ballesteros and others charged this group with racism, Lane said she was "deeply hurt" by the accusation and denied it. The city, she said, had many problems, and the gun-control movement could not solve all of them. "We live," she said, "in a vast area of 10 million people . . . a city divided, where people live in enclaves. I see this as an opportunity for as many people as possible to participate, by giving them two locations at two different times." Ballesteros, on the other hand, saw having two marches as "sad and ridiculous." Joyce Black, an African American woman who cofounded the group One Voice to mobilize mothers across racial lines, thought that having two separate marches was "insanity." "You cannot solve a problem with people marching off in different directions. If we do not march unitedly, we do not achieve a good end. It's just that simple." Joy Turner, an African American, tried to spin the conflict positively: "It's not the Westside march, or the downtown march. It's the Million Moms March. . . . It's just like a wedding. Everyone's mad now, but. . . . This is about preventing our babies from dying."[63]

Fabian Nunez's optimism was more tempered. The political director of the Los Angeles County Federation of Labor, Nunez thought that the attempt to bring these women together was clearly a breakthrough. "How often do you have concerned parents, mothers in particular, from different social classes coming together to tackle a common problem?" Still, Nunez understood that their effectiveness would depend on their ability to get along: "People always look at how do you deal with this from the perspective of the community where they reside, not how to deal with it from a broader, more holistic way." Joyce Black agreed with Nunez. Reflecting on the split, she said: "We have to understand that in order to solve this problem of gun violence, women have to unite with harmony. Our children are watching." What they saw on May 14 was one rally that began at 9:30 a.m. in Westwood, followed by an 11 a.m. march, and another rally that began in downtown Los Angeles at 12:30 p.m., followed by a march that started at 1 p.m.[64]

This incident speaks volumes about the dearth of black and minority women in the Million Mom March. Although many white women crossed racial boundaries to work with minority women, it was usually minority women who had to cross over to work with white women. The minority women had to educate white women, tell them that gang violence was gun violence, that gun violence in their communities was not always gang violence, that their children *were* children and deserved inclusion.[65]

Most white women, including Donna Dees-Thomases, came to the issue of gun control with little understanding of race. Her account of the Million Mom March, *Looking for a Few Good Moms: How One Mother Rallied a Million Others against the Gun Lobby* (2004), shows her commitment to universalism and demonstrates no structural analysis of American racial hierarchy. One searches in vain for a reference to race or even a suggestion that racial issues are involved in the gun-control fight. Race or ethnicity emerges only when Dees-Thomases describes Dana Quist, a Florida organizer, as pleading with a "singsong Puerto Rican accent" when she describes a meeting with the man she credits with teaching her about violence in African American neighborhoods, Lt. Eric Adams of 100 Blacks in Law Enforcement; and when she identifies Jacquee Algee, of Atlanta, as an African American.[66]

The incident that forced Dees-Thomases to identify Algee's race proved the rule of the universalist approach of the Million Mom March. It involved *The Oprah Winfrey Show* and a call made to the show threatening to boycott it and the Million Mom March because the African American community was not properly represented. According to Dees-Thomases, this created a mini-crisis because, as she put it, Oprah was "sensitive to any charges—founded or not—of being in any way unfair to African-Americans." When Dees-Thomases told the producer that Algee was black, the crisis passed. But the events surrounding this episode tell us a great deal more. According to Dees-Thomases, the woman who called the show belonged to a group of Million Mom March workers whom Dees-Thomases identified as "a small band of malcontents." They stirred up conflict and a lot of anxiety, particularly when it came to the purpose of the Million Mom March. Originally the march had used the slogan "Mobilizing for Commonsense Gun Control." Dees-Thomases subsequently changed the slogan to "Mobilizing for Commonsense Gun Laws." The so-called malcontents railed against this change and sent an e-mail to the entire Million Mom database, a message described by Dees-Thomases as "militant and uncompromising." According to Dees-Thomases, the e-mail caused her to lose two Connecticut organizers, one of whom was "an editorial writer for a conservative newspaper." Apparently the malcontents thought that Dees-Thomases had conceded too much to conservatives because the slogan was changed to appease southern women who were for gun safety but not for gun control. Like the decision made by suffragists to accept the disfranchisement of black women in return for southern support of woman's suffrage, this compromise had expediency written all over it.[67]

And Dees-Thomases compromised without a second thought. When the Violence Policy Center offered the Million Moms a grant if they would adopt the center's goal of banning handguns outright, Dees-Thomases refused: "I said I couldn't do it. The Southern moms already made it abundantly clear: They would bolt faster than a bullet if we changed our stance from regulating to banning handguns. One Southern mom had even told me that she'd have to start shopping at her Piggly Wiggly in disguise if our mission became to ban guns entirely."[68]

Whatever the race of the malcontents (Dees Thomases is careful not to reveal it), when it came to the difference between commonsense gun laws and gun control, and gun control and a ban on handguns, clearly the latter choice in each case was the more radical option, and minority women, particularly black women, would have been better served by it, most obviously because they suffered the most from gun violence.[69] Not only were their children, especially their male children, more likely to die by a gunshot, but the mothers themselves were more likely to be murdered by someone wielding a firearm. The disproportionate number of black male deaths and nonfatal gunshot wounds has overshadowed the fact that black women have a murder rate that is much higher than white women. Throughout the 1990s, black women, most of them in their mid-thirties, were murdered at a rate more than three times higher than that of white women. Black women also had a pregnancy homicide risk about seven times that of white women, and black women between the ages of twenty-five and twenty-nine were about eleven times as likely as white women in that age group to be killed when pregnant or in the year after childbirth. Most of these murders were committed with handguns. Since most of the handguns were stolen, registration laws and waiting periods—solutions offered by the Million Moms—would not have made much difference. Although statistics are vague about the type of guns used in suicides—which is highest for white males—all available data suggest that registration, waiting periods, and even gun locks would not bring down the suicide rate. Given these facts, clearly the more radical approach to gun violence would have made more sense to minority women.[70]

In 2002 Nancy Hwa, a spokeswoman for the Brady Campaign, said of mothers: "The moms are an early warning system. They let us know when something is happening in their communities."[71] If Hwa is right, then mothers are like the miner's canary that Lani Guinier and Gerald Torres use metaphorically to talk about race in America.[72] If, once in the mines, the canary died, miners knew that their lives were in peril. Guinier and

Torres use the canary to warn that the disabilities suffered by America's minorities foreshadow coming trouble for all Americans. This story of a millennium maternalism should be our canary. The Million Mom March was unable to sustain the momentum it gained from the initial event on May 14, 2000. By 2004, when the political scientist Robert Spitzer wrote about the Million Mom March, identifiable membership had shrunk, offices were closed, thirty out of thirty-five employees had been laid off, and the organization had folded into the Brady Campaign.[73] If we follow Hwa's lead and take the Million Mom March as an early warning system, or Guinier and Torres's lead and take it as a canary, there is indeed much to be troubled about.

The good news is that, like maternalist movements past and present, the Million Mom March allowed mothers to transform the maternal experience into political work and to reconceptualize their unpaid, often devalued labor. Million Mom mothers whose children had been victims of gun violence had felt not only grief but helplessness before they joined the march movement. Through the Million Mom March, they transformed personal pain into civic action. Women who had little or no experience speaking before large audiences, or organizing groups, found their voices and mobilized hundreds of thousands of mothers. For a time, they scared the National Rifle Association because they gave the nation a powerful counterimage to the masculine patriot: a dutiful, sorrowful, maternal citizen come to rescue the nation. The movement also brought women of different backgrounds together. Those who were willing to reach across America's racial and cultural divides learned that guns were indeed a great equalizer: guns felled both rich and poor, black and white, urban and suburban.

But unfortunately what the feminist philosopher Sara Ruddick theorized about maternalist movements—that like any politics they are always "limited by context, incomplete and imperfect"—held sway in the Million Mom March. Emotionalism has its uses in social movements, but here, as is often the case, it proved to be a double-edged sword. The visible suffering of mothers was a powerful mobilizer of both people and sentiment, but their public display of grief also evoked fear and disgust—fear that this maternalist movement would succeed in eliminating guns, a literal and figurative symbol of American masculinity; and disgust at the sentimentality that threatened to supplant masculine strength with feminine weakness.

The Million Mom March also faltered on what was meant to be its pillar of strength: its diversity. Race mattered in this gun-control movement, and the Million Moms' expectation that they could build an interracial movement without tackling the different ways and perceptions of black and white death was naive and impolitic. From the Revolutionary War patriot to the black beast rapist, the opposition delivered racially coded messages understood by all Americans, not just NRA sympathizers. Since the historical and contemporary face of American criminality is a black male, the Million Moms' color-blind approach proved just as much a double-edged sword as their public displays of suffering. On the one hand, as Dees-Thomases suggested, it might have increased the membership and contributed to *political* diversity—bringing both liberals and conservatives into the fold—but it also inhibited the development of an effective rebuttal to the racially coded pro-gun arguments, thus decreasing the likelihood of *racial* diversity. The Million Moms had no answer when their opponents, in typical right-wing nationalist fashion, evoked race and claimed that criminals, not children, were dying. To address the argument, the Million Moms would have had to address systemic racism and argue forcefully enough to arouse sympathy for black male children, who did, and still do, die disproportionately from gun violence. They would have had to become advocates for the many poor black mothers who, through what the political scientist Ange-Marie Hancock perceptively identifies as the "politics of disgust," have been devalued and stigmatized as unworthy, bad mothers.[74] In short, they would have had to tackle, head-on, the logic of William Bennett's assumption that black Americans are to blame for crime in America and are the real and legitimate source of white fear, a fear that the Million Moms themselves believed in and tried to capitalize on.[75]

These tall orders needed a much broader agenda than the one offered by the Million Mom March, and one wonders whether the Million Moms themselves could have overcome their own fears and prejudices and led a sustained movement against the historically rooted racial tropes of the bad black mother and the black criminal rapist. Although it is doubtful that turn-of-the-century maternalism would have survived any better than it did had it chosen to do so, the fact is that even without taking the more challenging tack, it did not survive and had only limited success.

While all of this speaks to the continued tragedy of race in America, it also makes one wonder about the kinds of coalition building that are possible among black and white women. If their dead children could not bring them together, one wonders what will.[76]

Notes

1. Million Mom March Transcript, Speeches by Gale Thorson, Madella Marsh-Williams, and Veronica McQueen; Million Mom March Profiles from the National MMM Web site, http://www.millionmommarch.org/mam/index.asp?record=28; Sheila Stroup, "Moms Vow to Continue Their March," *Times-Picayune*, May 18, 2000, metro edition.

2. Caitlin Liu, "Vigil Memorializes Gun Violence Victims," *Los Angeles Times*, December 11, 2000, metro edition, sec. B; Million Mom March Transcript, speeches by Yvonne Pope, Patty Nielson, and Dawn Anna.

3. Alexis Jetter, Annelise Orleck, and Diana Taylor, eds., *The Politics of Motherhood: Activist Voices from Left to Right* (Hanover, N.H.: University Press of New England, 1997), 3–20.

4. "Gun Deaths among Children and Teens Drop Sharply," National Center for Health Statistics, Centers for Disease Control and Prevention, http://www.cdc.gov/nchs/pressroom/00news/finaldeath98.htm. Statistics on the number of gun deaths vary depending on who is reporting them. Pro-gun advocates minimize the number, and gun-control advocates exaggerate them. This study uses statistics by government agencies such as the FBI, GAO, and CDC.

5. Monica L. Haynes, "Local Women Join Million Mom March Next Sunday to Fight Guns," *Pittsburgh Post Gazette*, May 7, 2000, local edition; Blake Morrison and Scott Bowles, "Do Marches Make a Difference," *USA Today*, May 12, 2000; Robin Toner, "The Nation Pulling Strings: Invoking the Moral Authority of Moms," Week in Review, *New York Times*, May 7, 2000; Jim Galloway, "When Mothers Get Mad," Perspective, *Atlanta Journal and Constitution*, May 14, 2000.

6. Alice Echols, *Daring to Be Bad: Radical Feminism in America, 1967–1975* (Minneapolis: University of Minnesota Press, 1989), 104–7, 369–77.

7. This is a long and complicated history. See, e.g., Benita Roth, *Separate Roads to Feminism: Black, Chicana, and White Feminist Movements in America's Second Wave* (New York: Cambridge University Press, 2004); and Dorothy Roberts, *Killing the Black Body: Race, Reproduction, and the Meaning of Liberty* (New York: Random House, 1997).

8. Toni Morrison, "What the Black Woman Thinks about Women's Lib," *New York Times Magazine*, August 22, 1971. According to the political scientist Melissa Harris-Lacewell, a poll taken of black women at the Black Women's Expo in December 2005 revealed that black women still hold similar negative opinions about white women. Fall 2005 presentation at the Woodrow Wilson International Center, Division of United States Studies.

9. Jeff Goodwin, James M. Jasper, and Francesca Polletta, "Why Emotions Matter," in *Passionate Politics: Emotions and Social Movements* (Chicago: University of Chicago Press, 2001), 1–24.

10. Donna Dees-Thomases with Alison Hendrie, *Looking for a Few Good Moms: How One Mother Rallied a Million Others against the Gun Lobby* (Emmaus, Pa.: Rodale, 2004), xxiii, 3–5.

11. Jen Sansbury, "Million Mom March: Georgia Marchers Urge Common Sense," *Atlanta Journal and Constitution*, May 15, 2000; Dees-Thomases, *Looking for a Few Good Moms*, 150.

12. Dees-Thomases, *Looking for a Few Good Moms*, 174, 78.

13. Ibid., 107; Galloway, "When Mothers Get Mad"; Thom Powers, *Guns and Mothers*, DVD (Brooklyn: First Run/Icarus Films, 2003).

14. Doni Pagano, "Moms See Bigger Picture about Guns," Viewpoints, *Buffalo News*, May 16, 2000; Carlos Illescas, "Moms Meet to Organize," *Denver Post*, September 16, 2000, Denver and the West; Paula Wolff, "Can Million Moms Be Wrong?" editorial, *Chicago Sun-Times*, May 19, 2000, Editorial; Dana Dratch and Shelli Liebman Dorfman, "Moms on a Mission," http://www.atlantajewsihtimes.com, May 12, 2000.

15. Janine DeFao, "Moms' March in Oakland Draws 5,000 People," *San Francisco Chronicle*, May 15, 2000; Laurel J. Sweet, "Some Stay Behind to Rally Troops Near Home," *Boston Herald*, May 15, 2000; Galloway, "When Mothers Get Mad."

16. Mary Beth Norton, "The Evolution of White Women's Experience in Early America," *American Historical Review* 89, no. 3 (1984): 617.

17. Million Mom March Transcript, speeches by Mieko Hattori and Rosie O'Donnell.

18. Linda Kerber, "The Republican Mother," in *Women's America: Refocusing the Past*, ed. Linda Kerber and Jane Sherron De Hart, 3rd ed. (New York: Oxford University Press, 1991), 87–95; Carl N. Degler, *At Odds: Women and the Family in America from the Revolution to the Present* (New York: Oxford University Press, 1980), 298–327.

19. See Gail Bederman, *Manliness and Civilization: A Cultural History of Gender and Race in the United States, 1880–1917* (Chicago: University of Chicago Press, 1995). For other instances of mother blaming, see Molly Ladd-Taylor and Lauri Umansky, eds., *"Bad" Mothers: The Politics of Blame in Twentieth-Century America* (New York: New York University Press, 1998).

20. Philip Wylie, "Common Women," in *Generation of Vipers* (1942; reprint, New York: Pocket Books, 1955), 184–96.

21. E. Franklin Frazier, *The Negro Family in the United States* (1939; reprint, Chicago: University of Chicago Press, 1966), 89–113, 209–24, 265, 256–67, 349–50; Office of Policy, Planning, and Research, U.S. Department of Labor, *The Negro Family: The Case for National Action*, by Daniel Patrick Moynihan (Washington: U.S. Government Printing Office, 1965).

22. Katha Pollitt, "Moms to NRA: Grow Up!" *Nation*, June 12, 2000; Charles W. Johnson, letter to the editor, *Geekery Today*, May 11, 2000, http:/radgeek.com/mt/

mt-tb.cgi/69; Jannie Dresser, "Lest We Forget the Contributions of Non-Moms," Outlook, *Houston Chronicle*, May 14, 2000.

23. For a lay history of the issues, see Elinor Burkett, *The Baby Boon: How Family Friendly America Cheats the Childless* (New York: Free Press, 2000), esp. 147–75. For a quick scholarly review and personal stories, see Irene Reti, ed., *Childless by Choice: A Feminist Anthology* (Santa Cruz: HerBooks, 1992). See also Jetter, Orleck, and Taylor, *Politics of Motherhood*, esp. 349–81.

24. See Dorothy Sue Cobble, *The Other Women's Movement: Workplace Justice and Social Rights in Modern America* (Princeton: Princeton University Press, 2004), 60.

25. Pollitt, "Moms to NRA: Grow Up!" See also Sara Ruddick, "Rethinking 'Maternal' Politics," in Jetter, Orleck, and Taylor, *Politics of Motherhood*, 369–81.

26. See, e.g., Rita Porter, editorial, "Moms Should Stay Home and Focus on Raising Kids," *Columbus Dispatch*, May 21, 2000; Scott Mooneyham, "NRA Women: We're Good Moms Too," *Chicago Sun-Times*, May 22, 2000; Margaret Bernstein, "Pro-Gun Women Plan Counterdemonstration," Everywoman, *Plain Dealer*, May 2, 2000.

27. Charles Sanborn, editorial, "Million Mom March—Where Do Comments Differ?" *Seattle Times*, May 14, 2000; Steve Kruse, editorial, "Public Pulse," *Omaha World Herald*, May 17, 2000.

28. Susan Stroupe, editorial, "Reader Responses: Million Mom March," *Atlanta Journal and Constitution*, May 16, 2000; Dallas Dlouhy, editorial, "Public Pulse," *Omaha World Herald*, May 17, 2000.

29. See the Urban Dictionary, http://www.urbandictionary.com/define.php?term=soccer+mom.

30. Suzanne Fields, "Moms Should Redirect Their March in Line with the Facts," Forum Opinion and Ideas, *Plain Dealer*, May 22, 2000; Sonja Monsen, letter, Letters, *Tampa Tribune*, May 30, 2000, Nation/World; Camille Paglia, "The Million Mom March: What a Crock!" http://www.salon.com/peope/col/pagl/2000/05/17/cpmillionmom.

31. Goodwin, Jasper, and Polletta, "Why Emotions Matter," 1–24,14–15.

32. See Temma Kaplan, *Taking Back the Streets: Women, Youth, and Direct Democracy* (Berkeley: University of California Press, 2003), esp. 1–14.

33. See, e.g., Andrew Guy Jr., "175 Gun Advocates Protest Group's Agenda at Hotel," *Denver Post*, September 16, 2000, Denver and the West.

34. Shane Brower, editorial, "Logic and Facts Necessary," *Pittsburgh Post-Gazette*, June 11, 2000.

35. "NRA Answers Moms Rally," *St. Louis Post-Dispatch*, May 22, 2000. See, e.g., Charlton Heston's speech before the Free Congress Foundation, December 7, 1997, http://www.vpc.org/nrainfo/speech.html.

36. Ellen Gammerman, "Million Mom March Evokes Power, Pathos," Telegraph, *Baltimore Sun*, May 15, 2000; Andrew Stuttaford, "Moms Away: The New Brand of Gun Nut; Million Mom March; Brief Article," *National Review*, June 5, 2000; Scott

Mize, editorial, "Reader Responses: Mom Marchers Ignoring Statistics," *Atlanta Journal and Constitution*, May 14, 2000.

37. See, e.g., Fields, "Moms Should Redirect Their March"; Stuttaford, "Moms Away."

38. Rusty Burroughs, "NRA Women: We're Good Moms, Too," *Chicago Sun-Times*, May 22, 2000.

39. Kevin McCullen, "Boulder Gun Debate Lures Crowd," *Denver Rocky Mountain News*, June 22, 2000.

40. Fields from Sonja Monsen; Kevin McCullen, "Boulder Gun Debate Lures Crowd," "Moms Should Redirect Their March," *Plain Dealer*, May 22, 2000; "Letter Hearing Held to Gather Comments," *Denver Rocky Mountain News*, June 22, 2000.

41. Julio Ochoa, "Moms Wrap Up Anti-gun Meeting, Gathering an Effort to Share Ideas, Grow," *Denver Post*, September 17, 2000, Denver and the West; Ronald W. Powell, "Area Mothers Rally for Gun Control," *San Diego Union Tribune*, May 15, 2000; Fields, "Moms Should Redirect Their March"; Dave Kopel, "Rapists Like Gun Control," *National Review*, April 14, 2000, http://www.nationalreview.com/comment/comment041400a.html; Jeff Jacoby, "Guns for Rapists, but Not for Potential Victims," *Capitalism Magazine*, October 6, 2002, http://www.capmag.com/article.asp?ID=1949; J. H. Huebert, "Open Fire on Chicago's Gun Law," *Chicago Maroon*, July 12, 2002, http://www.jhhuebert.com/articles/chicagoguns.html.

42. While some might think *manhood* and *masculinity* are synonymous, Gail Bederman reminds us that they are distinct. See Bederman, *Manliness and Civilization*, 5–10, 17–19.

43. To understand the racial and gender dynamics of rape, see George M. Fredrickson, *The Black Image in the White Mind: The Debate on Afro-American Character and Destiny, 1817–1914* (Hanover, N.H.: Wesleyan University Press, 1971), 256–82; Jacquelyn Dowd Hall, "'The Mind That Burns in Each Body': Women, Rape, and Racial Violence," in *Powers of Desire: The Politics of Sexuality*, ed. Ann Snitow, Christine Stansell, and Sharon Thompson (New York: Monthly Review Press, 1983), 328–49; Jacquelyn Dowd Hall, *Revolt against Chivalry: Jesse Daniel Ames and the Women's Campaign against Lynching* (New York: Columbia University Press, 1979).

44. Monica L. Haynes, "Local Women Join Million Mom March Next Sunday to Fight Guns," *Pittsburgh Post-Gazette*, May 7, 2000; James Hart, "Shooting Victim's Mother Fights for Tougher Gun Laws," *Kansas City Star*, October 12, 2000, Metro edition.

45. "Gun-Toting Mothers 'Want to Be Safe at Home,'" *Ottawa Citizen*, May 22, 2000.

46. Thom Powers, *Guns and Mothers* (Television Documentary, 2003); Fields, "Moms Should Redirect Their March."

47. Carole A. Stabile, *White Victims, Black Villains: Gender, Race, and Crime News in U.S. Culture* (New York: Routledge, 2006), 11–28, 177. See also note 43 above.

48. For a sociological study on white fears of young black males, see Elijah Anderson, *Streetwise: Race, Class, and Change in an Urban Community* (Chicago: University of Chicago Press, 1990), 163–89; *Media Matters for America*, September 28, 2005, http://mediamatters.org/items/200509280006.

49. Wahneema Lubiano, "Black Ladies, Welfare Queens, and State Minstrels: Ideological War by Narrative Means," in *Race-ing Justice, En-gendering Power: Essays on Anita Hill, Clarence Thomas, and the Construction of Social Identity*, ed. Toni Morrison (New York: Pantheon Books, 1992). See also Ruth Feldstein, *Motherhood in Black and White: Race and Sex in American Liberalism, 1930–1965* (Ithaca: Cornell University Press, 2000), 57, 98–102; Ange-Marie Hancock, *The Politics of Disgust: The Public Identity of the Welfare Queen* (New York: New York University Press, 2004); Dorothy Roberts, *Killing the Black Body: Race, Reproduction, and the Meaning of Liberty* (New York: Vintage Books, 1999), 104–49; Deborah Gray White, *Ar'n't I a Woman? Female Slaves in the Plantation South*, rev. ed. (1985; reprint, New York: W. W. Norton, 1999).

50. For example, when Emmett Till was murdered, his mother, Mamie Till Bradley, went to great lengths to raise sympathy for her son. See Ruth Feldstein, *Motherhood in Black and White*, 86–110.

51. Adrienne Young, quoted in Monica L. Haynes, "Local Women Join Million Mom March Next Sunday to Fight Guns," *Pittsburgh Post-Gazette*, May 7, 2000.

52. Editorial, "Marching for Little Tony: One of the Million Moms Has a Personal Reason to Take a Stand against Gun Violence," *Pittsburgh Post-Gazette*, May 10, 2000.

53. On the few minority women who participated, see Marie Cocco, "Moms Face a Stiffer Challenge after Their March," Viewpoints, *New York Newsday*, May 16, 2000, Nassau and Suffolk Edition; "Free for All," Op-Ed, *Washington Post*, May 20, 2000, final ed.; Mary Dejesvsky, "500,000 'Moms' Rally for Tougher Controls on Guns," *Independent* (London), May 15, 2000, Foreign News; Ellen Gamerman, "Moms and Minivans versus Lawyers, Guns, and Money," *Baltimore Sun*, May 11, 2000, Telegraph; Galloway, "When Mothers Get Mad."

54. Haynes, "Local Women Join Million Mom March."

55. Jessica Garrison, "Protest Takes Aim at Guns," *Los Angeles Times*, May 15, 2000.

56. Powers, *Guns and Mothers*.

57. Mary Leonard, "'Million Mom March' against Guns on Mother's Day, May 14," *Boston Globe*, May 14, 2000; Alison Gerber, "Bus Brings Moms Together for Rally," May 15, 2000; Karima Haynes, "Los Angeles: Mothers Push Fight against Gun Violence," *Los Angeles Times*, August 5, 2002, B3; see also Mike Harden, "Moms Take Anti-gun Fight on the Road," *Columbus Dispatch*, May 14, 2000; Mary Niederberger, "Million Mom March Group Continues Fight for Gun Control," *Pittsburgh Post-Gazette*, June 7, 2000, metro ed.; Julian Borger, "U.S. Faces Its Biggest Anti-gun March as Moms Say 'No More,'" *Guardian*, May 13, 2000.

58. Dratch and Dorfman, "Moms on a Mission"; Dees-Thomases, *Looking for a Few Good Moms*, 31.

59. Lynn Smith, "L.A. Moms Fighting on a Local Level," *Los Angeles Times*, May 1, 2000, sec. E, Southern California Living.

60. Haynes, "Local Women Join Million Mom March"; "The Million Mom Impact," editorial, *San Francisco Chronicle*, May 16, 2000.

61. "The Million Mom Impact"; Gamerman, "Moms and Minivans"; Galloway, "When Mothers Get Mad"; Dejevsky, "500,000 Moms Rally"; see also Karima A. Haynes, "Los Angeles: Mothers Push Fight against Gun Violence," *Los Angeles Times*, August 5, 2002, Metro.

62. Jessica Garrison, "Rift over Locations Yields Two Anti-gun Protest Marches," *Los Angeles Times*, May 12, 2000, Metro, sec. B.

63. Garrison, "Protest Takes Aim at Guns"; Garrison, "Rift over Locations"; Richard Simon and Nick Anderson, "Mothers March against Guns," *Los Angeles Times*, May 15, 2000.

64. Garrison, "Rift over Locations"; Lynn Smith, "L.A. Moms Fighting Guns on a Local Level," Southern California Living, *Los Angeles Times*, May 1, 2000; see also K. A. Haynes, "Los Angeles: Mothers Push Fight against Gun Violence"; Garrison, "Protest Takes Aim at Guns."

65. See Benita Roth, *Separate Roads to Feminism*, 195–200. Roth describes a similar phenomenon in the feminist movement of the 1960s and 1970s.

66. Dees-Thomases, *Looking for a Few Good Moms*, 56, 31, 158.

67. Rosalyn Terborg-Penn, *African American Women and the Struggle for the Vote: 1850–1920* (Bloomington: Indiana University Press, 1998), 107–35.

68. Dees-Thomases, *Looking for a Few Good Moms*, 156–59, 56–57, 79. Dees-Thomases also noted that the so-called malcontents, whom she euphemistically calls the 151s, consistently asked to be paid for their work and complained that moms were being pushed out of organizing as more and more professionals assumed greater responsibilities.

69. Statistics for other minority women are spotty at best. Even for Hispanic males, the stats are incomplete, as Hispanics are sometimes put in either the black or white group without distinguishing Hispanic origin.

70. The statistics on homicide and suicide for juveniles and for adults vary according to the agency doing the reporting. The facts in this paragraph are not disputed, although different agencies may give different numbers. See Office of Justice and Delinquency Prevention, "Promising Strategies to Reduce Gun Violence," http://ijjdp.ncjrs.org/pubs/gun_violence/secto1.html; "Homicide One of Leading Causes of Injury-Related Death among Pregnant Women, New Mothers, CDC Study Says," *Medical News Today*, http://www.medicalnewstoday.com/medicalnews.php?newsid=20316; U.S. Census Bureau, Statistical Abstract of the United States, 2000, http://www.census.gov/prod/2001pubs/statab/seco2.pdf; Shay Bilchik, *1999 National Report Series: Juvenile Justice Bulletin*; *Kids and Guns* (March 2000); CDC, "Methods of Suicide among Persons Aged 10–19 Years: United States, 1992–2001,"

Morbidity and Mortality Weekly Report 54, no. 22 (June 11, 2004): 471–74, http://www.cdc.gov/mmwr/preview/mmwrhtml/mm5322a2.htm.

71. Geraldine Baum, "The Nation: Mom Marches On to Keep Ban on Weapons," *Los Angeles Times*, May 9, 2004.

72. Lani Guinier and Gerald Torres, *The Miner's Canary: Enlisting Race, Resisting Power, Transforming Democracy* (Cambridge: Harvard University Press, 2002).

73. Robert Spitzer, *The Politics of Gun Control*, 3rd ed. (Washington, D.C.: CQ Press, 2004), 96–97.

74. Ange-Marie Hancock, *The Politics of Disgust: The Public Identity of the Welfare Queen* (New York: New York Press, 2004).

75. Stabile, *White Victims, Black Villains*, 153–89.

76. For histories of recent discordant relationships between black and white women, see Winifred Breines, *The Trouble between Us: An Uneasy History of White and Black Women in the Feminist Movement* (New York: Oxford University Press, 2006); and Benita Roth, *Separate Roads to Feminism*. Guinier and Torres suggest that it is possible for blacks, whites, and Hispanics to come together if a strategy of what they call political race is adopted. See Guinier and Torres, *Miner's Canary*, esp. 67–107. David Plotke suggests a tactic different from that suggested by Guinier and Torres; see his "Racial Politics and the Clinton-Guinier Episode," *Dissent* 42 (Spring 1995): 221–35.

Writing Women's History

A Response

—ANNE FIROR SCOTT

Only forty years ago it was possible to read all the books on women's history in the University of North Carolina library in a week. Now we all complain about the impossibility of keeping up with the flood of books and articles, conferences and sources. The rapid growth of the field of women's history in four decades may be unprecedented for a new field. The multiplication of such things also suggests that we need intelligent ways of separating the wheat from the chaff.

In the meantime, I have no hesitation in saying that these papers are good, sound wheat. At first glance, it appears that they cover a wide variety of different subjects, and indeed, in a narrow sense they do. Yet they also share connections and exhibit what I take to be significant trends.

I do not suppose that many of the writers were able to compare notes before presenting at the symposium, but perhaps you are struck, as I am, by the points at which they reinforce each other. After many studies that generalize about "southern women," we see in these papers a renewed attention to individual cases. Darlene Hine, for example, builds on the life experience of two unusual women nurses who managed to cross the race barrier. Excavating their history raises an intriguing question: is medicine one of the first places where real integration took place? Laura Edwards, dealing with working-class white women, concentrates on individuals who tangled with the law and thereby managed to create a record. Glenda Gilmore uses examples of women activists to make her case for the importance of context. Laurel Ulrich begins with the work of one woman.

Others deal with specific groups: women working for gun control, southern women who found themselves in the path of northern soldiers, colonial women who aspired to self-education.

It takes some chutzpa for me to undertake a comment covering so many areas—often areas in which the authors are far more knowledgeable than I will ever be. Since, however, I found the papers both enlightening and immensely stimulating, not one failed to give me ideas.

Laura Edwards's paper set my mind whirling. I wondered if the phenomenon she describes of women with no formal power quietly finding ways to influence the lives of their friends and neighbors is common in small communities where people know each other well. Put another way, she describes presumably powerless women devising ways to influence decisions that affect the whole community. I remember a citizen in colonial New England who, without apology, reported peering in the window of a neighbor's house to determine whether the neighbor was up to no good. If she did not like what she found, no doubt public opinion would soon bring the man to account. Would we find similar behavior in villages in England or Germany? Mormon women in the days of plural marriage certainly found ways to assert themselves. To take a contemporary situation, Muslim women in their burqas, I suspect, find similar ways of asserting some power despite the degree of male domination. *A Thousand Splendid Suns* (2007), Khaled Hosseini's novel about the horrors inflicted on women in Afghanistan, tells the story of a second wife choosing to murder an abusive man to allow the first wife to run away with her childhood lover. The second wife does this knowing that she will be hung for murder.

As I read Laura's paper, I wondered whether I could go back to the original characters in *The Southern Lady*, whom I discovered forty years ago in their personal documents, with an eye to the questions raised here. Should I have dug deeper when I found Gertrude Thomas complaining to an all-female group that a woman they were discussing would be ostracized for adultery, while the man was likely to be admired? Was she proposing that the group should ignore the expected behavior? And what experience led a minister to oppose separate female prayer meetings because "who knows what they might pray for?"

Crystal Feimster's paper, too, suggests things I could go looking for in those same sources—a fear that was dramatically illustrated in *Gone with the Wind* when Scarlett shot a marauding Yankee soldier whom she perceived as intending rape. The historians have not been so perceptive. Drew Faust, in her book about Confederate women, dwells at length on the possibility of white-black sex when husbands were away, and she has plenty of evidence of women who were disgusted with the failures of their men. I, however, could find no word about any fear of the Yankee soldiers on this score. The fear about which we hear a great deal had to do with the loss of food and silver and the presumed demoralization of enslaved people.

Since I am taking colleagues to task, I took the precaution of looking back to see whether I had done any better in the "war" chapter of *The Southern Lady*. The answer is, not much. I did describe Sherman's men "running wild" as they approached Savannah, and I included a specific case of the Jones women, mother and pregnant daughter, who were alone and felt great trepidation with no man to protect them. Otherwise I made no specific mention of the fear of rape. If Frances Newman was right that a southern lady was not supposed to know what a virgin was until she ceased to be one, chances are that the word *rape* had not made it into their vocabulary.

To an admirer of *A Midwife's Tale*, it is no surprise to discover that Laurel Ulrich again found material long available and uncovered implications no one else had seen. In this case, she was not deterred by the widely held assumption that the two quilts in question had been created by an unknown African American woman. I imagine Laurel reading that statement and saying to herself, "Well, now, let's see if the quilter is *really* unknown." Laurel's paper, dealing as it does with the African American tradition of quilting, is particularly apropos in Mississippi, where the Tutwiler Quilters and the Crossroads Quilters of Port Gibson are making names for themselves. A small coincidence increases my own curiosity, since Harriet Powers came from my hometown. Laurel's research reveals a great deal about Powers's art and the religion that infused her work.

Deborah White, among other things, raises an issue that has confronted presidents for the last four decades: how to deal with the National Rifle Association. Deborah argues that the ambitious effort of the multiracial Million Mom March against guns came a cropper because of the variety of motives among the organizers. Because the antigun activists based their argument on motherhood, the organizers gave the NRA a handle with which to attack them. What are *mothers* doing out here marching when they should be home taking care of their children? Whose fault is it if a child gets hold of a gun if not the mother's? And so on.

Of course, activist women and representatives of women's associations have used the motherhood argument since the early days of the Republic. And we have ample evidence that it has long been a double-edged sword. The first major postsuffrage legislative achievement was the Sheppard-Towner Maternity and Infancy Protection Act, a pioneering federal-state cooperative program. Adopted in 1921, the law brought great benefit especially to women and children in the South, which was short of welfare institutions. In Mississippi, for example, efforts evolving from the Sheppard-Towner Act drove the maternal death rate down by one-third in the African American community in only ten years. By the time the law came up for renewal in 1929, however, the opposition, led by the most vociferous opponents of anything that looked like an effort to limit child labor, had its attack in order. The law was not renewed. Perhaps the comment of a Kentucky newspaper in connection with an earlier effort to restrict child labor might well be applied to the Million Mom March: "There are times when one may gauge the need for one's activity . . . by the ungracious manner of one's reception" (*Lexington Herald*, May 9, 1923).

Mary Kelley goes over what we know about early women activists (though I miss Judith Sargent Murray), but the main contribution of her essay rests on the records of a long-continuing women's self-educating reading circle, one with aspirations to provide its members with the equivalent of higher education.* The Boston Gleaning Circle, as it was called, was made up of women from the "best families," and the members had a very high opinion of themselves. Their example was destined to be followed by thousands of such groups, some more sophisticated than others, but collectively responsible for an enormous amount of self-education and growing self-confidence. An ironic question raised by a nineteenth-century male supporter of women's rights—"Should women learn the alphabet?"—made the point of the degree of male skepticism regarding women's possibilities.

Glenda Gilmore, as is her custom, ranges over a wide terrain, drawing out the implications of her central idea—in this case, the importance of context in shaping what women are able to do in any time and place. Her suggestion that Pauli Murray and I came together ideologically to fight for women's rights and civil rights led me to a serious comparison of my efforts to promote the rights of women, and of minority women in particular, with what I have recently learned about Pauli's life. Though I wish it were otherwise, I do not think my part in either cause has been in the same class as hers.

Though I like to say I was born a feminist (as early as 1954, I called myself a "moderately militant" one), I came much more slowly to activism against racism. I cannot take much comfort from the reflection that I was like many of my generation when I remember that my friend Caroline

---

*Sheila L. Skemp, Clare Leslie Marquette Professor of History at the University of Mississippi, published *First Lady of Letters: Judith Sargent Murray and the Struggle for Female Independence* with the University of Pennsylvania Press in 2009.—Ed.

Ware, who was the link between me and Pauli Murray, born two decades before me, managed to be an unswerving supporter of equality for all human beings.

I was a feminist before I ever heard the word, but my relationship to the feminist *movement* was less one of political activism and more that of a teacher. From the time I began teaching American history in 1957, I included women in my assignments, in class discussions, and in tutorials. I have often told the story of how my interest in women as historical actors arose. As early as 1944, after seeing Greer Garson play Madame Curie in a film, I decided on the spot to write a history of women from Eve to the present. Nothing came of that prescient moment.

A few months later, however, I began working in Washington for the National League of Women Voters. There I was soon acquainted with a handful of magnificent survivors of the suffrage movement. There could be no doubt that they had helped to shape the history of the twentieth century. At the same time, I met contemporary league leaders in a dozen or more states and saw just how effective they were. Watching them, I could envision the glory days when the suffrage movement pioneered systematic public-interest lobbying. All of this reinforced my interest in women's past.

I was still working for the league when I met a young man who said, "Come marry me and go to Harvard," an offer I could not refuse. Once there, by a series of accidents, I found myself writing a dissertation with a scholar hardly older than I was who liked to question the conventional wisdom. When he pointed out that no one had examined the part southerners played in the so-called Progressive Movement, I thought it a subject that would engage my interest enough to sustain the work of writing a dissertation. I got off to a slow start, having at that point very little idea about how one should go about doing such a study. Oscar Handlin, though in some ways a wonderful mentor, was of the sink-or-swim school of thought. When I finally began to see a way to get into the subject, I soon discovered that the most effective progressives were women. Unfortunately I was too uncertain of myself—after all, no male historian had ever mentioned this interesting fact—to make it the theme of an otherwise unimpressive dissertation.

In due course, fate (and Andrew Scott) took me to Chapel Hill. There, as the only woman in the history department and a very temporary appointee, I somehow found myself scheduled to give a paper to the all-male faculty seminar. Searching for a topic, I remembered those women Progressives and took myself to the Southern Historical Collection (SHC) in search of their origins. I like to say that twelve years later I came out of the SHC with the manuscript of *The Southern Lady*. That joke distorts reality.

Born and raised in Georgia, I had grown up among southern ladies of various sorts, but it was only when I began reading the records from the nineteenth century that I began to understand those women. It did take years to finish the book, but in retrospect, the timing was lucky.

The book came out in 1970, just as a whole raft of young women were pounding on the doors of graduate schools. When they got in, they often undertook research in women's history. The papers we heard at the thirty-third Porter L. Fortune Jr. History Symposium, and the books from which they were drawn, are part of the result, a result that would have occurred even if I had never set foot in a library or published a word. I often reminded myself of the Englishman who pulled the plug in his bathtub just as the bomb fell—and he felt he must have caused it.

In more or less forty years of teaching undergraduates and a few graduate students, I managed to create quite a number of good feminists. There is no more persuasive way to increase their numbers than to encourage the study of women's past. As for civil rights, I can only wish I had not been so backward in realizing that race is the central social issue of our time.

It is true that when I was quite young, I became uneasy about the way black people in my hometown were forced to live. In college I was much influenced by a short story, written by Sara Hardt, in which two children—one white, one black—had been best friends until a visiting white child called the black child a nigger. Although that story shook me, I managed to go through college and graduate school without paying much attention to the strange absence of black students.

When I went to work at the League of Women Voters, an organization that described itself as devoted to the public interest, there was one staff member and one board member willing to take a stand in favor of integration. As late as 1952, when the league created the first televised presidential debate, I was assigned to arrange for questions from the audience. I found six members who were willing, one of whom was African American. Members of the board, when they heard, expressed dismay. "On television? The league sponsoring an African American questioner?" Only the league's president, Percy Maxim Lee, stood behind me and said that I had done the right thing. So the member asked her question, and the heavens did not fall. But imagine: that was only two years before the *Brown* decision. Six years later when the Scott family moved to Chapel Hill, the place was astir about the disgraceful election in which Frank Porter Graham had been defeated for the Senate by a man who was shameless about his use of what we now call "the race card."

When a black family applied for transfer of their children to the elementary school where my children were enrolled, the school board turned them down. I joined with three other mothers to circulate a petition asking the board to reconsider. It was a learning experience, for sure. Many doors were firmly closed when the people inside understood my purpose. Two of my companions were intimidated and gathered few signatures. I was held in place by a fearless neighbor who, despite midnight phone calls and the burning of a cross on her lawn, stuck with it. In the end we had a respectable petition. The board again turned us down, and the chairman, the dean of the UNC Law School, resigned in protest.

As the movement heated up in our town, I did manage to take not a very visible part. Again, as in the case of feminism, my major effort took place in the classroom. In those days there was little chance for specialization, so I taught many different things and integrated black history in all my courses. In one memorable year—1968—the president of the black student union appeared in my introductory American history course. In deference to him, I reorganized the syllabus to look at the American past from the black perspective. In the end, the black students went on strike, and he disappeared. But I had already embarked on the new syllabus, and to my surprise, the white students loved it. It was not the old movie they had heard since fourth grade, and they did more work than usual by a good deal. They worked hard on primary-source papers. The topics therefore took them to aspects of the past they had never before encountered. When I developed a course called "The Social History of American Women," I included black women as a regular part of my syllabi. When I published *Natural Allies* (1991), black women were treated as just a part of the story of women's associations in the shaping of American society. In time I developed a course called "One History or Two" and tried to make sure it had almost equal numbers from both sides of the racial divide.

It was only in 2002, when I began writing *Pauli Murray and Caroline Ware*, that I castigated myself for not having arranged to meet Murray—a meeting that Caroline Ware several times said was something we must do. Once I got into Murray's papers, I realized how much more complicated she was than the public persona most people saw. I also realized how much of this complication was related to her mixed heritage, as well as to her doubts about her sexuality. In any case, working in the Murray papers has been a chastening experience.

When I reflect on all of this, I must say that perhaps in a broad sense Pauli and I shared an ideology. In practical terms, she was a lion ready to fight every battle, while I was a mouse ready to turn every challenge into an opportunity for teaching.

I will end by thanking Elizabeth Payne and the Porter L. Fortune Jr. History Symposium committee for this extraordinary tribute. I can only promise to do my best to deserve it.

Contributors

Laura F. Edwards

Laura Edwards, professor of history at Duke University, received her B.A. from Northwestern University, followed by a Ph.D. from the University of North Carolina, Chapel Hill. She has taught at Duke University since 2000. Professor Edwards's publications, not unlike those spearheaded by Anne Scott, speak to the ways in which women's and southern history have come of age, largely through her deft reenvisioning of these fields. *Gendered Strife and Confusion: The Political Culture of Reconstruction* (1997) and *Scarlett Doesn't Live Here Anymore: Southern Women in the Civil War Era* (2000) have served to challenge conventional thought regarding gender status and roles within the nineteenth-century South. Positioning the household as the central institution within southern society, Edwards's research has punctuated the linkages between domesticity and civic, legal, and political rights.

This methodology is reminiscent of Scott's reminder of the importance of the domestic when considering the "great events" of history. Dr. Edwards's numerous articles, several of them prize winning, on varying aspects of southern history in the nineteenth century relate her interests in women, gender, and the law during slavery and emancipation. Her most recent book, *The People and Their Peace: The Reconstitution of Governance in the Post-revolutionary U.S. South*, explores the reconfiguration of ordinary citizens to the law and governance, with emphasis on changes in domestic relations, patriarchy, and the status of white women and enslaved women and men in the early nineteenth century. It won the American Historical Association's Littleton-Griswold Prize for the best book published in 2009 on the history of American law and society.

Dr. Edwards has won numerous fellowships and awards and has amassed a wide array of professional activities, including service as associate editor of the *Law and History Review*. Equally noteworthy (and appropriate to mention here) has been Dr. Edwards's steadfast commitment to the Southern Association of Women Historians (SAWH), of which she has been a member since graduate school and is a past president. The SAWH molded her development as a scholar of southern history and provided her with professional support, intellectual succor, and companionate research agendas. Indeed, she credits it as being the most important professional organization in her career.

It is with such professional and methodological grounding that Dr. Edwards here contemplates the legacy of Anne Scott, who skillfully documented the movement of southern women from the "pedestal" and into politics. Her essay considers the broad and nuanced implications of Professor Scott's scholarship on the field of southern women's history.

—ANGELA HORNSBY-GUTTING
University of Mississippi

Crystal N. Feimster

Crystal Feimster, a native of North Carolina, attended the University of North Carolina at Chapel Hill. During her undergraduate years at Chapel Hill, she became interested in women's activism. Her Ph.D. in history is from Princeton University, where her dissertation focused on the topic of her essay in this volume. From 2003 to 2010, Professor Feimster served as a member of the Department of History of North Carolina at Chapel Hill, a strong center of women's studies and history and of African American history. In fact, the departments of history at Chapel Hill and Duke University, and their cooperation, played a pivotal role in the establishment and evolution of southern women's history. She now teaches at Yale's Department of African American Studies.

Anne Scott's early examination of southern white women's activism during the Progressive Era exposed caverns of questions about southern women's history. She then spent the next half century pushing many of us into that abyss. Sometimes our excavations take us to dark places. Feimster's study of southern white women who further empowered themselves by literally igniting black men at "lynching bees" illuminates a very dark place. Other times our work takes us to beautiful places—arm-in-arm connections that reverberate across generations. Scott's study of the relationship between Pauli Murray and Caroline Ware, a black woman and white woman, and their shared vision of racial harmony and justice represents another side of history. These extremes of subject matter—the horrible and the hopeful—and the validity and veracity of both, keep us researching, writing, arguing, in a vital and sometimes heated dialogue. This intellectual and personal exposure is the heart of the study of southern women's history and a vital organ in the field itself. Feimster's book *Southern Horrors: Women and the Politics of Rape and Lynching in the American South* (Harvard University Press, 2009), from which her essay in this volume is derived, upholds the provocative traditions of the subversive sisterhood of Duke and University of North Carolina feminist scholars that Dr. Anne Scott made manifest over years of hard work, sustained by a great hope that this dialogue will make a difference in the future.

—SARAH WILKERSON FREEMAN
Arkansas State University

Darlene Clark Hine

Darlene Clark Hine is Board of Trustees Professor of African American Studies and professor of history at Northwestern University. Her writings focus on the alienation of African American women and its causes. She defines racism as beliefs and practices that result in an unequal racial distribution of power and resources. Hine writes about the reasons for, and effects of, racism and the means by which African American women have approached and struggled against inequality. Her work explores how black women have survived, even thrived, despite being devalued, politically disenfranchised, sexually exploited, professionally marginalized, and economically repressed. She examines the interiority through which they coped with assaults and repressed possibilities.

Acknowledging that the convergence of race, gender, and class created a complex gumbo of discrimination, Hine analyzes women's use of what was available. Between the late nineteenth century and the mid-twentieth, African American women worked within the frequently demeaning white power structure of philanthropic organizations and segregated educational institutions. Hine's extensive writing regarding black nurses reveals how sexism and racism posed major professional obstacles. White philanthropists established black hospitals and nursing schools generally based on racist social control and goals of white supremacy. African American nurses during the 1930s and 1940s were determined to transform their work into a means for social and professional change. After World War II they pressed for professional inclusion and increased employment opportunities. While traditionally highly respected members within black society, African American nurses were frequently perceived by whites as mere servants. Limited primarily to private-duty assignments in white homes, African American nurses were continually subjugated to low pay, racial insults, and gender abuses. The loftiest professional level that African American nurses could attain was found in the field of public health. Only after the 1970s did these women began to be accorded full professional inclusion and equal employment opportunities.

Hine analyzes the mechanism through which black women maintained a semblance of personal dignity that obscured exterior demons. They protected themselves from the overwhelming psychic pain of alienation, exploitation, and devaluation by adapting this strategy of dissemblance. Sexual exploitation, racial inequality, and repressed potentials certainly created rage. However, the psychological synergy and personal courage of African American women, and the interiority of their lives, afforded them power to maintain authenticity rather than to be ravaged by sexism and racism. Perhaps black women's greatest achievement is their historic refusal to define themselves as victims. Hine reveals how these women created their authentic selves and escaped their primal enemy, alienation.

—DIANE GLEASON
Arkansas Technical University

Glenda Elizabeth Gilmore

Glenda Elizabeth Gilmore is a graduate of the Ph.D. program in history at the University of North Carolina, Chapel Hill. She is presently the Peter V. and C. Vann Woodward Professor of History, African American Studies, and American Studies at Yale University.

Professor Gilmore's first book, *Gender and Jim Crow: Women and the Politics of White Supremacy in North Carolina, 1896–1920*, linked the history of African American women's organizing and suffragist activism to the broader story of New South political structures and the reconstitution and maintenance of white supremacist power. This history used African American women's perspectives to illuminate the intersections of gender, race, and class in the function of white supremacy at the inception of Jim Crow repression and its aftermath. The revelation of these intersections exposed the fissures through which African American women found access to agency and intervention in the structures of power both within and well outside of formal, recognized political arenas.

Gender and Jim Crow also insisted on the centrality of the story of black women's agency and activism to the historiography of U.S. and southern politics. Women's history, Professor Gilmore asserted—especially the history of oppressed women's interventions in political power structures—is vital political history. Just as gender was central to the function and ideologies of Jim Crow white supremacy, so are race and gender inextricably tied to the larger story of U.S. politics at every level.

For breaking new ground in linking women's and political historiographies, *Gender and Jim Crow* earned the 1997 Frederick Jackson Turner Award, the James A. Rawley Prize, and the Lerner-Scott Prize from the Organization of American Historians, as well as the 1997 Julia Cherry Spruill Prize from the Southern Association of Women Historians. Her second monograph, *Defying Dixie: The Radical Roots of Civil Rights, 1919–1950*, published in January 2008, investigates radical challenges to segregation in the South before the civil rights movement. Left-wing activists like Pauli Murray, Gilmore argues, laid the foundation for the midcentury movement that would ultimately eliminate established Jim Crow structures of power and privilege. *Defying Dixie* was an American Library Association Notable Book of 2008, one of the *Washington Post*'s Best Books of 2008, and won Honorable Mention, Gustavus Myers Center for Human Rights Book Award.

In her essay in this volume, Gilmore is inspired by conversations about Pauli Murray she had with Anne Scott as Scott did research for *Pauli Murray and Caroline Ware: Forty Years of Letters in Black and White*. In "From Jim Crow to Jane Crow, or How Anne Scott and Pauli Murray Found Each Other," she argues that African American civil rights and women's rights converged during the 1940s and early 1950s to set the stage for an international human rights movement.

—ERIN CHAPMAM
George Washington University

Mary Kelley

Mary Kelley's forty-five years of pathbreaking scholarship have made her a leading historian in the areas of early American women, nineteenth- and twentieth-century intellectual history, and American culture and women's studies. Dr. Kelley is the Ruth Bordin Collegiate Professor of History, American Culture, and Women's Studies at the University of Michigan, Ann Arbor. Her contribution to academia and her sensitive analysis of American women and their place in American culture helped earn her the position as past president of the American Studies Association and the Society of Historians of the Early Republic.

Kelley is the author of numerous books and scholarly articles describing the intersection of women, education, and the struggle of gender roles in society. In *Woman's Being, Woman's Place: Female Identity and Vocation in American History* (1979), Kelley presents a collection of essays on the diverse experiences of women in reform movements, education, and labor. Within each of these experiences, she emphasizes the common thread of wifehood, motherhood, domesticity, and women's lives in the public and private spheres. Kelley's *Private Women, Public Stage: Literary Domesticity in Nineteenth-Century America* (1984) analyzes the lives and work of twelve middle-class female authors who sought public recognition in a male-dominated field while, paradoxically, maintaining their domestic roles in the private sphere. Her critical textual analysis of the authors' published works, diaries, journals, and private letters articulates Kelley's keen ability to examine and share the lives of those she describes as "literary domestics."

In her most recent publication, *"Learning to Stand and Speak": Women, Education, and Public Life in America's Republic* (2006), she analyzes the role of schooling at female academies and seminaries, describes how women moved from the private to public sphere, and measures the significance of women's individual and social identities. Detailed research based on personal documents, letters, and curriculum catalogs adds texture to her notion of women's centrality in the creation of a civic culture through teaching. Kelley's commitment to better understanding the place of educated and literary women continues to broaden the field of American women's historiography and to provide further insight to the challenges women endured in antebellum America.

Unwavering dedication to understanding and explaining the intellectual development of antebellum women and the paradox of their role as educators in a male-dominated society makes Kelley a leading scholar in the field of early American women, culture, and intellectual history. Her ability to challenge conventional assumptions about women and their relationship to education, as well as to reveal new evidence and interpretations, makes Kelley's work a starting point for rethinking gender roles and better understanding the lives of early American women.

—AMANDA M. MYERS
University of Mississippi

Anne Firor Scott

In a charming memoir that Anne Scott wrote on the occasion of her eightieth birthday, she reflected on the many "contingencies" that set her on the course of becoming a professional historian. She began with the fact that her parents instilled in her nothing to suggest that her future should be limited by her gender. With the coming of new wartime opportunities for women (and Scott wrote that she had "a wonderful war"), she learned to look at the past in new ways as she worked for the League of Women Voters. Her close association with some of the old suffragists and her daily engagement with the ways intelligent women were changing the world alerted her to contributions that male historians did not yet consider fit subjects for serious historical study.

Then, as she struggled with her dissertation on southern Progressivism while she had three babies, she came to the realization that the most interesting Progressives were women whose stories had not made their way into the history books. After soldiering through two temporary appointments, Anne Scott secured a position that she held for the next thirty years, eventually winning the appointment as W. K. Boyd Professor of History and becoming chair of the department. With the appearance of her pathbreaking study *The Southern Lady* in 1970, just as the women's movement was gaining steam, Scott established herself as one of the foremost authorities in an area that suddenly needed a history.

Contingency played a part in Anne Scott's life, as it does for all of us, but Anne is far too modest when she suggests it is the first explanation for her success. Instead, her own intellectual honesty, her courage in being willing to think outside the box, her compassion for her historical forebears in life's journey, and especially her tenacity in not giving up or giving in to the conventions of a male-dominated profession made it possible for Anne Scott to craft a career that enabled all of us to see the past in new ways.

Anne saw the interface between the public and the private in women's documents, and she reconstructed ordinary life for women on their own terms. She chose a different path in her research—valuing the previously unheard—and in doing so, she unleashed an avalanche of work on women that has expanded the common understanding of what kinds of subjects deserve serious historical consideration.

When I was in Chapel Hill in the early 1970s, Anne was a legend among the female graduate students, and I was terrified of her. But George Tindall always told me that she was the genuine article, so I admired her from afar and read her work with enthusiasm. When she noticed me at the Southern Historical Convention in Memphis in 1982 and spoke to me, I felt that I had arrived as a professional. That moment made such an impression on me that I have a vivid memory of the room, the speakers, and even what I was wearing. That was, by the way, the same convention where I met Elizabeth Payne—all things considered, a momentous convention!

I did not have the privilege of being taught or mentored by Anne Scott, but she came alive to me in a new and meaningful way at a long-ago meeting of the Southern Association for Women Historians. I had been president of SAWH when we decided to create the Willie Lee Rose and Julia Cherry Spruill Prizes, and Anne had graciously consented to lead the fund-raising effort for the Spruill Prize. When she reported her successful efforts to the association, she told us a little of her love for Julia Cherry Spruill, the brilliant woman whose work had been devalued by her male colleagues, the dutiful daughter who had put aside her career to care for her aging parents. Overcome by the frustration and the waste of the story she was telling, the Anne Scott I had seen as formidable, no nonsense, and all business burst into tears. I was stunned and moved, and I realized that once again Anne Scott was showing me how to combine being a sensitive woman with being a serious academic.

I am thankful for all the kinds of people my career has brought into my life. I am grateful for the male professors and colleagues who have set high standards and encouraged me to reach for the bar. I am especially thankful for the academic women who have expanded so dramatically my understanding of what I could do and who I could be. I will be eternally grateful to Anne Scott for the example of her life and for the doors she has opened for all of us.

—ELIZABETH JACOWAY
Newport, Arkansas

Laurel Thatcher Ulrich

Laurel Thatcher Ulrich, Harvard University's 300th Anniversary University Professor and previously professor of history at the University of New Hampshire, is one of the most creative historians whose work I have ever had the pleasure to read. Ulrich's first book, *Good Wives: Image and Reality in the Lives of Women in Early New England, 1650–1750*, published in 1982, was a tour de force. It made every previous argument about early American women almost irrelevant. Two words serve as a shorthand explanation of why *Good Wives*—and the rest of Ulrich's work—is special: "Deputy Husband." It's hard to believe that until 1982, we had never heard that expression. It means, quite simply, that in certain circumstances colonial women stepped outside their ordinary domestic realm, stood in their husbands' place, and did "his" job, without losing their femininity or their standing as good wives.

But in Ulrich's hands, the expression means so much more. It allows early American historians to transcend that tired debate about the "golden age." They no longer ask if women were "better off" in the seventeenth century than they were later on. It indicates that notions of women's equality and independence in the seventeenth century are anachronistic and meaningless. Both men and women were "dependent" in this period, but as Ulrich points out, dependence did not mean servility. Nor did it mean—as it would eventually—that what was unusual for women was impermissible. Women did not *ordinarily* pick up a gun or a plow handle—but they could.

This is just one example of the impact Ulrich's corpus of work has had on the study of early American women. Ulrich continually changes and expands our focus. She seldom talks directly about political rights. She never confines her work to elite women. She tells us that we can understand ordinary women's lives if we only think creatively. Whether she is looking at a wood carving or a pocket, a cupboard or a quilt, or a journal that historians once dismissed as inconsequential, Ulrich's insights about the lived lives of all women are breathtaking. Ordinary women, after all, not just the wives of merchants and planters, were "deputy husbands."

Ulrich's second book, *A Midwife's Tale: The Life of Martha Ballard Based on Her Diary, 1785–1812*, published in 1990, received the Pulitzer Prize in 1991. The following year, she won a MacArthur Foundation Fellowship and used the time in part to create a PBS documentary on Ballard's life. The book and documentary took a diary previously described as containing "just trivia" and created a compelling picture of a woman on the Maine frontier who performed domestic work, delivered babies, and healed the sick while at the same time astutely observing politics and religion.

Ulrich has forced historians to reevaluate much of what they thought they knew about this period. She argues that even in the eighteenth century, women were more religious than secular. She describes gender not as an identity but as a role or performance. She claims that seventeenth-century women thought in terms of "responsibilities," not "opportunities." If they picked up a gun, they did not see this as an advance "for women." It was just another duty. Ulrich has moved the discussion of women beyond notions of victimhood and power, opportunities and limits. Above all, she has encouraged us to do what historians should always do: to understand these women as they would have understood and recognized themselves.

—SHEILA SKEMP
The University of Mississippi

Deborah Gray White

It is easy to forget just how far the field of southern women's history has come in a relatively short time. It was, for instance, little more than two decades ago that Deborah Gray White profoundly shifted the focus of the study of slavery. In 1985, when she published her seminal work *Ar'n't I a Woman*, the subject of slave women had not yet been awarded a book-length treatment. While scholarship on slavery flourished in the 1960s and 1970s, it was largely male slaves, it seemed, who were making their own worlds and were positioned at the center of their communities. Women were relegated to the periphery of studies on the peculiar institution.

What Dr. White did in her two-hundred-page volume was remarkable and forever changed the way scholars study and teach the history of enslaved black women. In her examination of slave women's life and work, White revealed that slavery was a fundamentally different system for women than for men. It was she who so decisively articulated what to us is now such a fundamental point: that slave women suffered doubly, as both their sex and their state of bondage made them vulnerable to sexual exploitation. Dr. White also clearly illustrated, however, that slave women were, in many ways, able to transcend the circumscribed racial and gender roles that whites cast for them: the "Jezebel" on one hand, and the "mammy" on the other. They were able agents, capable of defining themselves and their lives.

Much of Dr. White's subsequent work has moved up in time into the twentieth century, but she has continued to revisit many of the themes present in *Ar'n't I a Woman*. In works such as *Too Heavy a Load: Black Women in Defense of Themselves, 1894–1994* and in her current project, which focuses on political gatherings in the 1990s, she explores how black females have struggled with sometimes conflicting identities as African Americans and as women. She has, with great skill and imagination, captured their efforts to combat stereotypes, form female networks, and shape their own destinies both collectively and as individuals.

Dr. White is Board of Governors Professor of History at Rutgers University, where she continues her impressive research.

—Anne E. Marshall
Mississippi State University

Index

abortion, 117, 143
absolute rights. *See* rights
abstinence, 117
activism, 21, 117–18, 123, 145, 173, 175–76, 206–7
Adams, Eric, 189, 192
Adams, Monni, 91
Addams, Jane, 99
"Advantages of Education," 13
affirmative action, 178, 180
African American folklore, 88
African American women. *See* women
African Americans, 21, 54–55, 85, 91–92, 102, 104–5, 118–19, 122, 131, 153–54, 156, 165, 186, 192
"African Influence on the Art of the United States," 82
agriculture, 21
Aiken, South Carolina. *See* South Carolina
Alabama Scottsboro case, 185
Algee, Jacquee, 192
alienation, 128
American Association of University Women, 162
Ames, Jessie Daniel, 145–46
Amspaugh, Lisa, 177
American Dilemma, An, 150
anger, 66, 128, 176–77, 188
Ansonville, North Carolina. *See* North Carolina
Antebellum America, 3, 7, 19, 21–22
Antebellum civil society, 20, 22
Antebellum period, 30
antigun laws. *See* law

apathy, 128
appellate decisions, 31–32
appellate law. *See* law
appliquéd quilt, 82, 83, 89, 91, 93
Asking Saves Kids (ASK), 176
Athens, Georgia. *See* Georgia
Athens Women's Club, 98, 100–101, 115
Atlanta, Georgia. *See* Georgia
Atlanta Cotton States and International Exposition, 102
authority: governing, 33; husbands', 43, 50; legal, 36; masculine, 50; moral, 122

babies, 117–18, 134–36, 179, 186, 191
Bacon, Alice, 104
Baker, Frazier, 120–21
Ballesteros, Victoria, 190–91
Banks, Anna De Costa, 118, 120–29, 131
Benberry, Cuesta, 84, 93
benevolence, 9, 13, 16, 19, 22
Bennett, William, 186, 195
Berlo, Janet, 93
Bilbo, Theodore, 159
Black, Joyce, 191
Black Codes, 54
black consciousness, 133
black matriarchy, 179
black mobilization, 133
black motherhood. *See* motherhood
black professional life, 118
black women. *See* women
Blek, Mary Leigh, 176, 185
Bock, Diana, 188
bodies, 39, 46, 49, 117–18, 136
Boston Gleaning Circle, 206

Brady Campaign, 175, 193–94
Brown, Lucy Hughes, 118, 120–23, 127–28, 131
Brown, Nicole, 184
Brown v. Board of Education, 146, 149, 162
Bryan, Mary, 93–94
Butler, General Benjamin, 70
business, 31, 117, 136; black, 130; health care, 120
business cycle, 44
businessmen, 101, 104, 136, 162

Callen, Maude, 118, 123, 133–36
capitalism, 21
caste system, 120
Cavallo, Adolph, 82
Chapone, Hester, 4
Charleston, South Carolina. *See* South Carolina
Charlotte, North Carolina. *See* North Carolina
Chicanas, 174
children's rights. *See* rights
Christianity, 20, 72, 91, 101, 122–23, 127
circuit courts, 31–33
citizenship, 20, 153, 175, 177
civic action, 194
civil rights. *See* rights
civil rights movement, 118, 145, 164–65
civil society, 7–9, 11, 19–20, 22
Civil War, 3, 5, 20, 29–31, 47, 53–55, 64–67, 69, 78, 85, 100, 148, 184
class, 36, 122, 174; middle, 114, 144, 146, 179; planter, 75, 78; professional, 123, 128; social, 143, 191; working, 173, 179, 203
coalition building, 195
coalitions, 173–74, 180, 195
Cobb, T. R. R., 100
Cold War, 145

Columbia, South Carolina. *See* South Carolina
Columbia Clinic movement, 132
Columbine High School (Colorado), 173, 175, 181, 188, 190
Commission on Interracial Cooperation, 146, 149
"Communication," 13–14
community building, 118, 128
Confederacy, 66–67, 70, 76, 100
convict lease system, 98, 105
cooperation, between black women and white women. *See* women
coverture, 42
Covington, Georgia. *See* Georgia
"credit," as reputation, 35–36, 45, 50–52, 101
creditors, 44–45
crime rates, 181, 186
cruelty, as crime, 51, 53
cultural capital, 5
cultural surrender, 91
cultural survival, 91
curriculum, 3–4, 6–7
customary norms, 30

daughters, 5, 9, 14–17, 21, 40–41, 64–65, 67–68, 73, 77, 148–49, 161, 173, 178
Daughters of the American Revolution, 99
Daughters of the Confederacy, 100
Davis, Frances, 176, 188
decentralized government, 31
Dees-Thomases, Donna, 175–76, 180, 189, 192–93, 195
dehumanization, 118
desegregation, 147, 149–50, 152, 161–62
discrimination, 118, 158, 162
dissemblance, 117
Diver, Lorene Curtis, 87–88, 96–100, 104, 107, 110, 115
divorce cases, 38–40, 42–43, 46, 51, 53, 55

Index

domestic violence cases, 38–39, 43, 46–47, 49–50
Durham, North Carolina. *See* North Carolina

economic conditions, 132
economic instability, 44
economic justice, 54
economic volatility, 44
Edgeworth, Maria, 4, 18, 20
Elements of Moral Science, 13
elite planters, 4, 15, 21, 65
elite white women. *See* women
emancipation, 9, 29, 54, 85, 96, 148
emotionalism, 182, 194
emotions, 175, 181–83, 187, 194
enslaved women. *See* women
Escobedo-Steele, Maggie, 176
evangelical Protestantism, 18–20
Evans, Matilda A., 118, 122–23, 129–33
Evans, Sara, 145, 164
exclusion, 31, 118, 127, 179

family resources, 42–44, 53
family networks. *See* networks
Fayetteville, North Carolina. *See* North Carolina
Felton, Rebecca, 65–69, 72, 74–75, 77–78
female academies, 4–6, 11–14, 16, 22–23
female learning, 11–12, 14, 16–17, 19, 22
female networks. *See* networks
female seminaries, 18
feminism, 145, 175, 178, 180, 183–84
feminist movement, 174, 184, 207
feminists, 145, 174, 179–81, 208
Finch, Lucine, 87–89, 97–99, 104, 107
First Amendment, 183
Fitzgerald, Cornelia Smith, 148, 159
folklore, 84, 88, 90
folkways, 146–47, 149, 151–52
Fourteenth Amendment, 54, 163
Frazier, E. Franklin, 179

free black clinic movement, 131
freedpeople, 54
freedwomen. *See* women
Freeman, Roland, 84, 92
Friedman, Kathy, 189
Fry, Gladys, 82, 84–85, 109–11, 114

Gaines v. Canada, 150
gender, 4, 16, 33, 57, 136. *See also* race: and gender
gender bias, 129
Generation of Vipers, 178
Georgia, 7, 18, 65–67, 69, 71, 76, 84, 91, 93, 100, 104, 133, 146, 148, 161–62, 208; Athens, 82, 85; Atlanta, 136, 175, 189; Covington, 74; Macon, 6; Marietta, 175; Rome, 72; Sandtown, 73
Gilcher, William, 94
global network. *See* networks
gossip networks. *See* networks
governance, 30, 38, 54–55
governing authority. *See* authority
government, 8, 31–34, 54, 56–57, 73, 118, 165, 181–83
Graham, Frank Porter, 208
grand juries, 31, 35, 47
Grant, Zilpah, 7, 13
Great Depression, 132, 146
Greensboro, North Carolina. *See* North Carolina
Guinier, Lani, 193–94
gun control, 173–77, 179–81, 183–87, 190–94, 203; color-blind approach to, 185, 187, 195
gun violence, 172–73, 175–76, 180, 185, 187–91, 193–95

Halbwachs, Maurice, 182
Hall, Reverend Charles Cuthbert, 89–90, 99
Hall, Jacquelyn Dowd, 145
Hamilton, Clare, 100

Hamilton, Shikha, 176
Hancock, Ange-Marie, 195
Handlin, Oscar, 207
Hardt, Sara, 208
Harris, S. F., 101
Harrison, Evangeline Banks, 124, 126
Hastie, William, 150, 160
Hawes, Bessie, 125
Haynes, Monica, 187
health care, 118, 120, 122–23, 125, 127, 130–36, 141
health professionals, 117, 122, 127, 133
Hester, Al, 95
Heston, Charlton, 183
Hicks, Kyra, 96, 105, 109–10, 115–16
higher education, 3, 23, 136, 206
historians, 3, 10, 20, 29–31, 35, 50, 55, 65, 84, 91, 98, 149, 165, 173, 177, 204
Hodges, Luther, 162
Holmes, Catherine, 95
Holmes, Emma, 76
Holsey, Martha, 100–102
Hospital Herald, 126, 128, 131
hospitals, 119–21, 124–30, 133, 136, 142, 176
hostility, 128
Howard University, 153, 155, 159
Humes, Mary, 4, 23
husbands' authority. *See* authority
husbands' rights. *See* rights
Hwa, Nancy, 193–94

Ileto, Lillian, 188
imprisonment, of black men, 186
Independent, 100–101
Indians, 21, 92
individual rights. *See* rights
indolence, 43
inequalities, 34, 123, 152
infanticide, 117
influence of women. *See* women
in-laws, 40

intellectual independence, 15
interracial cooperation, 98, 100, 118, 126, 146, 149, 189
intimacy, 19, 118
intragender and interracial mediation, 124

Jane Crow, 142, 145, 160, 163
Jim Crow, 118, 123, 126, 130, 135–36, 142, 145, 151
Johnson, Guion, 142–50, 152, 158–59, 162–65
Johnson, Mordecai, 158–59
Jones, Alfred, 130
Jones, Susie, 162
Joyce, Jane Wilson, 90

Kentucky, 6, 14, 17, 73, 206
Kershaw District, South Carolina. *See* South Carolina
Kingsley, Carol, 177
kinship networks. *See* networks
Kopecky, Cathie, 185, 189

Ladies Benevolent Society, 124, 126
ladyhood, 9, 15
Lane, Ann Reiss, 190
law: antigun, 177; appellate, 53; common, 32; discriminatory, 163; gun, 176–77, 184, 192–93; and government, 31–32; Jim Crow, 130; localized, 32, 35, 39, 40, 45, 48, 52–53; "Twenty-Nigger," 68; property, 32–33, 40, 42, 45; segregation, 133, 154, 162; state, 32, 56, 152; statute, 53
lawyers, 32–33, 45, 104
leaders: black, 132; cultural, 22; female, 105; male, 104; national, 104; Negro, 150; political, 44, 66; religious, 130, 155
League of Women Voters, 180, 207–8
Lee, Barbara, 177
Lee, Melinda, 188

Lee, Percy Maxim, 208
legal authority. *See* authority
legal process, 34, 39
legal system, 31, 35, 46, 49, 54–55
legitimacy, 39, 52, 179
Lewis, Edmonia, 104
Lieb, Loren, 188
Life, 134
Link, Arthur, 161
Lipscomb, Mary Ann, 100–101
Litchfield Female Academy, 3, 5, 9
literary societies, 6, 10–13, 17–21
lobbying, 177, 179, 192
local administration, 32
local communities, 32, 35, 45, 52
local court records, 30, 63
local custom, 32, 39, 49
local governance, 55
localized law. *See* law
localized systems of governance, 38
Looking for a Few Good Moms: How One Mother Rallied a Million Others against the Gun Lobby, 192
Lucy Cobb Institute, 85, 100
lynching, 68–69, 130, 145–48, 151, 161
Lyon, Mary, 5, 9, 11, 16
Lyons, Mary E., 92

Macias, Carolyn, 188
Macon, Georgia. *See* Georgia
MADD (Mothers against Drunk Driving), 177
magistrates, 32, 34–36, 46–47, 51, 61
male heads of household, 33
mammy, 100–101, 107–8
Manly, Charles, 8, 148
manufacturing, 21
March on Washington Movement, 153, 155–56, 158
Marietta, Georgia. *See* Georgia
marital separation, 14, 17, 38–42, 51, 53, 60, 63

Marks, Jane Barnham, 10–11
Marks, Julia Pierpont, 8, 16
Marshall, Thurgood, 153, 156, 162
masculine authority. *See* authority
masculinity, 178, 182, 184, 194
maternalism, 173, 175, 180, 184, 186, 189, 194–95
McClennan, Alonzo, 120–21, 126–27, 131
Methodists, 68, 99, 161–62
middle class. *See* class
midwife training, 134
midwives, 133–36, 141
Miller, Thomas E., 119
Million Mom March, 172–73, 175–80, 185, 187, 189–92, 194–95, 205–6
Mills, Janet, 175
miscegenation, 118–19
mission schools, 9
missionaries, 18, 161
Mississippi, 6–7, 15, 18, 71, 76, 84, 104, 146, 159–60, 205
modernity, 85
"momism," 178, 181
moral authority. *See* authority
moral motherhood. *See* motherhood
morality, 117, 177
More, Hannah, 4, 18
Morrison, Toni, 174
Moss, Robert, 185
mother blaming, 178
motherhood, 175, 177, 190, 205; and activism, 173; black, 179; essentialist understanding of, 177; moral, 178, 180; republican, 178
mothers, 15–17, 28, 40–41, 46, 70, 73, 91–92, 96, 118, 133, 135, 160, 172, 205, 209; angry, 179; Antebellum, 16; bad, 179, 188, 195; black, 179, 186, 188–89, 195; minority, 188; mourning, 181–82; negligent, 186; patriotic, 67; poor, 125; republican, 177–78; single, 126, 144;

slave, 91; urban, 173, 179; white, 173–74; working, 101; working-class, 179
Mount Holyoke Seminary, 4–5, 7–9, 11, 16, 21
Moynihan, Daniel Patrick, 179
Muhammad, Brenda, 176, 189
Murray, Judith Sargent, 206
Murray, Pauli, 142, 145, 148–65, 167, 206–7, 209
Myrdal, Gunnar, 142, 150

NAACP (National Association for the Advancement of Colored People), 149–51, 153–54, 156, 159–60
national economy, 21
national networks. *See* networks
nationalism, 19
Negro Family in the United States, The, 179
Negro Health Journal, 131
networks: family, 44; female, 3; global, 18; gossip, 36; kinship, 44; national, 7, 18, 106; patriarchal, 42; social, 17–19, 49, 51
New England, 5, 18, 20–21, 204
New Enlightenment, 165
New Hampton Female Seminary, 9, 17
New Orleans, Louisiana, 70–71, 74, 99, 172
"new woman," 3, 86, 99, 163
nonviolence, 154
North Carolina: Ansonville, 5; Charlotte, 154, 157; Durham, 136, 143–44, 148, 163; Fayetteville, 69, 76; Greensboro, 12, 19–20; Wilmington, 127
NRA (National Rifle Association), 174, 179, 183, 185, 194–95, 205
Nunez, Fabian, 191
nurses: black, 100, 118–20; student, 121, 124–26, 128–29; white, 124

O'Donnell, Rosie, 177
Odum, Howard, 143–49, 151–52

100 Blacks in Law Enforcement, 189, 192
One Voice, 191
Oprah Winfrey Show, 192
Orangeburg, South Carolina. *See* South Carolina
organizational life of American women. *See* women

Paley, William, 4, 8, 13
panopticon, 144
patriarchal order, 30, 33, 37–39, 50
patriarchal networks. *See* networks
patriarchy, 38
Pearsall Plan, 162
Perry, Regenia, 92
Personal Politics: The Roots of Women's Liberation in the Civil Rights Movement and the New Left, 145
Pierce, Sarah, 3–6, 9, 23
Pineville, South Carolina. *See* South Carolina
"pistol-packin' mama," 183
plantation mistresses, 28, 30, 65, 67
plantations, 38, 66–69, 71, 78
planter class. *See* class
Plessy v. Ferguson, 149
political democracy, 54
political diversity, 195
political rights. *See* rights
political system, 31
politics, 29, 32, 53, 56, 119, 136, 173, 175, 177, 180, 194; local, 136; maternalist, 175; party, 30, 55; state, 119, 136; women's, 173, 180
"politics of disgust," 195
Popkin, Renae, 175
Porter, Sarah, 10, 13
postemancipation social order, 54
postrevolutionary America, 10, 21
power: black, 120; formal, 204; gender, 122, 130; racial, 130
power dynamics, 90, 130

Powers, Harriet, 82, 83, 84–85, 87–88, 90–99, 101–2, 104–5, 106, 108–10, 205
Price, Carole, 176
Principles of Moral and Political Philosophy, 4, 13
private matters, 4, 13
private property, 46
privilege, 22, 146
professional class. *See* class
Progressive Era, 98, 145, 157
progressivism, 161
pro-gun advocates, 180–82
property claims of wives, 39–40
property law. *See* law
prostitution, 70, 173, 178
protection of southern women. *See* women
Proud Shoes, 164
public arenas, 30, 136
public culture, 30
public health, 122, 131, 133–34
public interest, 34, 85, 207–8
public life, 3, 22, 145
public matters, 30, 34, 38
public opinion, 4, 9, 15, 19, 22, 47, 204
public order, 30–31, 35, 47, 54
public protest, 66

quilting, 84, 91–92, 97, 205
Quist, Dana, 192

race, 21, 36, 73, 77, 85, 98–99, 101–2, 122–23, 125, 128–30, 142–47, 150–52, 156–57, 160–64, 174–75, 184–87, 192–95, 202–3, 208–9; and gender, 36, 66, 85, 98, 115, 122–23, 128, 130, 143–44, 184, 199
"race card, the," 209
race riots, 156
racial diversity, 195
racial equality, 54
racial segregation. *See* segregation

racially coded messages, 195
racism, 28, 145, 185, 191, 206; systemic, 195
Ransom, Leon, 153, 155, 159
rape, 64–66, 68–74, 76–77, 117, 142–43, 148, 155, 184–85, 204–5; fear of, 66, 205
rationality, 182
Rayborn, April, 176
reading, 6, 9–12, 18, 29, 96, 99, 206
Reconstruction, 118, 151
Reed, Isaiah R., 119
religious culture, 90, 98
republican motherhood. *See* motherhood
Revels, Susie, 104
rights: absolute, 45; children's, 188; civil, 102, 104, 137, 148–49, 154–57, 165, 206, 208; husbands', 39, 45–46; individual, 31–32, 39–40, 49, 54; political, 31, 53–55, 163; women's, 9, 21, 145, 157, 160, 164–65, 206
Rome, Georgia. *See* Georgia
Roosevelt, Eleanor, 155–57, 159, 163, 165
Rosewood, Florida, 185
Ruddick, Sara, 194
rumor mill, 37
rural communities, 51, 125
Rutherford, Mildred, 100
Rykard, Antonio, Jr., 187

Sandtown, Georgia. *See* Georgia
Schofield, Martha, 129–30
Scott, Anne Firor, 3, 23, 28–31, 55, 64, 85, 98, 100–101, 105, 117, 129, 142, 145, 147, 157, 160–61, 163–65
scripture, 89–90, 97
Second Amendment, 183
Second Amendment Sisters, 184
second-wave feminism, 145
sectionalism, 20
Segal, Karen, 175

segregation, 102, 105, 118, 120, 123, 126, 133, 138, 149, 151–52, 154, 161–62, 174
segregation laws. *See* law
self-confidence, 11, 206
self-defense, 66, 182–83
self-education, 203, 206
self-examination, 14
sexism, 145, 153, 163, 174
sexual assault, 47–48, 50–51, 61–63, 66, 68, 77–78, 155
sexual violence, 65–66, 68, 70–71, 73–74, 77
Sheppard-Towner Maternity and Infancy Protection Act, 205–6
Sheriff, Hilla, 134
Sigourney Club, 19–21, 26
Sinko, Dawn, 189
Sirius Mystery, The, 92
sit-ins, 154–59
slave insurrection, 68
slave rebellion, 68
slave revolt, 66, 68
slave women. *See* women
slavery, 28, 31, 53–54, 65, 68, 73, 78, 85, 96, 100–101, 104, 117, 173, 178, 186
slaves' reproductive labor, 117
Sleeper, Sarah, 9, 17–18
Smalls, Robert, 119
Smith, Jennie, 85, 90–91, 96–98, 108, 110
Smith, W. Eugene, 134
Smithsonian, 82, 83, 84–85, 87
"soccer moms," 181
sociability, 9, 15
social capital, 5
social change, 147–48
social class. *See* class
social connections, 38
social construction of gender, 144
social construction of race, 144
social justice, 54, 164
social movements, 182, 194
social network. *See* networks

social order, 32, 34, 38, 46–47, 53–54, 122
social reform, 16, 22, 30, 117, 159
social relationships, 30, 32
social structure, 29
social welfare institutions, 105, 136
Sorrels, Mary, 93, 95
South Carolina, 7, 19–20, 30–31, 36, 42, 56, 65, 67, 71, 76, 117–18, 120, 123, 126–31, 134–36; Aiken, 129; Charleston, 120, 126; Columbia, 72, 129; Kershaw District, 47; Orangeburg, 130; Pineville, 133
South Carolina Female Collegiate Institute, 5, 8, 10
Southern Association of Women for the Prevention of Lynching, 161
southern history, 28, 30–31, 55, 62, 117
southern ladies, 28–30, 55, 208
Southern Lady: From Pedestal to Politics, 1830–1930, The, 28–30, 64, 204–5, 208
southern womanhood. *See* womanhood
sovereign body, 33
Stanton, Lucy, 107, 108
States' Laws on Race and Color, 162
statutes, 31, 53, 56, 120
Steffen, Lincoln, 99
stereotypes, 108, 115, 117, 131
Stevens, Thelma, 161–62
subjectivity, 3, 7, 11–12, 16
suburban women. *See* women

Taylor, Carol Ann, 188
teaching, 5, 7–9, 13, 155, 207–8, 210
Temple, Robert, 92
Thompson, Javon, 187
Thompson, Melissa, 130
Thompson, Robert Farris, 82, 109
Thurman, Howard, 159
Till, Emmett, 185
Tillman, Benjamin, 119
Torres, Gerald, 193–94
Troy Female Seminary, 3, 5, 7–8

tuberculosis, 131
Turner, Joy, 190–91
twentieth-century quilt revival, 85
"Twenty-Nigger Law." *See* law

United Nations, 161–62
University of North Carolina, 5, 142, 146–50, 160, 203
urban women. *See* women

vagrancy, 36–37, 43, 46
Van Prooyen, Anne, 176
Violence Policy Center, 192
Virginia, 4, 12, 18, 42, 74, 76–77, 106, 150; Hampton, 124; Leesburg, 15, 73; Lexington, 14; Sperryville, 73
Vlach, John Michael, 91, 111
voluntary organizations, 3, 19, 98–99, 106, 122, 136, 163
Voorhis, Horace Jeremiah (Jerry), 157
vulnerability, 66

Wahlman, Maude, 92, 111–12
Walker, Alice, 82, 84
Ware, Caroline, 155, 161, 163–65, 209
Washington, Booker T., 102, 104
Washington, D.C., 6, 154, 172
Wayland, Francis, 13
Webb, Millie, 177
Whipper, William J., 119
White, Deborah Gray, 117, 122
white hegemony, 90
white supremacy, 122, 130–31, 148, 150, 155, 159
white women. *See* women
Wigg, James, 119
Willard, Emma, 3, 5, 7–8
Wilmington, North Carolina. *See* North Carolina
wives, 18, 28, 35–36, 38–53, 61–62, 68, 70, 73, 77, 147–48, 178
wives' families, 40–42, 44

wives' labor, 46
womanhood, 8, 70, 77, 179, 183; southern, 65–67, 71, 78; white, 185
women: African American, 53–55, 100, 105, 107, 174, 187, 189; black, 28, 30, 66, 72–73, 98, 100–101, 106, 117–20, 122–24, 127–29, 131, 133–34, 136, 164, 174, 186, 189–90, 192–93, 196, 202, 209; cooperation between black women and white women, 98, 100, 118, 126; elite white, 8, 66, 75, 77, 122, 130; freed, 54; influence of, 31; middle-class white, 114; organizational life of American, 85; poor white, 77; protection of southern, 65–66, 68–78, 184; slave, 30–31, 34, 37–38, 73–74, 117; suburban, 173; urban, 173, 179; white, 9, 29–31, 35, 55, 64, 68–77, 85, 98–101, 108, 120, 122, 124, 129, 136, 145–46, 163, 174, 184–85, 187–93, 195; working-class white, 203
Women against Gun Violence, 190
women's associations, 3, 98–101, 117, 128, 130, 132, 147, 180, 205, 209; African American, 105; black, 98, 101; white, 101, 163
women's education, 3, 178; and the importance of books, 4, 8–12
women's history, 3, 28, 117, 144, 164, 174, 203, 208
women's rights. *See* rights
women's roles, 8, 15, 22, 30–31, 34, 38, 40, 42, 53, 67–68, 126
women's subordination, 29, 37–38, 49–50, 53, 138
Woodward, C. Vann, 146, 161
working class. *See* class
writing, 6, 11–12, 14, 28, 68, 75, 160–61, 207, 209
Wylie, Philip, 178

Yankee invasion, 66, 68
Young, Adrienne, 187, 189

www.ingramcontent.com/pod-product-compliance
Lightning Source LLC
Chambersburg PA
CBHW030341240426
43661CB00052B/1705